THE KITCHEN DETECTIVE

A CULINARY SLEUTH SOLVES
COMMON COOKING MYSTERIES, WITH
150 FOOLPROOF RECIPES

Christopher Kimball

PHOTOGRAPHY BY CARL TREMBLAY
AND DANIEL VAN ACKERE

America's
TEST KITCHEN

BROOKLINE, MASSACHUSETTS

America's Test Kitchen
17 Station Street, Brookline, MA 02445

ISBN: 0-936184-70-1
Library of Congress Cataloging-in-Publication Data
Kimball, Christopher
The Kitchen Detective: A Culinary Sleuth Solves Common Cooking
Mysteries, with 150 Foolproof Recipes
1st Edition

ISBN 0-936184-70-1 (hardback): $24.95
I. Cooking. I. Title
2003

Manufactured in the United States of America
Distributed by America's Test Kitchen
17 Station Street, Brookline, MA 02445

Designed by Julia Sedykh

For Whitney, Caroline, Charlie, and Emily

CONTENTS

ACKNOWLEDGMENTS

Every cookbook author has help, and I am no exception. Jeanne Maguire has been my long-term test cook and culinary advisor, performing literally thousands of recipe tests over the years. She has made this book, as well as my weekly newspaper column, the "Kitchen Detective," not only possible but enjoyable. A very warm and genuine thank you is in order.

My wife, Adrienne, does the "final test" for each of my recipes, making them for the family, often an unrewarding task given the culinary preferences of four-year-olds. They are fed beet soup when their heads are filled with visions of grilled cheese sandwiches. Since hers is a thankless task, I wish to thank her publicly for all of her careful note taking and practical suggestions.

Thanks to Jack Bishop, who edited this book with intelligence and wit, rare commodities in today's book business.

I have worked with art director Julia Sedykh since 1998, when she designed my second book, *The Yellow Farmhouse Cookbook*. She is Russian, brilliant, and has an ear for editorial as well as an eye for design. It is a great pleasure to work with an art director who grew up on Dostoyevsky and Tolstoy instead of MTV.

Carl Tremblay shot the cover and chapter openers, and Daniel Van Ackere captured my testing process in dozens of step photographs. Erin McMurrer organized the photography shoots.

Thanks also to the following people: Melissa Baldino, Ron Bilodeau, Barbara Bourassa, Steven Browall, Hugh Buchan, Rich Cassidy, Sharyn Chabot, Shekinah Cohn, Julia Collin, Mary Connelly, Cathy Dorsey, Connie Forbes, Julie Gardner, Jason Geller, Lori Galvin-Frost, Larisa Greiner, Rebecca Hays, India Koopman, David Mack, Helen Martineau, Jim McCormack, Jen McCreary, Nicole Morris, Henrietta Murray, Adam Perry, Jessica Lindheimer Quirk, Jean Rogers, Mandy Shito, Diane Unger-Mahoney, Jacqui Valerio, Jonathan Venier, and Elizabeth Wray.

PREFACE

A kitchen detective is anyone who is curious about cooking. That could mean you, me, or your 10-year-old who wants to know the difference between baking powder and baking soda. It's natural to ask the question "Why?" What is surprising is that so many of us have cooked for so long without really knowing why we do what it is that we do.

We were quite happy to believe that searing meat seals in juices, that braising mysteriously tenderizes meat fibers, that milk must be scalded before it can be thickened with a roux, and that pork must be cooked to 160 degrees. That's why I started asking questions back in the 1970s, when I signed up for my first professional cooking lessons. (I had started my cooking education in Vermont in the 1960s, in the capable hands of an old-time country baker named Marie Briggs.) I rarely received a satisfactory answer and was most often simply told to do it "my way." It turns out that "my way" is often the wrong way.

That begs the obvious question. Are the recipes in this book the last word on these dishes? Absolutely not. I have researched, tested, and retested to determine what I think are the best methods given the desired outcome. You may disagree. I may discover a better method a year from now. I may find someone who knows something I don't. (This happens not infrequently.) I can state for the record that these recipes are, in the words of a country cook, "pretty good" and reasonably foolproof. I can't help you if your oven needs calibrating and the temperature is off by 50 degrees, if you substitute cake flour for all-purpose, or if you use salted instead of unsalted butter. Otherwise, though, these recipes should be worth making more than once. At least that's my goal.

Here are the answers to a few other questions that might come up as you look over this book.

Why is this book called The Kitchen Detective?
That term clearly describes my approach in the kitchen and my weekly newspaper column of the same name.

How do you test recipes?

I start with a few sample recipes for a particular dish to decide what I like and don't like. Then I come up with a long list of things to test — ingredients, methods, cookware, and so forth — and I taste the results as I go along. This helps to eliminate the bad techniques and ingredients and focus on the better approaches.

Does anyone help you in the kitchen?

Yes. Jeanne Maguire, my long-time test cook, has been instrumental in developing most of these recipes, as has my wife, Adrienne, who performs the final recipe test by cooking these dishes for our family weeknight dinners. If my eight-year-old eats it, it's a winner.

Are these healthy recipes?

Wholesome ingredients prepared properly are always healthy in moderation (as are butter and salt). Prepared shelf-stable foods, fast foods, and the habit of snacking are the bane of the American diet. If you don't eat between meals and do exercise moderately, then you can eat real cheesecake instead of the low-fat kind. (You know you'll eat two pieces of the low-fat version anyway.)

Do you have a favorite recipe in The Kitchen Detective?

These are the recipes (out of hundreds that I have developed over the last six years) I actually make for my family and friends both in Boston and Vermont. I wanted my favorite "go to" recipes all in one book. In essence, this is the *Best of the Kitchen Detective*. Okay, you still want specific recipes. Try the Roasted Tomato and Red Pepper Soup and the Clam, Bean, and Potato Soup with Bacon and Tomatoes — I serve both constantly. Steaks with Sherry-Shallot Pan Sauce are very quick and flavorful. Rich, American-Style Soda Bread is easy to make and (I think) better than similar recipes since it is a bit richer. Try the Best Bran Muffins for breakfast since they are easier and lighter than most. For dessert, Quick, Creamy Rice Pudding is simple and delicious. Granola Bars with Fruit Filling are a bit of work and full of butter but worth every calorie.

Are these "gourmet" recipes?

For the most part, no. A few are fancier than others, but most qualify as American home cooking, the type of food most folks really cook at home.

Are these "quick" recipes?
They are as quick and easy as I could make them given a certain level of taste. Short ribs worth eating take hours to cook, not minutes. I don't mind spending time cooking if the results are worth it.

Do I need to be an experienced cook to use The Kitchen Detective*?*
No. Even a beginning cook should be able to follow these recipes.

Is there any difference between recipes created by The Kitchen Detective *and those created in the* Cook's Illustrated *test kitchen?*
Yes. There are a handful of recipes in this book that were developed both in the *Cook's* test kitchen and also independently in my home kitchen in my role as Kitchen Detective. These recipes are usually quite similar; mine reflect the opportunity I had to exercise my own personal judgment about taste and texture. The *Cook's* test kitchen is a democratic, one-cook-one-vote process; this book is more of a personal cookbook based on the classic *Cook's* approach to step-by-step testing.

— Christopher Kimball
Boston, 2003

Being prepared in the kitchen means gathering all your ingredients before you start to cook. Chefs call this practice *mise en place.* I call it common sense.

A jelly roll pan is a common and portable tray for your ingredients. The *Cook's* test kitchen often uses disposable plastic bowls, but I prefer small glass bowls, which are cheap and, of course, reusable. To save on bowls and to make cooking easier, combine ingredients as they are called for in the recipe. (If chopped onions, carrots, and peppers are added at once in the recipe, put them all in one bowl instead of three.)

The Boy Scout Rule:
Be Prepared

Let me put this as simply as I can: Never start cooking a recipe before *all of the ingredients have been measured and prepped.* Beginners often make the mistake of starting a recipe without reading it, without having the ingredients on the counter, without having measured them, without having chopped, diced, or minced them, and without having checked to make sure that they have the proper equipment. Don't start looking for that 9-inch tube pan *after* the angel food cake batter is ready to go!

How many times have you started a recipe only to find that you don't have Dutch-processed cocoa, or that your cake pan is an 8-inch instead of a 9-inch, or that your head of garlic has gone soft and sprouted? How many times did you start a cake recipe only to find that the butter and eggs have to be at room temperature? Or, perhaps you have prepared a batter only to discover that you haven't buttered and floured the cake pan. I have made all of these mistakes and many more just like them.

The technical term for all of this is *mise en place.* At *Cook's Illustrated,* ingredients are measured and prepared, placed into bowls (small glass bowls work well), and then placed on a jelly-roll pan so that they can be easily moved. A copy of the recipe is also placed on the tray. Everything is prepped, everything is accounted for, everything is ready to go. Cooking is the easy part, but it does take concentration. If you are worrying about mincing garlic, measuring chicken stock, and finding that expensive package of fresh thyme while you are also sautéing, the results will be unpredictable at best.

I also suggest that you read the recipe long before you have to make it. And when I say "read" it, I mean really read it. Make sure that you have the ingredients, the proper cookware, and that everything is at the proper temperature before beginning. Sometimes a bowl has to be chilled in the refrigerator or a dessert has to be chilled for four hours before serving. That's an unpleasant discovery if your guests are expected in an hour. Or, perhaps you need 10-ounce ramekins and you only have the 6-ounce variety. Or, you need parchment paper to line a baking sheet and you discover that you are fresh out. (You try to substitute waxed paper with disastrous results.)

Be smart. Plan ahead. Do the prep. Clean the kitchen. Be prepared.

The good and bad news about chicken noodle soup is chicken stock. The bad news is that, when made with commercial chicken broth, this soup is not worth eating. The flavor is dull, often sour, and always one-dimensional. The good news is that when made with homemade stock, the results are extraordinary: fragrant, light, and alive with flavor. ▶◀

The problem for the home cook is that most chicken stock recipes start with bones that are often roasted and then cooked for hours in a stockpot along with vegetables. This is fine for a restaurant kitchen, but beyond the pale for time-pressed home cooks who have but an hour to put dinner on the table. While writing *The Cook's Bible*, I tested five different techniques for producing homemade chicken stock. The best method is to roast the bones and then simmer them for three hours. This is also a good technique even if the bones are not roasted. Simmering just the bones for one hour produces inferior stock, and simmering an entire chicken carcass overnight in a very low oven produces dull, tasteless dishwater. Although the long-simmering of a whole chicken does produce a lot of flavor, I found that simply simmering a chicken along with carrots and onions for 25 minutes in about 2½ quarts of water (at this point the chicken is cooked) yields a light, flavorful stock that is ideal for soups (see page 8).

So the simple answer to the best chicken noodle soup is to start with a whole chicken cut into 10 pieces. (I find it is best to cut each breast half in half again. This speeds up cooking and makes the pieces more manageable.) Instead of simply simmering the parts, I found that I could increase the flavor of the stock by first browning the chicken in a Dutch oven before simmering. Along with the chicken, I add large pieces of onion, carrots, celery, bay leaves, and cloves. After 25 minutes or so, when the stock has taken on a lot of color and flavor, I strain it through cheesecloth and reserve the chicken. Next, I add finely chopped onion and carrots and simmer briefly before adding back the chicken meat plus sherry, noodles, and frozen peas, all of which are cooked for a final seven minutes. I also tested whether it is necessary to skim off the brownish foam that rises to the surface as the stock simmers and found this to be unnecessary. Just strain it through cheesecloth before adding the vegetables.

Chicken Noodle Soup

SERVES 4 TO 6

If you want to make this recipe ahead of time, complete step 2, remove the chicken, strain the stock, and let both cool in the refrigerator. When ready to serve, remove the fat floating on top of the stock and proceed with the rest of step 3.

1	(3- to 4-pound) chicken, cut into 10 pieces (each breast should be cut in half)
	Salt and freshly ground black pepper
3	tablespoons unsalted butter
1	large onion, quartered and peeled
3	medium carrots, coarsely chopped
3	medium celery ribs, coarsely chopped
2	bay leaves
12	whole cloves
1	tablespoon sherry
½	cup finely chopped onion
½	cup finely chopped carrot
4	ounces egg noodles
1	cup frozen peas
¼	cup finely chopped fresh flat-leaf parsley

1. Rinse the chicken pieces and pat dry with paper towels. Season liberally with salt and pepper.

2. Heat the butter in a 6- to 8-quart stockpot or large cast-iron Dutch oven over medium-high heat until the foam subsides. Brown the chicken parts on both sides in 2 batches, about 10 minutes for each batch. Pour off excess fat, leaving no more than 2 tablespoons. Return all parts to the pot, add 2½ quarts cold water along with the quartered onion, coarsely chopped carrots, celery, bay leaves, and cloves and bring to a boil. Reduce the heat to a simmer and cook until the chicken is cooked through and the stock is nicely colored and flavored, about 25 minutes.

3. Remove the chicken and reserve. Strain the soup through a double layer of cheesecloth into a bowl and then return it to the pot. Add salt and pepper to taste. Bring back to a simmer. Add the sherry, finely chopped onion, and finely chopped carrot and cook until the carrots are barely tender, 3 to 4 minutes. Meanwhile, chop the chicken into bite-size pieces, discarding the skin and bones. Add the noodles, the peas, and the chicken and simmer until the noodles are cooked, 5 to 7 minutes. Stir in 2 tablespoons of the parsley and serve with a sprinkling of more parsley on top.

The Secrets of Chicken Stew

A stew made from chicken is usually problematic. The chicken is overcooked, the liquid is thin and bland, and the flavors are dull and one-dimensional. Some cooks, to make this dish more appealing, resort to extreme measures, poaching ingredients from foreign cuisines that have never met and should, in my opinion, remain strangers. ▶◀

My first step was to determine whether browning the chicken was necessary. Not only did browning turn out to be important for flavor development, but I also found that most of the fat in the skin can be rendered during sautéing, which makes this a much leaner dish. I have tried a number of different pans for this technique and found that a large cast-iron Dutch oven is preferred. Cast iron is vastly better than any other material for maintaining heat and therefore works faster and better. Instead of taking 10 or 12 minutes to brown chicken parts, a hot cast-iron pan can do the job in half that time. In addition, such a pot costs about $30, a real bargain when you consider that the premier brands go for well over $100 for a 6-quart Dutch oven.

Next, I was looking for a technique for adding flavor to the stew. As is common in some Italian recipes, sautéing the chicken liver along with the onions provides much depth of flavor, turning this into a more interesting dish. It also appeals to my frugal nature, as the liver, along with the rest of the giblets, is usually discarded. Thick-cut smoked bacon, cloves, and fresh sage combined well with the liver to give this simple stew a lot of punch. (I tested mincing the bacon versus using larger pieces and found that when minced the small bits blended nicely into the sauce.) For liquid, I use a combination of chicken stock and wine, the latter providing a cleaner, brighter taste that cuts through any of the fattiness in the stock. I tested various quantities of wine and settled on ⅔ cup; greater amounts overpowered the other flavors. In order to further reduce any greasiness in this dish, I pour off the sauce into a fat separator after the chicken is cooked. You can also place it in any large measuring cup; the fat will rise to the top after just a few minutes, at which point it can be spooned off.

Finally, I have discovered that the chicken cooks very quickly after a good sauté. If you use enough heat when browning the chicken parts, the pieces will be about half cooked before they are simmered in the stew. This means that some pieces are almost cooked through after a mere 15 minutes of simmering. Watch this closely, because chicken quickly becomes tough and dry when cooked to a high internal temperature.

Chicken Stew
with Sage and Bacon

SERVES 4 TO 6

This is a very flavorful stew because the chicken liver gives it depth. Be sure to sauté the chicken pieces over medium-high heat. This will render as much fat as possible from the skin, which is then discarded. The chicken breasts need to be halved in order to provide uniform pieces for cooking. Serve this dish with mashed potatoes.

    2   slices thick-cut bacon, minced
    1   (3- to 4-pound) chicken, cut into 10
        pieces (each breast should be cut in
        half) with liver reserved and minced
        Salt and freshly ground black pepper
    1   large onion, sliced into thin rounds
    1   tablespoon tomato paste
    2/3 cup white wine
    1 3/4 cups chicken stock
    1   tablespoon minced fresh sage

1. Heat a large, heavy Dutch oven (cast-iron preferred) over medium-high heat. When hot, add the bacon bits and cook until brown and crisp, stirring frequently. Drain the bacon bits on paper towels and reserve. Meanwhile, season the chicken with salt and pepper. Pour off all but 3 tablespoons of the fat from the pot. Add the chicken pieces, in batches if necessary, and cook until deeply browned on all sides. (Use lots of heat and render as much of the fat from the skin as possible.) Remove and reserve the chicken.

2. Pour off all but 2 tablespoons of the fat. Add the onion and chicken liver and cook over medium heat until the onion is soft and translucent, 7 to 8 minutes. Add the chicken and bacon pieces back to the skillet. Add the tomato paste and 1/3 cup of the wine and stir to coat the chicken. Add the remaining 1/3 cup wine and the chicken stock and scrape the browned bits from the bottom of the pan with a wooden spoon. Simmer, stirring occasionally, for 10 to 20 minutes, or until the thighs reach an internal temperature of 165 degrees measured on an instant-read thermometer. Add the sage and salt and pepper to taste. Remove the chicken to a bowl and cover to keep warm. (At this point, you can degrease the sauce if you like by straining it into a fat separator or by letting it sit for a few minutes in a glass measuring cup and spooning off the fat that rises to the top.) Simmer the sauce another 8 to 10 minutes or until thickened. Remove the skin from the chicken and then add the pieces back to the pot; heat through and serve at once.

The Truth about Chicken Stock

The truth is sad, but here it goes: Most canned, frozen, or dried chicken stock doesn't taste like it ever got anywhere near a chicken. At *Cook's Illustrated,* we have done more than a few tastings over the years and have found most brands to be either flavorless or with a flavor that one can only describe as metallic, sour, salty, or much like bad beef stock. The brand we recommend is Swanson's Natural Goodness chicken broth, which is "pleasant and perfectly fine" but nothing like the real thing.

So, what are you going to do, make your own stock? The truth is that for the vast majority of recipes, even the best cooks use canned stock. However, for certain recipes — a simple soup that's based on chicken stock, for example — you really ought to make your own. The question is how to do it quickly and easily.

I have tested just about every method (roasting the bones, cooking for hours, etc.) and find that the best method is simply to simmer a chicken in cold water for 30 to 40 minutes. That's it. Add other ingredients if you like, but that is the basic concept.

Here is a recipe that takes just one hour from start to finish. It does include other ingredients, but the concept is the same.

Quick-Cook Chicken Stock

MAKES ABOUT 1½ QUARTS

Cut up the chicken and vegetables to maximize the flavor during the short cooking time. Once the chicken has been cooked, it can be saved and used in another recipe.

- 1 (3½- to 4-pound) chicken, cut into pieces
- 1 large onion, coarsely chopped
- 1 medium carrot, coarsely chopped
- 1 bay leaf
- 6 sprigs fresh thyme, oregano, or rosemary or 1 teaspoon dried
- 6 whole cloves
- 2 medium celery ribs, coarsely chopped
- 4 large sprigs fresh flat-leaf parsley, coarsely chopped
  Salt

1. Place the chicken, onion, carrot, bay leaf, thyme, cloves, and 2 quarts water in a large pot and bring to a boil. Simmer, uncovered, for 30 to 40 minutes or until the chicken is cooked through. Don't bother skimming the fat and foam as it rises to the surface; the stock will be strained after cooking. Remove the chicken pieces and use in another recipe.

2. Add the celery and parsley and simmer for an additional 20 minutes. Remove from heat. Strain. (A quadruple thickness of cheesecloth works best.) Lightly salt to taste, being careful not to overseason, especially if the stock will be reduced later for another recipe. The stock can be used now or immediately refrigerated and used within 2 or 3 days. (Freeze if you intend to hold it longer.) If the stock is chilled, remove the congealed fat layer on top before reheating.

Dressing Up Chickpea Soup

Chickpea soup, especially when made with canned chick-peas, is often an uninspired and insipid mess, reminding one of peas porridge from the nursery rhyme. The question was how to add flavor and freshness to what should be a simple and delicious pantry soup. ▶◀

I made lots of recipes, including one from *The Naked Chef* by Jamie Oliver, which I liked a lot, and others from regional cookbooks, such as the Wedding Soup from *Sultan's Kitchen* by Ozcan Ozan. The former recipe combined chickpeas with potatoes and a pile of leeks. This unlikely trio worked well, though I did find room for improvement: The balance of ingredients was skewed toward the leeks, there was not enough liquid, and the soup needed a sharp garnish to offset its rather subtle flavors.

My first question, however, was whether canned chickpeas are a suitable substitute for dried. The answer was an unequivocal no. Canned chickpeas lack the complex and earthy quality of the dried variety. However, dried chickpeas come in many different types and sizes; I purchased organic and conventional, prepackaged and bulk. I also found that cooking times varied from 45 minutes to 1½ hours, though this did not correlate to the size of the peas themselves. For best results, I found that the chickpeas needed to be soaked overnight and then cooked in lightly salted water. Prescribed cooking times were irrelevant, so I simply cooked them until tender.

Although Jamie Oliver's recipe calls for five leeks, I found that one leek was sufficient. This was plenty to impart lots of flavor. I also tried using onion in its place or in combination with the leek and found that the leek by itself was best. Also, if the leeks were added to the pot without being sautéed, the soup tasted slightly flat.

For the potatoes, I tried russet, Yukon Gold, and red varieties. The red potatoes were too waxy and didn't offer enough flavor for this recipe. I liked the russet, but the buttery flavor of the Yukon Gold was my clear favorite. Two medium potatoes, peeled and cut into ½-inch dice, were just right. I used 3½ cups homemade chicken stock for most of the testing of this recipe. While low-sodium, store-bought is an okay substitute, the cleaner, fresher taste of the homemade was my preference.

After the soup was cooked, I wondered if some of it required pureeing. This is a matter of personal taste; if you do puree some of the soup, 2 cups is enough. Return the pureed soup to the pot to simmer for a couple of minutes, otherwise it will remain foamy. (The pureed version is heartier; the regular version has a clearer, cleaner flavor and texture.) The soup benefited from a pinch of sugar. I topped it with a drizzle of olive oil and some grated Parmesan cheese.

Still, the soup needed some sort of garnish to provide a counterpoint to its earthy, simple flavors. I tried combinations of bold ingredients such as diced tomato, olives, capers, parsley, chives, tarragon, anchovies, scallions, garlic, and shallot. I also went the other route and tried a knob of butter, a dollop of sour cream, or a bit of heavy cream. I finally settled on lemon rind combined with chopped parsley and garlic, a common culinary mixture called a gremolata, which is often served with osso buco (braised veal shanks). Now I had a Saturday night soup made with Tuesday night ingredients.

Chickpea Soup with Leeks, Potatoes, and Lemon Zest

SERVES 4

Do not use canned chickpeas for this soup. It will not be worth eating. This soup is best made with homemade chicken stock (page 8).

1	cup dried chickpeas (about 6 ounces), rinsed, picked over, and soaked overnight in a bowl of cold water
3/4	teaspoon table salt
1	tablespoon unsalted butter
1	tablespoon olive oil
1	leek (about 1¼ inches thick), white and very light green parts only, halved lengthwise, rinsed, and thinly sliced (about 2 cups)
3½	cups chicken stock
2	medium Yukon Gold or russet potatoes, peeled and cut into ½-inch dice
	Pinch sugar
	Freshly ground black pepper
¼	cup fresh flat-leaf parsley
	Zest from 1 medium lemon
1	medium garlic clove
	Extra-virgin olive oil
	Freshly grated Parmesan cheese

1. Bring the chickpeas, 5 cups water, and ¼ teaspoon of the salt to a boil in a medium saucepan over medium heat. Reduce the heat to maintain a gentle simmer. Cover and cook until just tender, 45 minutes to 1½ hours, depending on the age of your chickpeas.

2. Place the butter and olive oil in a soup pot or large saucepan over medium heat. Once the butter has foamed, add the leek and sauté until soft but not at all colored, about 5 minutes. Drain the chickpeas and add them to the pot along with the chicken stock, potatoes, sugar, and remaining ½ teaspoon salt. Cook until the potatoes are tender, about 20 minutes. Adjust the seasonings with additional salt, if needed, and pepper. If desired, puree 2 cups of the soup in a blender or food processor and return it to the pot to simmer for 1 to 2 minutes or until the foam has subsided.

3. Meanwhile, coarsely chop the parsley with the lemon zest and garlic or use a mortar and pestle to combine the flavors and break up the parsley. Ladle the soup into bowls and garnish with a teaspoon of the parsley mixture along with a drizzle of olive oil and some Parmesan cheese.

Improving Vegetable Soup

Perhaps the most useful recipe in a home cook's repertoire is vegetable soup. Yet how many do you know who make a good one? The broth is made from flat-tasting canned broth, and the vegetables are undercooked or overcooked. *Lackluster* hardly begins to describe the outcome. ▶◀

The first question was how to develop a basic chicken stock base that was easy but delicious. (Vegetable stocks are time-consuming, require more than a dozen ingredients, and, at the end of the day, don't—in my opinion—taste as good as chicken stock.) There are two basic approaches: doctoring canned broth with additional ingredients or simmering a cut-up chicken in water for a half hour or so. I tested both approaches and preferred the latter; it is not much more work, and it produces a much deeper, richer flavor.

Starting with the chicken itself, I tested a whole, cut-up chicken as well as chicken thighs. I found that you can get almost as much flavor—although slightly less interesting—from the thighs as you can from a whole chicken. You will need to use eight thighs for 8 cups of water. I also found that removing the skin before simmering produced a less-fatty stock—a good outcome for a light, bright vegetable soup.

Because this was to be a vegetable soup, I wanted the chicken stock to be a backdrop for lots of vegetable flavor. One onion and one leek were good for starters, adding sweetness and a bit of sophistication, but scallions and shallots were lost in the mix. I used a carrot in the stock but didn't care much for celery. I found that a ripe tomato thrown into the pot added bright flavor and color. Mushrooms can add depth to stocks, but I wanted a light vegetable soup so decided to omit them. For herbs and spices, a couple of garlic cloves added flavor, as did a bay leaf, a couple of sprigs of thyme and parsley, and peppercorns instead of cloves (a common stock ingredient).

As for the vegetables in the soup, I tested leeks, carrots, potatoes, green beans, asparagus, snap peas, Brussels sprouts, scallions, mushrooms, spinach, escarole, Swiss chard, and, from the freezer aisle, peas. I thought the leeks and potatoes were keepers right off the bat. They were both earthy and satisfying, and the potatoes made the soup seem more substantial. I used red potatoes for their color and ability to remain in neat cubes after they are cooked. I also liked the sweetness carrots added. I cut them into thin slices instead of dice, as it is easier and the carrots cook more quickly. Green beans and asparagus failed to impress, so I tested the addition of spinach or Swiss chard.

Baby spinach was tender and a winner. I also liked the frozen peas, which couldn't be easier — no peeling, cutting, or washing. The snap peas and Brussels sprouts were coals to Newcastle — there was no vacancy in the stockpot at this point. Finally, I tried using rice or pasta in place of the potatoes. Depending on your mood, either would do the trick, but, again, they take extra preparation. (Whether using rice or pasta, you need to fully cook it first and then add it to the bowls before serving.) To finish the soup, I added a bit of salt and freshly ground pepper and a generous pinch of fresh parsley. The soup is light and still hearty enough to serve at dinnertime.

Really Good Vegetable Soup

SERVES 6

Yes, you do have to make a chicken stock for this recipe for the best flavor, but it takes only 40 minutes. A canned broth variation is also listed below, but it's not as good as the real thing. If baby spinach is not available, you may use mature leaves, but be sure to remove the tough stems and tear the leaves into bite-size pieces.

FOR THE STOCK

1 (3½- to 4-pound) chicken or 8 chicken thighs
1 medium onion, coarsely chopped
1 medium leek, coarsely chopped and rinsed
1 medium carrot, coarsely chopped
1 ripe tomato, quartered, optional
2 garlic cloves, smashed
1 bay leaf
2 sprigs fresh thyme
4 sprigs fresh flat-leaf parsley
8 black peppercorns

FOR THE SOUP

2 medium red potatoes, cut into ¾-inch chunks

Salt and freshly ground black pepper
2 medium leeks, white and light-green part only, halved lengthwise, cut into ½-inch slices, and rinsed well
2 medium carrots, peeled and thinly sliced
1 cup frozen peas
2 cups baby spinach
3 tablespoons chopped fresh flat-leaf parsley

1. For the stock: Cut the whole chicken into 9 pieces (legs, thighs, breast halves, wings, and the backbone) or purchase chicken pieces at the supermarket. Remove and discard the skin from the thighs and breasts and cut away any large pieces of fat. If using thighs, skin and remove excess fat from each piece. Add all of the ingredients to a large pot or Dutch oven along with 2 quarts cold water. Bring to a simmer and cook with the cover ajar for 40 minutes, adjusting the heat to maintain a simmer. Strain the stock through a triple layer of cheesecloth. Reserve the chicken for another use. Use the stock immediately or, even better, chill overnight and remove the layer of fat that forms on the surface before using.

2. For the soup: Bring the stock to a simmer in a large saucepan over medium heat. Add the potatoes and ½ teaspoon salt; simmer for 5 minutes. Add the leeks and carrots and simmer 5 minutes more or until the vegetables are tender. Add the peas, spinach, and parsley and cook for 1 minute. Season with salt and pepper to taste and serve immediately.

VARIATION
Vegetable Soup with
Canned Chicken Broth
Omit the chicken in the stock recipe. Substitute 8 cups low-sodium canned chicken broth for the water. Simmer for 20 minutes and strain. Proceed with the soup recipe.

Watch Those Substitutions

Some substitutions are simple enough. I will substitute water for, say, chicken stock if a recipe calls for an odd amount such as 2¼ cups. (Use 2 cups of the stock and ¼ cup of water, as canned stock often comes in 2-cup increments.) If I need 2 tablespoons of cognac, I might substitute bourbon, scotch, or rum—whatever is on hand.

But many home cooks are much too freewheeling in their use of alternative ingredients. Cake flour and all-purpose flour, baking powder and baking soda, buttermilk and regular milk, brown sugar and white sugar, light cream and heavy cream, yogurt and sour cream are all quite different and can dramatically affect the outcome of a recipe. Parsnips, white turnips, and rutabagas are all quite different in taste. Lemon juice and lime juice are not the same thing. Kosher salt and table salt are completely different in strength when measured by volume.

Let me give you an example from the *Cook's Illustrated* test kitchen. We asked seven subscribers to come to our offices and make Chicken Marsala so we could observe how home cooks use our recipes. In the recipe development process, it turned out that sweet Marsala was significantly better than the dry version (based on a blind tasting), but we provided bottles of both sweet and dry, just to see if everyone would follow the recipe exactly. We soon discovered that some of our subscribers reached for the dry Marsala, thereby producing an inferior dish. When we asked why, they simply said that the dry version sounded like it would produce a better product.

My suggestion is to stick to the recipe the first time out, and then make changes. Give the cookbook author a chance!

Minestrone with Flavor

I have made at least a dozen different recipes for minestrone, and the vast majority of them exhibited very
little flavor indeed. Maybe fresh Italian vegetables have
a lot more flavor than our rather dull supermarket varieties, but who wants to assemble a soup with 20 ingredients only to find that it tastes like pasta water? ▶◀

To refresh my memory, I made soups from *Essentials of Classic Italian Cooking* by
Marcella Hazan, *Trattoria Cooking* by Biba Caggiano, and *The Joy of Cooking.* I used
different combinations of onion, pancetta, carrot, celery, potato, cabbage, spinach,
tomato, green beans, dried beans, water, chicken stock, beef stock, zucchini, Parmesan
rind, parsley, and olive oil and was disappointed in the results (although the recipe
from *Trattoria Cooking* was the best). My conclusions were that pancetta was crucial for
flavor, that green beans and zucchini added nothing, that dried beans were vastly better
than canned (dried beans add a creaminess to the soup), and that soups using just
water and no stock have little flavor.

In addition to the pancetta, dried beans, and chicken stock, I liked olive oil, onion,
carrot, celery, garlic, tomato, rosemary, Savoy cabbage, and potato — a manageable
ingredient list. To make the soup, I started with 4 tablespoons olive oil and 2 ounces
pancetta. I browned the pancetta then added the onion, carrot, and celery and softened
them for about 5 minutes. Next I added the garlic and cooked the mixture for an additional 2 minutes. In went the beans, stock, tomato, and rosemary. I let this mixture
simmer for 45 minutes (or until the beans were soft but not totally cooked) then added
the cabbage and potato and let the soup cook for 20 minutes more.

This soup was my hands-down favorite, but it still needed work. First, the beans
were tough, because I added the tomato too soon. (I have found that dried beans
cook very slowly in an acidic liquid.) The next time, I added the tomato later in the
process — with the cabbage and potato — and the beans were more tender. I had
started with a full cup of beans but knocked that back to 2/3 cup, a better quantity to
serve eight as a main course. I tried substituting both bacon and salt pork for the
pancetta but liked neither, although the lean portion of salt pork will do in a pinch.
It turned out that garlic was also important to flavor development (no surprise there),
even though I intended to add freshly made pesto as a garnish. Fresh rosemary also
boosted the flavor nicely.

For the tomato, I had better luck mincing whole tomatoes packed in their own juices (use Muir Glen or Progresso canned tomatoes; never use tomatoes packed in puree, which have a processed "cooked" flavor) than using canned diced tomatoes, since the latter consists of rather large pieces. Savoy cabbage is not a new ingredient in minestrone, but it does add a lot of flavor. (Neither spinach nor Swiss chard contributed enough body.) I also liked the addition of waxy red potatoes, which made this a real main course soup. It adds a hint of sweetness and also works well with the rosemary. Chicken stock is essential for flavor, although a ratio of 4 cups canned broth (I use Swanson's) to 2 cups water seemed right. This isn't, after all, a recipe for chicken soup. Many cooks use Parmesan rind for flavoring. In this case, I prefer adding it grated as a garnish, finding the flavor of the rind cooked in this soup a bit overpowering.

Minestrone almost always includes pesto for flavoring and pasta for flavor and texture. I found that when added directly to the soup, the pesto lost some of its punch. I like its sweet, garlicky bite concentrated in a dollop on top of each serving. For the pasta, it is never a good idea to add it directly to the soup pot, as leftovers are then impossible. The pasta will swell like a children's sponge toy — in the morning the pasta is ready to jump out of the pot! I cook it separately and add it to individual serving bowls. Leftover soup can then be stored safely.

Hearty Minestrone

SERVES 8

If you want to skip the pesto, top off each serving with minced parsley and a splash of fruity olive oil. The soup, pasta, and pesto keep well if covered and stored in the refrigerator (in separate containers, of course). The flavor of this soup improves the second day.

FOR THE SOUP

¼ cup olive oil

2 ounces pancetta or the lean meaty portion of salt pork, finely diced

1 medium onion or 2 medium leeks, cut into ¼-inch dice (about 1 cup)

1 large or 2 medium carrots, cut into ¼-inch dice (about 1 cup)

1 small celery rib, cut into ¼-inch dice (about ⅓ cup)

2 large or 3 medium garlic cloves, finely minced

⅔ cup dried cannellini or navy beans, rinsed and picked over

1 tablespoon finely chopped fresh rosemary leaves

4 cups chicken stock, homemade preferred

1 (28-ounce) can whole tomatoes, packed in juice (Muir Glen or Progresso preferred), strained with juices reserved and tomatoes chopped fine

¼ small head Savoy cabbage, core removed and thinly sliced (about 2 cups)

4 medium red potatoes, cut into ¾-inch dice (about 2 cups)

Salt

Freshly ground black pepper

3 cups loosely packed fresh basil leaves

½ cup extra-virgin olive oil

2 medium garlic cloves, roughly chopped

¼ cup pine nuts

¼ teaspoon table salt

½ cup freshly grated Parmesan cheese

4 ounces small soup-size pasta, such as ditalini, cooked, drained, and tossed with 1 tablespoon olive oil
Freshly grated Parmesan cheese

1. For the soup: Heat the oil in a large soup pot over medium heat. Add the pancetta or salt pork and cook until slightly browned, about 3 minutes. Add the onion, carrot, and celery and cook until the onion has softened but the vegetables have not browned, 5 to 7 minutes. Add the garlic and cook for another 2 minutes. Add the beans, rosemary, chicken stock, and 2 cups water and bring to a boil. Reduce heat to maintain a simmer. Cover and cook, stirring occasionally, until the beans have softened but are not completely cooked, about 45 minutes.

2. Add the tomatoes and their juices, the cabbage, potatoes, and ½ teaspoon salt and simmer, uncovered, for another 20 minutes, stirring occasionally. Adjust the seasonings, adding pepper and more salt if necessary.

3. For the pesto: Place all of the ingredients except the cheese in a food processor. Process until smooth and transfer to a medium bowl. Stir in the cheese.

4. To serve: Place about 2 tablespoons of the cooked pasta in the bottom of each soup bowl. (I find shallow soup plates work best for this recipe.) Ladle the hot soup into each bowl. Add a dollop (no more than a tablespoon) of pesto to the center of each bowl. Add a bit of freshly grated Parmesan and a couple of grinds of pepper. Serve immediately.

A Word about Salt

Restaurant chefs use lots of salt. Home cooks are afraid of it. That is one key reason people enjoy eating out—the food is properly salted. Use more salt than you think you need and check the salt level when a complete dish is assembled. (For example, a pasta sauce should taste a bit too salty on its own, because it is later tossed with pasta. Sauces, in general, should be boldly flavored, because they are always served as a complement to another food.) Also, taste for salt five, six, even ten times during cooking. Don't be afraid to add salt in numerous small pinches. Keep at it until you get it right.

There is one other problem with salt and home cooking: Most people don't know that 1 teaspoon table salt and 1 teaspoon kosher salt, for example, are not the same thing. In fact, they are *very* different. The teaspoon of table salt weighs about 7 grams, and the kosher salt weighs only three to four grams. That means that table salt is a lot saltier by volume than kosher salt. Why is that? It's simple. How a particular type of salt is produced affects the size of the crystals. Morton's table salt, for example, comes from underground salt deposits, and the process of extracting it produces finer crystals than those produced by a sea salt producer such as Maldon or Fleur de Sel. The bigger the crystal, the less salt by weight fits into a specific volume. Hence, table salt is "saltier" by the teaspoon than any sea salt. Here is a simple chart to help you make substitutions.

SALT EQUIVALENCY CHART

Most cookbook authors use regular table salt (such as Morton's) as their standard. If you are using another variety—a kosher salt, for example—the chart below indicates how much salt you will need per teaspoon of table salt.

One Teaspoon	One-and-a-Half Teaspoons	Two Teaspoons
Morton Table Salt	Morton Coarse Kosher Salt	Diamond Crystal Kosher Salt
	Fleur de Sel	Maldon Sea Salt

One other thought: Be sure to find out what type of salt the recipe writer was using. If it is not expressly stated in the recipe (e.g., 1 teaspoon table salt), look in the front matter of the book. This information is usually buried somewhere. If you are still not sure, use a light hand with the salt, adding less than the recipe calls for and adding more as you go. This, of course, doesn't work for baking but will for most other recipes. I assume that an author is using table salt unless otherwise noted. (In my recipes, I use table salt unless otherwise indicated.)

Really Good Pasta and Bean Soup

Pasta e fagioli is, at heart, peasant food and should therefore be simple, rustic, and well balanced in flavor. The basic recipe starts with sautéed aromatic vegetables, beans, liquid, optional meat, and tomato, which are then finished with pasta. The problem? Many pasta and bean soups are watery with mushy beans, while others have an unpleasant starchy liquid and an overbearing porky flavor. ▶◀

First, I wondered if canned beans were acceptable, as they would greatly simplify this recipe. They turned out okay but not nearly as creamy and earthy tasting as dried beans. Next, I wondered if the beans had to be partially precooked. The answer was a resounding yes. Cooking raw beans in with the other ingredients produced a muddy, starchy liquid, and the beans themselves were inferior in taste and texture. Finally, I found that precooking the beans with a small onion or shallot, a couple of cloves that I pushed into the onion, a bay leaf, and ½ teaspoon salt was beneficial. (Some cooks swear that salting the water makes beans tough and split apart. I did not find this to be true. In fact, cooking beans in unsalted water left them with a dull, insipid flavor.)

As for the other ingredients, I found that one large diced carrot, one medium diced onion, and three large or four medium minced garlic cloves was about right. As for meat as a flavoring component, I tested pork chops, prosciutto, pancetta, ham hocks, ham bone, and bacon. Pork chops provided little flavor, the subtle flavor of prosciutto boiled away in the pot, and pancetta was sweet and meaty, although it is sometimes hard to find. Ham hocks, ham bone, and bacon were all overpowering. The answer was that the soup fared well without any meat, although a bit of pancetta was a nice addition.

For the tomatoes, one 28-ounce can of whole peeled tomatoes, not packed in puree, was just fine. In addition, 4 cups chicken stock was necessary to provide enough liquid. (Water resulted in soup that was flat tasting.) If you are lucky enough to have one, this is a great time to use a Parmesan rind, which adds a great deal of flavor. Now the pot is set to simmer for about 40 minutes or so, until the beans are just tender and the ingredients have married. Finishing touches include fresh sage and rosemary.

The pasta should be cooked separately and added to bowls just before ladling the soup. For this amount of soup, I used ½ pound of ditalini or another small tubular pasta. The final issue was pureeing. A blender or food processor adds air to the mixture — it also requires cleaning an appliance. I found that simply crushing some of the beans with a potato masher worked just fine. (If you have a food mill, you can use that instead of a masher.) However, the amount of mashing you do is a matter of personal preference — some prefer a thick soup, others like more of a clear broth. Once the pasta is placed in the bowls, about ⅓ cup in each, and the soup is ladled over, the soup must be topped with a drizzle of best-quality extra-virgin olive oil and freshly grated Parmesan cheese.

Pasta and Bean Soup

SERVES 10 TO 12

The easiest way to finely chop pancetta is to freeze it for about 45 minutes or until it becomes firm. When reheating the soup for leftovers, you will find it has thickened and additional stock will be required.

- 1   pound dried white beans, navy or cannellini, rinsed and picked over
- 2   whole cloves
- 1   small onion or 1 shallot
- 1   bay leaf
- 1   teaspoon table salt
- 1   (28-ounce) can whole tomatoes packed in juice, Muir Glen preferred
- 2   tablespoons best-quality extra-virgin olive oil, plus more for drizzling over the finished soup
- 1   medium onion, cut into ½-inch dice
- 1   large carrot, cut into ½-inch dice
- 2   ounces pancetta, finely chopped, optional
- 3   medium or 4 large garlic cloves, finely chopped or pressed
- 4   cups low-sodium chicken broth (if using homemade stock, use 2 cups stock and 2 cups water)

Freshly ground black pepper
- 1   Parmesan rind, optional
- 1   tablespoon finely chopped fresh sage
- 1   teaspoon finely chopped fresh rosemary
- ½   pound small tubular pasta
     Freshly grated Parmesan cheese

1. Place the beans in a medium saucepan and cover with 2 inches of water. Stick the cloves into the onion or shallot and add it to the pot along with the bay leaf and ½ teaspoon of the salt. Bring to a simmer and cook, covered, for 30 minutes for the navy beans and 40 minutes for cannellini or until the beans have begun to soften but remain firm.

2. Drain the tomatoes, crush them with your hands, and reserve. Place the oil in a soup pot over medium heat. Add the onion and carrot (and optional pancetta) and sauté for about 7 minutes or until the onion is translucent and softened. Add the garlic and sauté an additional 2 minutes. Remove and discard the clove-studded onion and bay leaf from the bean pot. Drain the partially cooked beans and add them to the onion mixture. Add the tomatoes, chicken broth or stock-water combination, the remaining ½ teaspoon salt, several grinds of black pepper, and the optional Parmesan rind and stir to combine. Bring to a simmer, cover, and cook for about 40 minutes or until the beans are just tender. Add the sage and rosemary and simmer an additional 10 minutes or until the beans are creamy. Adjust the seasoning with salt and pepper if necessary.

3. Bring 4 quarts of salted water to a rolling boil in a large pot over high heat. Add the pasta and cook until just done but still firm and toothsome. Drain and, if not using immediately, add 2 tablespoons olive oil and stir to coat pasta. Cover to keep warm if necessary. Remove the optional Parmesan rind from the soup pot. If desired, you may use a potato masher to puree some of the beans. (If pureeing some of the beans, you may wish to add additional chicken broth to adjust the consistency of the soup.)

4. Place about ⅓ cup pasta in the bottom of each soup bowl. Ladle the soup over the pasta and top with a generous drizzle of best-quality olive oil and freshly grated Parmesan cheese. Serve immediately.

VARIATION

Quick Pasta and Bean Soup

With minimal loss of flavor and texture the soup can be made with four 15½-ounce cans cannellini beans. Skip step 1 in the main recipe. The beans should be drained and added to the pot as stated in step 2.

Simplifying Lentil Soup

The appeal of lentil soup is the subtle flavor of lentils, yet many recipes call for all sorts of extra ingredients — ham hocks, parsnip, and turnip to name a few — which may, in fact, not serve the best interest of the soup: to convey the unique flavor of the lentils. So which ingredients complement the lentils and which are unwelcome competition? ▶◀

First, the basic method, used to make most soups, is to sauté onion, garlic, and vegetables, add lentils and liquid, and then simmer until done. My first test was to determine whether some sort of meat — I tested ham hocks, ham, pancetta, and bacon — might improve the recipe. I found that the flavor of the lentils was lost and the recipe became too close to the flavor of split pea. So, meat was out. For the vegetables, I tested parsnip and turnip, both of which were too strong for the lentils. The same was true of either red or green peppers. Next, I wondered if I could skip the initial sautéing of the onions, carrot, and celery and found that the resulting flavors were a bit flat and the onion did not soften properly. For herbs, bay leaves contributed an unpleasant flavor, and I also did not like the addition of thyme, sage, rosemary, and parsley, either fresh or dried. The main ingredient, lentils, cannot stand much flavor competition.

As for the lentils themselves, I tested French lentils, which are small with a dark green color, and found that they had a smoother texture and flavor than the flatter, browner lentils most Americans are familiar with. If you have a choice, go with the French variety. (I also found that old, dried-out lentils of any color have almost no flavor.) I also liked the addition of tomato in this recipe but found that a half cup was all that was needed — any more overpowered the lentils. Good canned tomatoes, such as Muir Glen or Progresso, work just fine.

I wondered if beef broth might work here, so I tested the soup using a homemade beef stock, but this was too much work and the flavor was overpowering. Chicken stock is a better companion for subtle lentils. Canned broth was good, but homemade stock was clearly better.

The one ingredient missing from the soup was a starch. I tested grating potatoes into the soup, but the soup both looked and tasted muddy. However, one finely diced potato made a nice addition. But it was even easier to simply add uncooked rice to the soup, which I actually found to be preferable to the potato.

Finally, I felt that some sort of green would balance out the tastes and textures of this simple soup. Kale was too bitter, Swiss chard was too tough, and escarole was too flimsy. Oddly enough, frozen spinach worked just fine. Of course, fresh spinach is even better. I also found that a dash of vinegar punched up the flavor. Balsamic vinegar is my first choice, with rice vinegar a close second, due to its low acidity level. I would pass the bottle around, allowing guests to add their own according to their taste.

Lentil Soup with Spinach and Rice

SERVES 8

For the tomato, I prefer Muir Glen diced tomatoes or Progresso tomatoes packed in juice, not puree.

- 2 tablespoons unsalted butter
- 2 tablespoons olive oil
- 1 large onion, cut into ½-inch dice
- 2 carrots, cut into ½-inch dice
- 1 celery rib, cut into ½-inch dice
- 2 garlic cloves, minced
- 1 cup lentils (green preferred over brown), rinsed and picked over
- 6 cups chicken stock
- 4 cups water
- ½ cup chopped tomato (canned is fine)
  Salt and freshly ground black pepper
- ¼ cup uncooked rice
- ½ pound fresh or frozen spinach (stem, wash, and dry fresh; thaw frozen)
  Freshly grated Parmesan cheese, optional
  Balsamic vinegar, optional

1. Place a heavy-duty stockpot or Dutch oven over medium heat. Add the butter and oil. When the butter stops foaming, add the onion, carrots, and celery and sauté until the vegetables soften, 8 to 10 minutes. Add the garlic and cook another 2 minutes, stirring frequently. Add the lentils, chicken stock, water, and the tomato. Cover and simmer 45 minutes or until the lentils are very soft.

2. Add ½ teaspoon salt, pepper to taste, and the rice. Cover and simmer 15 minutes. The soup will have thickened a bit, and the rice should be tender. Check seasonings and add salt if necessary. Stir in the spinach, cover, and cook another 2 to 3 minutes or until the spinach is fully cooked.

3. Ladle the soup into bowls and serve with a dusting of Parmesan and a few drops of balsamic vinegar in each bowl, if desired.

Clam Chowder Light

Although I have experienced the combination of dairy
and shellfish in even the best of four-star restaurants,
I have never understood it. Shellfish, especially clams,
oysters, and mussels, have a clean, briny tang to them
that ought not to be muddied by the addition of milk
or cream. So I set out to create a clam chowder that
was clean, refreshing, and yet substantial enough for
a one-pot supper.

I didn't have to look far. In Jasper White's excellent book *50 Chowders,* there is a
terrific recipe for Clam, White Bean, and Potato Chowder. Having made it a half dozen
times, I found the end result to be virtually flawless but decided to go through each
step of the recipe to see if I could simplify or streamline anything.

The first issue was the clams. Jasper calls for small quahogs or cherrystones. Well,
quahogs are virtually impossible to find at the markets I shop at, and cherrystones are
not widely available either. Fortunately, littlenecks are easy to find and make delicious
chowder, although they are the most expensive variety of the three. I thought that the
recipe could be greatly simplified by purchasing canned clams, but the processing
removed all of their sweetness and added a slightly metallic aftertaste, so fresh clams
were a must.

The second major ingredient is the beans. Canned beans were a disappointment—
they were flat, mushy, and metallic tasting. I then tried a superior brand of canned
beans (Goya), and they were better but still not nearly as good as the dried variety.
Simple navy beans are fine, and they cook more quickly than the large lima beans recommended by Jasper. (You can also use cannellini beans.) The original recipe calls
for pureeing half the beans to thicken the soup. I found that leaving all of the beans
intact makes a thinner chowder but one that has a more distinctive clam flavor, which
I liked. The beans should not be salted, because they absorb the saltiness of the clam
juice when they are simmered in the chowder.

Although Jasper would cringe at the notion of NOT using salt pork in a chowder—
this ingredient is the one common thread in almost all chowder recipes—I found that
much salt pork in the supermarket is too fatty or too salty. Good bacon is easier to find,
and I liked the notion of sprinkling cooked bacon over each bowl before serving.

As for the vegetables, I dumped the celery, because I felt that the chowder was better without it. I thinly sliced the onion instead of dicing it, for better texture. As for the tomatoes, I liked 1½ cups instead of 1 cup, and I found that canned tomatoes didn't add much to this dish. Fresh, good-quality seasonal tomatoes are great, however. During the rest of the year I would just skip them. For the potatoes, I preferred Yukon Gold to red potatoes — they seem to be the only variety of potato that really has good flavor these days.

For herbs, I agree with Jasper that two bay leaves are a nice addition. I increased the thyme to four sprigs but dumped the fresh basil near the end of cooking, because I thought it was an odd combination with the other ingredients. I cut the crushed red pepper in half (to ¼ teaspoon), and the chowder needed little or no extra salt, as the clam broth was plenty briny.

Making this chowder a day ahead of time does improve its flavor as Jasper suggests, although more than one day in the refrigerator turns the potatoes mushy. If you make this recipe for a crowd and double it, note that you will have a vast amount of clams to cook — either you will need a huge lobster pot or you should cook them in two batches.

Clam, Bean, and Potato Soup with Bacon and Tomatoes

SERVES 6 AS A LIGHT SUPPER

This recipe is very similar to one published by Jasper White in 50 Chowders. *I highly recommend the book and this recipe. Also note that the bigger the clams, the easier it is to make this recipe, although the flavor of littlenecks is superior. If making this recipe ahead of time, refrigerate the chowder once the tomatoes and beans are added.*

- 8 ounces dried white beans such as navy or cannellini, rinsed and picked over
- 8 pounds littlenecks, cherrystones, or quahogs, scrubbed clean
- 4 pieces thick-cut bacon, cut crosswise into ¼-inch pieces
- 2 tablespoons olive oil
- 1 large onion, quartered lengthwise and thinly sliced
- 2 bay leaves
- 4 sprigs fresh thyme
- ¼ teaspoon crushed red pepper
- 2 medium garlic cloves, minced or pressed
- 2 medium Yukon Gold potatoes, peeled and cut into ½-inch dice (about 2 cups)
- 2 medium ripe tomatoes, peeled, seeded, and cut into ½-inch dice (skip this ingredient if tomatoes are flavorless)
  Salt and freshly ground black pepper
- ¼ cup chopped fresh flat-leaf parsley

1. Place the beans in a saucepan with 6 cups water over high heat. Bring to a boil and simmer for 40 to 60 minutes or until tender. (Do NOT undercook the beans.) Drain and set aside.

2. Place the clams in a large pot with 2 cups water and set over high heat. When the water boils, cover the pot and cook for 4 minutes. Remove the cover and quickly (but gently) stir the clams. Cook an additional 4 minutes or until most of the clams have opened. Remove the open clams to a large bowl. Continue cooking a few minutes until almost all of the clams have opened; discard any unopened clams. Drain the clam broth into a large measuring cup. When the clams cool, remove the meat (you should have 2 cups) and refrigerate.

3. Meanwhile, cook the bacon in a large pot until brown and crispy. Remove and reserve. Pour off all but 1 tablespoon of bacon fat and add the olive oil. Add the onion, bay leaves, thyme, and red pepper and stir to coat. Reduce the heat to medium-low, cover, and cook for 8 minutes or until the onion is translucent. Add the garlic and cook for 2 minutes. Add the reserved clam broth, being careful not to pour off any grit that has settled to the bottom. Add the potatoes, stir, bring to a simmer, cover, and cook for 10 minutes. If you like, mash or puree half the beans (for a thicker chowder) and add the whole beans, the pureed beans, and the tomatoes and cook for an additional 10 minutes. Remove the bay leaves. Roughly chop the clams. Remove the pot from the heat, add the clams, and let sit for 2 minutes covered. Taste for salt and pepper. Serve with a sprinkling of reserved bacon and chopped parsley.

A $90 Electric Knife Sharpener?

One of the best cooks I ever met, Marie Briggs, was a Vermonter who had only about $200 worth of cookware. Yet, I do admit, a few kitchen gadgets are indeed worth the money. Here is my short list of kitchen tools that I have come to rely on almost every day.

ELECTRIC KNIFE SHARPENER

The three-stage **Chef's Choice Diamond Hone Professional Sharpener, model 110**, is the essential kitchen gadget. (See page 144 for more information.) It retails for around $90. Do NOT purchase the cheaper two-stage model that costs only $60 — it doesn't regrind the knife blade, a step that is crucial when your knife edge is really dull.

GARLIC PRESS

Mincing garlic can be a labor- and time-intensive, difficult chore. The garlic is sticky and will cling to your cutting board, knife, and fingers. A possible way to solve this dilemma is the garlic press. This tool can deliver speed, ease, and a comfortable separation of garlic from fingers. The use of a garlic press also enhances the flavor, since the finer a clove is cut, the more flavor is released from its broken cells. A good garlic press breaks down the cloves more than an average cook would with a knife and should ensure a consistently fine texture, meaning a better distribution of garlic within a dish.

My favorite garlic press, the **Zyliss SUSI DeLuxe Garlic Press** ($7.99), comprises two handles connected by a hinge. At the end of one handle is a small, perforated hopper; at the end of the other is a plunger that fits snugly inside that hopper. The garlic cloves in the hopper get crushed by the descending plunger when you squeeze the handles together, and the puree is extruded through the perforations in the bottom of the hopper. This garlic press has a classic design and is light, effective, easy to handle, and comfortable for all users. It also consistently produced the finest, most even garlic puree and handled unpeeled garlic and small chunks of fresh ginger without incident.

THERMOMETER/TIMER

A great gadget for roasting is the **Polder Cooking Thermometer/Timer** ($24.99). This item has a probe that is designed to be left in a roast as it cooks. A long wire connects the probe (lodged in the food, in the oven) to the base unit (which is either sitting on a nearby counter or attached to the outside of the oven door via a magnet). This gadget allows you to monitor the internal temperature of the food you're cooking without having to open the oven door. You can preset a target temperature using the alarm feature, and it will beep loudly when that temperature is reached. For other uses, it can also be left in pots of hot oil or sugar syrup, providing a precise temperature readout to its base unit, sitting a safe distance away. This item has Fahrenheit and centigrade readouts, outstanding readability, and a reasonable price. For an instant-read thermometer (without a timer), the best model is the **Thermapen**, which retails for a whopping $79.95 (contact www.kingarthurflour.com for more information). It handles reading temperatures higher than 500 degrees and has a huge half-inch-high digital readout; the last ⅛ inch of the probe tip provides temperature readings. The probe folds into the body of the thermometer, and when it hinges open, it turns the digital readout on. You can't buy a more useful kitchen tool.

PLASTIC MANDOLINE/SLICER

I bought a French mandoline back in the 1970s from Charles LaMalle in New York City. It is a work of art but, in my opinion, hard to use. (A mandoline contains a metal or plastic trough that has a variety of slicing blades inserted into it. The food is moved down the trough over the blade. The mandolin produces very thin slices and can also cut foods into julienne, french fries, ripples, and lattices. The latter two are used for garnishes.) These days, there are a variety of manufacturers (Joyce Chen, Börner, etc.) who make plastic mandolines that cost from $10 to $50. I have a German model (**GSD**), which works very well. They are indispensable for thinly slicing foods such as potatoes.

ELECTRIC KNIFE

Did I say essential? Well, you can live without this item, but I have grown quite fond of it after it won a testing at *Cook's Illustrated*. It carves meat, as you might expect (I remove entire sections of turkey breast at Thanksgiving and then slice them with this gadget), but it also delicately slices pecan pie, quesadillas, cakes, and pastries. The winner in our testing was the **Black & Decker Ergo Electric Knife** (now referred to as model EK550), which sells for about $27.

MICROPLANE GRATER/ZESTER

The **Microplane Grater/Zester** looks like a rasp with a black plastic handle. It has a narrow blade and fine teeth that do an excellent (and quick) job of grating everything from lemon zest to ginger. It also removes the zest (the outer peel) of the lemon/lime/orange without including any of the bitter pith. At less than $15 ($13.95 or so), this gadget is a must. Note that Microplane makes quite a few graters, some with larger blades and others with no handle at all. I recommend the grater/zester as an all-purpose kitchen tool.

CORN SOUP, TWO WAYS

CORN SOUP #1

A corn stripper quickly turns fresh ears of corn into a smooth,
milky puree that is my preferred base for making soup.
The finished soup has bits of onion and ginger and a great corn flavor.

CORN SOUP #2

If you don't have a corn stripper, you can cut the whole kernels off the cob
with a chef's knife. The soup must be pureed before serving because the kernels
are still pretty tough. The corn stripper method, however, produces a richer, more
luxurious soup since only the corn "milk" (the inside of the kernel) is used.

Rethinking Corn Soup

Corn soup and corn chowder are only worth making for a few weeks out of the year, when corn is so fresh and plentiful that one gets tired of simply eating it freshly boiled on the cob. But I am no fan of complicated recipes for corn soup, as the very essence of corn is no-nonsense simplicity. My goal, therefore, was to pare this recipe down to its bones and then add in a flavor or two to make it more than a bowlful of cooked, pureed kernels. ▶◀

I rarely demand that home cooks perform a task that requires a special tool, but, in this case, I am going to make an exception. After much testing, I have found that "milking" the kernels, thus leaving the tough outer skins still attached to the cob, produces a vastly superior soup. The only really practical method for achieving this is to purchase an inexpensive corn "stripper," a foot-long metal or wooden trough that has metal teeth that pierce the kernels as you slide the cob down the chute. A dozen ears can be milked in three or four minutes. (A variation on the recipe using whole kernels has also been included.)

Next, I had to decide between a chowder and a soup. The former includes diced potatoes; the latter doesn't. Having tried the recipe both ways, I found that the potatoes were an unwelcome complication; they need to be washed and diced, and their texture and flavor simply competed with the corn. So, soup it was.

Now I had a simple working recipe: milked corn, diced onion, half-and-half, chicken stock, salt, and pepper. I sautéed the onion very briefly in a bit of butter, added the rest of the ingredients, and simply heated them. It was good, but I wanted to make the recipe a bit more interesting. I added some minced ginger along with the onion, and this made for a nice pairing. Finally, to give the broth more depth, I added 1 cup coconut milk. This was too much, so I stepped it back to ½ cup, which was just right. After many test soups, I also dumped the half-and-half—it simply dulled the flavor of the corn. A final garnish of snipped chives added color and a fresh accent.

The whole recipe can be made in about 15 minutes, and it is special enough to serve at a fancy dinner party.

Corn Soup with Coconut Milk and Ginger

There is a lot of confusion about coconut milk, coconut cream, and cream of coconut. Cream of coconut is a sweetened product used primarily for making drinks; it contains thickeners and emulsifiers. Coconut milk and coconut cream are made by steeping coconut in water or milk, respectively. These are unsweetened products and are somewhat interchangeable in terms of commercial nomenclature. I use Thai Kitchen Pure Coconut Milk, which is available in supermarkets nationwide. An easy way to mince chives is to snip them with scissors. Be sure to simmer this soup GENTLY, as overcooking can cause the mixture to curdle.

2	tablespoons unsalted butter
1	small onion, chopped fine (about ½ cup)
2	cups milked corn (from about 8 ears of corn)
2	teaspoons minced ginger
½	cup coconut milk or coconut cream (NOT cream of coconut)
1	cup chicken stock
	Salt and freshly ground black pepper
¼	cup snipped or minced chives

Heat a 12-inch skillet or large saucepan with the butter over medium-low heat. When the butter is melted, add the onion and cook for 4 minutes, stirring frequently. Do NOT brown the onions. Add the corn, ginger, coconut milk, and chicken stock; simmer gently for 2 minutes. Add salt and pepper to taste. Serve garnished with chives.

VARIATION
Whole-Kernel Corn Soup

If you don't have a corn stripper, use this variation.

2	tablespoons unsalted butter
4	cups fresh corn kernels (from about 6 large ears)
1	cup diced onion
1	cup coconut milk or coconut cream (NOT cream of coconut)
2	teaspoons minced ginger
2	cups chicken stock
	Salt and freshly ground black pepper
¼	cup snipped or minced chives

1. Heat a 12-inch skillet or large saucepan over high heat for 2 minutes. Add the butter. When the butter has melted, add the corn kernels and onion and sauté over medium-high heat for 3 minutes, stirring frequently. Add the coconut milk and simmer for 2 minutes. Add the ginger and puree the mixture in a blender or food processor until smooth.

2. Rinse out the pan and return the mixture to it. Add the chicken stock, bring back to a simmer, and cook gently for 5 minutes. Add salt and pepper to taste. Serve garnished with chives.

Beet Soup Worth Eating

I say "beet soup" and you say, "no thanks." Well, maybe that is because you have had a particularly dreadful version of borscht, a recipe that ranges from a cold, lifeless puree to a hearty, workingman's meat soup. When I think of beet soup, however, I think of the jewel of root vegetables — bright in color and flavor and uniquely suited to exciting ingredient combinations. ▶◀

The first question was how to cook the beets. So I roasted the first batch and then simmered the second round in chicken stock. The roasted beet variation had a deeper and more intense flavor. Now I wanted to perfect the method. I found that peeling the beets first and then cutting them into 1-inch chunks allowed the juices to caramelize in the high-heat oven, thus producing more flavor. I tested salting them before cooking, which also improved the taste. Covering the beets for most of the cooking time prevented them from drying out, although a brief period uncovered toward the end of baking concentrated their flavor. As for oven temperature, 425 degrees was best; at higher temperatures, the beets took on a dark, roasted flavor that was overpowering.

Thinking that the soup would need some thickening, I tried adding half of a cooked, starchy potato as well as cooked rice. Neither was necessary; the soup was fine on its own. As for aromatics, I tested onion, celery, carrot, garlic, leek, and shallot and settled on just the onion for a simple, nonintrusive flavor. As for other flavors, cumin seeds paired with ginger were a perfect marriage with the beets — vibrant, earthy, and sharp. Toasting the cumin seeds in a small skillet really boosted the flavor. I also added lime juice and honey to further enhance the competition between sweet and sour.

Since borscht is usually served with sour cream, I wanted to test the addition of dairy. Yogurt was too tart. A half cup of heavy cream was nice — it adds a velvety smoothness — but I also liked the soup without it. For a garnish, sour cream does work well, as suggested by thousands of classic recipes.

Beet Soup with Toasted Cumin and Ginger

SERVES 6

Smaller beets tend to have more flavor than larger ones, although they take a bit more time to peel.

2	pounds beets, about 10 medium (2 inches in diameter)
2½	tablespoons vegetable oil
½	teaspoon table salt
1½	teaspoons cumin seeds
2	medium onions, roughly chopped
2	tablespoons minced ginger
6	cups chicken stock
1½	tablespoons honey
2	tablespoons lime juice
½	cup heavy cream, optional
	Freshly ground black pepper
	Minced chives for garnish, optional
	Sour cream for garnish, optional

1. Heat the oven to 425 degrees. Rinse the beets, trim the tops and bottoms, then peel and cut them into 1-inch chunks. Toss the beets in a roasting pan with 1 tablespoon of the oil and sprinkle them with ¼ teaspoon salt. Cover with aluminum foil and roast for 30 minutes. Remove the foil and continue to cook for about 10 minutes or until the beets are cooked through.

2. Place the cumin seeds in a nonstick skillet and toast over medium heat until they darken and are very aromatic, about 3 minutes.

3. Heat the remaining 1½ tablespoons oil in a soup pot or large saucepan. Add the onions and cook, stirring frequently, for about 5 minutes, until they have softened but not browned. Add the ginger and toasted cumin seeds and cook for an additional 2 minutes. Add the stock and the remaining ¼ teaspoon salt and bring to a boil. Reduce the heat to maintain a simmer, cover, and cook for 15 minutes. Add the beets and simmer for 5 minutes.

4. Puree the soup in a blender or food processor in batches. Return it to the pot and add the honey, lime juice, and optional heavy cream and bring back to a simmer. Adjust the seasonings with salt and pepper to taste. Ladle the soup into bowls and garnish with chives and sour cream, if desired.

Better Tomato Soup

If your childhood memories include Ed Sullivan, Hayley Mills, and Fred MacMurray, you probably associate tomato soup with Campbell's. Unfortunately, Campbell's was judged in a *Cook's Illustrated* blind tasting as bland and hardly worth the effort of opening the can. I wanted big tomato flavor with complexity, a soup that could be eaten on its own without a sandwich to make it interesting. I also wanted a recipe that could be made in the dead of winter with canned, not fresh, tomatoes. ▶◀

In the November/December 1999 issue of *Cook's Illustrated,* we published an excellent recipe for cream of tomato soup. The trick was roasting canned tomatoes with a sprinkling of brown sugar. Still, as good as it was, I was searching for a pairing of flavors that would give the soup a more complex flavor profile. The solution? Well, since I had to roast tomatoes in a hot oven, I decided to roast a red pepper as well, which gave the soup a wonderful smoky flavor and a sweetness that reduced the sugar in the recipe to just ½ teaspoon. The technique was simple enough: I used a very hot oven (500 degrees), lined a jelly-roll pan with foil, and roasted the peppers skin-side down after cutting them into 1-inch strips. When the skin was black and had blistered (which takes less than 15 minutes), I removed the peppers from the oven and folded up the foil to let them steam in their own heat. (This facilitates removal of the dark, bitter skins.) I then roasted the tomatoes in a similar manner, which took only 20 minutes.

Wanting still more flavor, I added onion to the recipe, sautéing it till softened but not browned, along with a garlic clove. All of the above ingredients were then simmered in tomato juice and chicken stock for about 20 minutes. To add a bit of contrast, I decided to add an herbaceous accent to the soup. After some experimentation, I settled on a garnish of simple pesto made from basil leaves, olive oil, and salt.

Roasted Tomato and Red Pepper Soup

This recipe is best made with canned tomatoes, which have more flavor than most fresh tomatoes you will find in the supermarket.

- 1 red bell pepper, seeded and cut into 1-inch strips
- 2 tablespoons olive oil
- 2 (28-ounce) cans whole tomatoes, packed in juice, drained and seeded, 3 cups liquid reserved
- 1 medium onion, cut into ½-inch dice (about 1½ cups)
- 1 garlic clove, finely chopped or pressed
- 1½ cups chicken stock
- ½ teaspoon sugar
- 1 tablespoon finely chopped fresh marjoram or tarragon
  Salt and freshly ground black pepper

1. Adjust an oven rack to the upper-middle position and heat the oven to 500 degrees. Line a jelly-roll pan or rimmed cookie sheet with foil (heavy-duty is best). Toss the pepper strips with 1 tablespoon of the olive oil and place them skin-side down on the pan. Roast until they have softened and large black blisters appear on the skin side, 12 to 14 minutes. Remove the pan from the oven and carefully pull up the ends of the foil around the peppers to make a closed package. Transfer the package to a plate and allow to cool. Once again line the pan with foil. Spread the tomatoes in a single layer. Roast for about 20 minutes, or until the liquid has evaporated and the tomatoes have started to brown (this will tend to be on the side in contact with the pan rather than the top). Open the foil packet with the pepper and remove the blistered skin.

2. Heat the remaining 1 tablespoon oil in a heavy nonreactive saucepan over medium heat. Add the onion and stir to coat with the oil. Reduce the heat to low and cook, covered, for 10 to 12 minutes, stirring occasionally, or until the onions are soft. Add the garlic and cook for an additional 2 minutes. Add the prepared tomatoes, the red pepper, reserved tomato juice, chicken stock, and sugar and cover; increase the heat and bring to a boil. Reduce the heat to low and simmer, covered, for 20 minutes. Add the marjoram and cook for an additional 5 minutes. Season to taste with salt and pepper and serve immediately, adding a dollop of Rough Pesto to each portion.

Rough Pesto

This "pesto" contains no pine nuts or Parmesan to dull the flavor of the basil.

- 2 cups tightly packed fresh basil leaves
- 6 tablespoons extra-virgin olive oil
  Salt

Using a food processor or mortar and pestle, crush the basil, oil, and salt to taste to form a rough paste.

The Case of the Dull Asparagus

Most of us simply steam asparagus and serve it as an unadorned side dish. I wanted to find a cooking method that would enhance its full flavor while adding a quick, light sauce that would complement rather than obscure its subtle taste. ▶◀

Most vegetables, especially root vegetables, can be cooked in a very hot oven in a roasting pan. I opted for a skillet, as I also wanted to throw together a quick pan sauce. Working with 1½ pounds asparagus (enough for four to six people), I found that a 12-inch skillet was necessary, although the spears did not all fit in one layer. I quickly determined that oven temperature was key. At 400 degrees, it took the asparagus a full 20 minutes or more to cook; at 450 degrees, that cooking time was almost halved, and the asparagus gained a great deal of flavor. (Higher temperatures dried out the tips.) I found it helpful to purchase asparagus that is of a relatively even diameter to promote even cooking. Also, most of my testing was done with moderately thin stalks — neither the hulking tree trunks nor the pencil-thin varieties often seen in stores at the height of the season.

For the sauce, I wanted to keep it light and simple. I removed the asparagus from the skillet (be VERY careful not to burn yourself; the skillet handle will be EXTREMELY hot), put it on a warmed plate, and then started cooking. I started with a tablespoon of olive oil and then added 1½ cups diced tomatoes (about 3 medium). I quickly discovered that it is very important to keep the dice small, because they cook faster that way. For flavorings, I tried vinegar, lemon juice, onion, shallots, and garlic. The only winner was the lemon juice. For herbs, I tested basil, parsley, tarragon, chives, mint, and marjoram, with basil and parsley emerging as the only strong candidates.

Now I had the simplest, freshest possible sauce. Add olive oil to the hot skillet over medium heat, sauté the diced tomatoes with a bit of salt for two or three minutes, remove the skillet from the heat, and add lemon juice, basil, pepper, and a tablespoon of good olive oil. Check the seasonings and pour the sauce over the asparagus — and you're done.

Finally, a combination of anchovies, capers, and olives also worked well with the asparagus. This variation is included, as well.

High-Roast Asparagus with Fresh Tomato-Basil Sauce

SERVES 4 TO 6 AS A SIDE DISH

Moderately thin stalks are best, neither pencil-thin nor large lumber-size. Keep in mind that the thickness of the asparagus will affect roasting times. Use firm, ripe tomatoes.

1½	pounds asparagus, rinsed and tough ends snapped off
3	tablespoons best-quality olive oil
¼	teaspoon table salt
3	medium tomatoes, cored, seeded, and cut into ½-inch dice (about 1½ cups)
1	tablespoon lemon juice
2	tablespoons chopped fresh basil or flat-leaf parsley
	Freshly ground black pepper

1. Heat the oven to 450 degrees and warm a serving plate in the oven as it heats up (remove when hot). Place the asparagus in a heavy-duty, ovenproof 12-inch skillet. Toss with 1 tablespoon of the oil and ⅛ teaspoon of the salt. Roast in the oven until the asparagus is just tender, 10 to 15 minutes depending on the thickness of the stalks.

2. Carefully remove the skillet from the oven (it's VERY hot), turn the asparagus onto the warmed plate, and cover to keep warm. Place the skillet over medium heat. Add 1 tablespoon of the oil and swirl the pan to coat the bottom. Add the tomatoes and the remaining ⅛ teaspoon salt. Cook, stirring occasionally, until the tomatoes have heated through and softened slightly and started to exude juice, 2 to 3 minutes. Off heat, stir in the lemon juice, basil, a few grinds of pepper, and the remaining 1 tablespoon oil. Taste for seasoning, adding salt and pepper if needed. Spoon the tomato mixture over the asparagus and serve immediately.

VARIATION

Asparagus with Tomatoes, Anchovies, Capers, and Olives

Add 1 large or 2 small chopped anchovies to the pan when adding the initial table-spoon of olive oil in step 2. Cook until the anchovies start to break down, about 1 minute. Add the tomatoes and 1 table-spoon drained capers but omit the salt in step 2. Off heat, add 6 coarsely chopped oil-cured or Kalamata olives along with the other ingredients.

Fresh Creamed Corn

Every summer, I plant almost a full acre of sweet corn in a small field just off the dirt road that heads toward town. Given my large supply of summer corn, I have developed recipes for chowders, salsas, simple soups, and even fritters. Recently, however, I wanted to perfect a recipe for creamed corn — a recipe that has been abused over the years, reduced to a pudding-like consistency, sweetened, and made virtually inedible. I knew that when prepared properly, creamed corn is a delicate, died-and-went-to-heaven dish made from just-picked corn with a little butter, a dash of cream, salt, and a few grindings of black pepper. ▶◀

I soon discovered that the key to this recipe is milking the kernels. If you simply trim off the kernels whole, none of the corn milk (the liquid inside the kernels) will be liberated. The easiest method is to use a "corn stripper," which both removes the kernels and milks them at the same time. A corn stripper is made of either metal or wood and looks like a foot-long trough with small metal teeth that slice open the kernels, pressing out the milk. If you don't have one, you're out of luck, as using a knife to perform this task is too much work even for me.

I tested the use of butter and cream, finding that 4 tablespoons butter to ½ cup cream is about right with a dozen ears of corn. Cooking time has to be short, eight minutes being just enough time to eliminate a raw flavor but long enough to meld together the simple ingredient list. The use of salt and pepper is crucial here. I find that freshly ground black pepper (or a pinch of cayenne) is essential to perk up the smooth, creamy taste of the creamed corn. Don't bother making this recipe with old, store-bought corn. It has to be fresh, juicy, and delicate.

Fresh Creamed Corn

As with the corn soup on page 30, a corn stripper is necessary to make quick work of the corn. By the way, milked corn can be frozen successfully in freezer bags and then used for creamed corn or corn soup. I put away about 5 gallons every August.

12	ears fresh-picked corn, husked and silked
4	tablespoons unsalted butter
½	cup heavy cream
¾	teaspoon table salt
	Cayenne pepper or freshly ground black pepper

Using a corn stripper, milk the corn (see page 38) into a large bowl. Cut off the kernels and add them to the bowl. Melt the butter in a large skillet. Add the corn, all of its liquid, and the cream. Cook over medium heat, stirring occasionally, until the mixture thickens and bubbles, and the corn no longer tastes raw, about 8 minutes. Add the salt and a pinch of cayenne or plenty of black pepper to taste. Serve.

VARIATION

Creamed Corn with Onion and Bacon

If the corn is very fresh and very sweet, don't bother with this variation. If, however, the corn needs some help, this version adds flavor.

Cook 4 pieces of thick-cut smoked bacon in a skillet. Remove to paper towels and pour off all but 1 tablespoon bacon grease. Add the butter to the pan plus ½ cup chopped onion. Sauté for 5 minutes over medium-low heat. Proceed with the master recipe, but crumble the reserved bacon and stir it into the corn mixture just before serving.

Dressing Up Mashed Potatoes

One could easily make a case for leaving well enough alone when it comes to mashed potatoes, but our family eats them at least once per week, and variations on the theme are always welcome. In particular, I wanted a dish that would be a bit dressy for company (as a side for prime rib, for example) but not so starched-collar that the potatoes lose their earthy root vegetable appeal. There is nothing worse than a bowl of mashed potatoes that have lost their culinary roots in pursuit of star power. ▶◀

I began with the most basic issue: how to cook the potatoes. At *Cook's Illustrated,* we swear by the notion of boiling potatoes in their jackets and then peeling them hot. This seems outright persnickety to me, so I usually peel, cut, and then boil the potatoes in pieces. To be fair to the *Cook's* method, however, I did a side-by-side tasting and was indeed won over by the in-the-jacket method, despite having to peel hot potatoes just before serving. I then wondered, as I did not relish the notion of peeling hot potatoes at the last minute, whether mashed potatoes could be made ahead of time. It turns out that they can indeed be made up to an hour ahead of time. Once the half-and-half has been added, place a clean kitchen towel between the pot and lid and set the pot aside. About 10 minutes before serving, remove the towel and lid and place the pot over low heat. Cook, stirring often, until very hot. Taste for seasoning. Add a speck more butter and half-and-half if the potatoes seem dry.

Now I wanted to go back and fill in the details on the basic mashed potato recipe before adding other root vegetables to the mix. In terms of potato variety, russets (dry, fluffy, and earthy) and Yukon Gold (sweet, creamy, and flavorful) were my top two choices. Salting the cooking water seemed to promote skin cracking, which made the potatoes soggy in spots (and did not seem to improve the flavor of the potatoes either), so unsalted water was fine. At *Cook's,* we suggest adding melted butter to the hot, peeled potatoes before adding any other liquid. This turned out to be very good advice, because the starch molecules become coated with fat, preventing them from turning soggy. Room-temperature butter works just fine, so there is no need to melt the butter unless it is cold. For additional liquid, half-and-half was best; cream was overwhelming, and milk or stock was too thin. Adding cold liquid proved to be a bad idea, because it cooled off the potatoes. So either bring the half-and-half to room temperature or warm it in a saucepan before adding. As far as ratios go, I found that 3 pounds potatoes worked best with 12 tablespoons butter and 1½ cups half-and-half. Now it was on to the other vegetables.

First of all, I quickly decided that the other vegetables would have to be peeled and cut before cooking, as they are very difficult to peel once cooked. Testing showed that carrots add a light, sweet flavor and beautiful color to the potatoes. I found that they worked best when added at a proportion of 50 percent (by weight) of the potatoes. Any more than that and the mix was too sweet and lost its rich texture. They cook in about 10 minutes and should be added to the cooking pot once the potatoes have cooked for about 15 minutes. Surprisingly, I didn't need to adjust the butter or half-and-half. Parsnips, one of my favorite root vegetables, worked well and should be used in the same manner as carrots. White turnips are bitter and thin, but yellow turnips (often referred to as rutabagas) are much better. They work well when added in equal proportion to the potatoes. Yellow turnips should be peeled and cut into 1¼-inch chunks that cook in the same amount of time as the potatoes, about 25 minutes. Once again, the butter and half-and-half remained the same. Celery root is interchangeable with the turnips in terms of technique and cooking time.

The vegetables need to be drained after cooking and should rest until you can bear to hold the potatoes in a double layer of paper towels as you peel them with a paring knife. The peeling is easy; the skins come off in big pieces. If you prefer a smooth, refined texture, use a ricer or food mill — the rest of us are perfectly happy with a potato masher. With the mashed vegetables in the warm cooking pot, add the butter and stir until melted and combined. Add the salt, pepper, and half-and-half and turn the burner to its lowest setting. Stir often until the potatoes are piping hot.

If you want to dress up this recipe, use the onion mixture that follows as a topping.

Mashed Potatoes with Carrots or Parsnips

SERVES 6

Mashed potatoes will hold for up to an hour and therefore do not have to be made at the last minute. See the variation on page 42 that uses yellow turnips or celery root.

2	pounds russet or Yukon Gold potatoes, unpeeled and scrubbed
1	pound carrots or parsnips, peeled and cut into 2-inch lengths, the thickest pieces halved or quartered lengthwise
12	tablespoons (1½ sticks) unsalted butter, at room temperature
2	teaspoons kosher salt

Freshly ground black pepper
1½ **cups half-and-half, at room
    temperature or warmed**

1. Place the potatoes in a large saucepan with enough water to cover by 1 inch. Bring to a boil over high heat. Reduce the heat to maintain a simmer and cook, covered, for 15 minutes. Add the carrots or parsnips and continue to cook until just tender (a paring knife or skewer can be poked in and out with little resistance), 10 to 15 minutes more. Drain.

2. When the potatoes are cool enough to handle through a double thickness of paper towel, remove the skins using a paring knife and cut into quarters. Pass the vegetables through a ricer or food mill back into the warm saucepan, or return the vegetables to the warm saucepan and mash with potato masher. Add the butter and stir gently until fully melted and well combined. Add the salt and pepper to taste and the half-and-half and stir gently to combine. Place over low heat and stir often until the potatoes are very hot, 2 to 4 minutes depending on the width of your saucepan. Taste for seasoning, adding salt and pepper if necessary. Serve immediately.

VARIATIONS

Mashed Potatoes with Yellow Turnip (Rutabaga) or Celery Root
Reduce the potatoes to 1½ pounds and omit the carrots or parsnips. Place 1½ pounds yellow turnip (I prefer small yellow turnips rather than the huge

rutabagas sold at some supermarkets) or celery root, peeled and cut into 1¼-inch pieces, in the water with the potatoes and cook both vegetables until just tender, 25 to 30 minutes. Continue with step 2.

Make-Ahead Mashed Potatoes
Once the half-and-half has been added in step 2, place a clean kitchen towel over the pan and cover with the lid. Let sit for up to 1 hour. About 10 minutes before serving, remove the lid and towel and place the pan over low heat, stirring often, until piping hot. If the potatoes have stiffened or dried out a bit, add a small amount of butter and half-and-half.

Onion-Anchovy-Parsley Topping
Don't be afraid of the anchovies. They add flavor but not a fishy taste. Spoon this topping over the mashed potatoes just before serving.

2 **tablespoons high-quality olive oil**
2 **tablespoons unsalted butter**
2 **anchovy fillets**
3 **medium onions, coarsely chopped**
¼ **teaspoon table salt**
2 **tablespoons chopped fresh flat-leaf
   parsley**

Heat the oil and butter in a large skillet with a lid. When the butter foam subsides, add the anchovies and cook for 2 minutes over medium-low heat. Add the onions and salt, cover, and cook for 20 minutes. Stir in the parsley and keep warm until needed.

Steamed Potatoes Made Simple

The simplest recipes are often the best, especially when it comes to a vegetable side dish, which should display the essence of the main ingredient without unnecessary folderol. In the case of potatoes, it's best not to bury the scented, loamy taste of freshly dug potatoes with an excess of butter, cream, or cheese. Small red potatoes, if treated with respect, also do a very nice job of showing off the main dish, playing an important but purely secondary role. Loyal subjects know it's dangerous to dress better than the king. ▶◀

The first test, of course, was which type of potatoes is best for steaming. I tried russet, Yukon Gold, and red potatoes, the russets being too dry and crumbly for this preparation. The Yukon Gold potatoes were also on the dry side, but the red potatoes held their shape nicely and were moist and creamy to boot. Be warned that there is more than one type of red potato in the market. For this recipe, I preferred golf-ball-size or smaller potatoes, often referred to as red creamers, which can be halved and then steamed in just 12 minutes. If you can find only larger specimens, cut them into 1-inch dice before cooking. I tested steaming versus boiling and preferred the former, as the steamed potatoes were more likely to maintain their shape.

The next question was how to dress steamed potatoes. I wanted to be able to serve this dish hot, warm, or at room temperature, and butter was out because it would solidify as it cooled. Olive oil, therefore, was the lubricant of choice. For herbs, I experimented with rosemary, oregano, thyme, parsley, chive, marjoram, cilantro, tarragon, basil, and arugula. Many of these herbs proved to be too powerful for simple steamed potatoes, so I ended up with a combination of chives and parsley. As for other additions, I tried mustard seed, celery seed, prepared mustard, garlic, anchovies, chopped olives, and pesto, but they were all either too strong or a bit too flamboyant. I didn't want a dressy salad; I wanted a simple dish of steamed potatoes. Shallots, however, were a nice addition as were salt and pepper. This is one recipe where simplicity is paramount.

Steamed Potatoes with Chives, Shallots, and Parsley

SERVES 6 AS A SIDE DISH

Although this dish can be served hours after cooking, I found that dressing the spuds while hot and then serving them immediately was ideal, because hot potatoes absorb the flavors of the herbs and oil.

2   pounds red potatoes, golf-ball-size or smaller, washed and halved (if using larger red potatoes, cut them into 1-inch dice)

¼   cup best-quality olive oil

¼   cup finely chopped fresh chives

3   tablespoons finely chopped fresh flat-leaf parsley

1   medium shallot, finely chopped (about 2 tablespoons)

½   teaspoon table salt
    Freshly ground black pepper

Place the potatoes on a steamer rack in a pot above boiling water, cover, and steam for 10 to 12 minutes or until fork-tender. Transfer the potatoes to a large bowl and add the remaining ingredients. Toss well and serve immediately or allow to cool to room temperature.

Rutabagas and Other Mysteries

When I decry the state of home cooking in America, someone always brings up the huge variety of vegetables available in most supermarkets. True, kiwis were not widely distributed in 1965. But I was curious to find out if anyone actually purchases some of the more obscure vegetables. As a test case, I chose rutabagas (think yellow turnips), because they have been around a long time and are available everywhere, and I have never seen anybody buy one.

Let's start with market share. In the root vegetable marketplace, potatoes are king, but the market share of rutabagas peaked in 1933, and things have been going downhill ever since. The good news for rutabaga boosters is that there are other roots and tubers that get even lower market shares, including beetroot, celeriac, kohlrabi, salsify, and others that I cannot even pronounce, including skirret, scorzonera, rampions, and scolymus.

Canadians (who actually like rutabagas, at least compared with Americans) consumed only 1.48 pounds of rutabagas apiece in 2000, down from 2.12 pounds in 1997. Here in the United States, we consume 46 pounds of potatoes each per year, but only a small fraction of a pound of rutabagas. Even parsnips at 0.11 pound, endives at 0.2 pound, and papaya at 0.1 pound do considerably better.

So, my conclusion? There may be a lot of diversity in supermarkets, but the real question is whether Americans are eating anything but the mainstream foods. The answer, based on the dismal sales of rutabagas, is no.

Quick-Cooked Root Vegetables

Is there a quick and easy way to cook root vegetables that also enhances their flavor? You can roast or bake them, of course, or boil and then mash them, but I was looking for a quicker and easier method, a side dish that could be thrown together at the last minute. I also wanted a method that preserved the taste and texture of the vegetables without drying them out. ▶◀

My first thought was to put together a variation on a stir-fry but without the Chinese flavorings. I cut the vegetables into small (½-by-½-by-2-inch) pieces and cooked them in a large skillet over high heat with oil. I tried potatoes, beets, and rutabagas cooked in this manner. The potatoes overcooked on the outside before the inside was tender, beets made a huge mess and overpowered the other ingredients, and the rutabagas were quite large and a bit difficult to cut into small pieces. Carrots, turnips, and parsnips, however, worked well, although each required a different amount of cooking time. (The carrots went in first, followed by the parsnips and then the turnips.)

My next thought was to skip the stir-fry method and cook the vegetables over high heat with water, butter, salt, and sugar until the liquid reduced and created a nice glaze. The small amount of water steams/boils the vegetables and then, as the liquid evaporates, the pan is drier and the contents are sautéed. Sure enough, this worked. Now that I had plump, tender, and browned vegetables, I wanted to try to develop a couple of quick variations with lots of flavor. My favorite combination was equal amounts of lime juice and honey—2 tablespoons of each are added after the vegetables are cooked. I also developed a more traditional Asian variation with ginger, soy sauce, sherry, and sugar or maple syrup.

Ten-Minute Root Vegetables

SERVES 4 AS A SIDE DISH

You can use just one of the vegetables or any combination.

2 medium carrots cut into
  ½-by-½-by-2-inch sticks (about 2 cups)

1 tablespoon unsalted butter
1 teaspoon sugar
½ teaspoon table salt
2 small parsnips cut into
  ½-by-½-by-2-inch sticks (about 1 cup)
1 small turnip cut into ½-by-½-by-2-inch
  sticks (about 1 cup)
  Freshly ground black pepper

Bring the carrots, butter, sugar, salt, and ½ cup water to a boil over high heat in a large skillet and cook for 2 minutes. Add the parsnips and cook an additional 2 minutes. Add the turnips and continue cooking, stirring about every minute, until all of the liquid is evaporated and the vegetables are tender, browned, and shiny, about 6 minutes longer. Adjust the seasoning with salt and pepper to taste and serve immediately.

VARIATIONS

Lime and Honey Root Vegetables
In a small bowl, stir together 2 tablespoons fresh lime juice (from 2 limes) and 2 tablespoons honey. Once the vegetables are tender and browned, add the lime-honey mixture and cook, stirring constantly, for another 30 seconds or until the vegetables are evenly coated with the mixture, which will be reduced to a glaze.

Soy, Ginger, and Maple Syrup Root Vegetables
In a small bowl, stir together 2 tablespoons soy sauce (light preferred), 2 tablespoons sherry, and 1 tablespoon maple syrup or granulated sugar. Substitute 1 tablespoon vegetable oil for the butter. Once the vegetables are tender and browned, make a well in the center of the skillet. Add 1 tablespoon finely minced ginger and 1 teaspoon peanut or vegetable oil and mash with the back of a spatula or wooden spoon. Cook until fragrant, about 5 seconds, and stir into the vegetables. Add the soy sauce mixture and cook, stirring constantly, until the vegetables are evenly coated and the mixture is reduced to a glaze, about 30 seconds longer.

Better Lentils and Greens

Lentils and greens are an ancient culinary duo, yet many recipes for this classic pairing are lackluster — watery, underseasoned, or diluted with unnecessary ingredients. I wanted simplicity itself, a dish that perfectly highlights the marriage of earthy lentils to fresh greens. ▶◀

There are two types of lentils generally available: brown lentils (light brown in color and found in all grocery stores) and the smaller, dark green French, or indigo, lentils (usually available in more upscale markets). A taste test revealed that the French lentils were more intensely flavored and a bit sweeter than the earthier, duller, "brown" lentils found in grocery stores. The prices are similar — $1.19 per pound for French lentils and $0.99 per pound for brown lentils — so purchase the French lentils if you can find them.

Although most lentil recipes do not call for soaking, I wanted to determine whether soaking improved their texture. Although the soaked beans were plumper than the unsoaked (and took just 15 minutes to cook versus 25 minutes), the difference in taste and mouthfeel of the lentils was negligible. My next question was whether or not to salt the cooking water. I found that cooking 1 cup lentils in 3 cups water with ½ teaspoon salt resulted in flavor that was superior to that of lentils cooked in unsalted water. I also tried adding a bay leaf, garlic cloves, or a clove-studded onion and found that the lentils were best left to their own devices so that their subtle flavor would easily come through. Finally, I tried cooking the lentils in stock instead of water and found no improvement.

Many authentic recipes call for borage — a green that is generally unavailable in the United States — so I tested escarole, kale, mustard, and even rabe and found the taste of spinach to be my favorite, with Swiss chard a close runner-up. In particular, I thought the iron-rich taste and tender leaf of spinach was a great match with the lentils. The stems need to be removed and chopped into about 1-inch pieces.

Next, I tried several additional ingredients that might enhance the flavor of the dish. Sautéed onion was a winner, as was minced garlic. Italian recipes in particular often pair lentils with sausage or pancetta. I tried crumbled sausage as well as browned bacon in the recipe. Truthfully, the texture and flavor were overpowering, and I preferred the dish in its simplest form.

WHICH GREENS WORK BEST WITH LENTILS?

SPINACH

Iron-rich flavor and tender texture. My top choice.

SWISS CHARD

The runner-up in my testing.

ESCAROLE

Okay but not great.

MUSTARD GREENS

Chewy and bitter.

BROCCOLI RABE

Overpowered the lentils.

KALE

Too tough and too assertive.

My last test was to determine exactly how to put the greens and lentils together. I found that sautéing the greens and then adding the lentils was preferable to adding the greens to the pot of lentils. Salt and freshly ground pepper are crucial to the dish — both the beans and greens are crying out for plenty of both.

Lentils with Spinach and Onion

SERVES 4 TO 6

This dish is good as a side dish to a roast or chops but is great as a simple supper served over rice with a squeeze of lemon, which is a nice counterpoint to the deep, earthy flavors.

1	cup lentils, French (dark green) preferred, rinsed and picked over
	Salt and freshly ground black pepper
1	tablespoon unsalted butter
1	tablespoon olive oil
1	medium onion, halved and thinly sliced
1	medium garlic clove, minced or pressed
12	ounces fresh spinach or Swiss chard, thoroughly washed, stems removed and cut into 1-inch pieces
	Lemon wedges, optional

1. Place the lentils in a medium saucepan with 3 cups water and ½ teaspoon salt. Bring to a boil and lower the heat to maintain a simmer. Cook until the lentils are tender and absorb most of the liquid, 25 to 30 minutes.

2. Heat a large heavy-duty skillet over medium heat. Add the butter and olive oil. When the butter stops foaming, add the onion and sauté until the edges of the onion are light golden brown, about 7 minutes. Add the garlic and cook for an additional 2 minutes. Add the spinach and sauté until completely wilted and tender, 2 to 4 minutes. Add the lentils and fold the ingredients together with a spatula or wooden spoon. If there is too much liquid, raise the heat to high for 1 to 2 minutes. Adjust the seasoning with additional salt and pepper to taste. Serve with a squeeze of fresh lemon juice, if desired.

A Bottle of Italian Olive Oil in Every Kitchen?

I am now going to blow the whistle on Italian olive oil. You've seen the ads, read the magazine articles, and made the recipes that use olive oil as if it were some sort of culinary elixir. Well, here is how all of that happened: Many years ago, the Italian Olive Oil Commission started inviting food editors and writers for tours of Italy. Mind you, these were FREE tours. The unstated quid pro quo was that articles would appear in American publications about Italian cooking, especially about the virtues of Italian olive oil. Some of the best-known names in the business went on these boondoggles. That's one good reason why in the United States, imports of Italian olive oil rose from 64 million pounds in 1982 to 366 million pounds in 1998.

The next thing you should know is that much "Italian" olive oil contains a blend of oils from various countries, including Spain, Greece, and Tunisia. (A recent ruling by U.S. Customs may require that the true country of origin be listed on the packaging.) In fact, the word *Italian* on the label simply means that the oil was blended in Italy—it doesn't necessarily have to be from Italian olives. This does not necessarily imply lower quality, but it is clearly a marketing ploy. Would you pay more for Italian or Tunisian olive oil?

As far as cooking goes, when you heat olive oil, most of the delicate flavors are lost. When sautéing, for example, you aren't going to find a big difference between an inexpensive and an expensive olive oil or, in many cases, even a cheap vegetable oil. The heat will see to that. (Don't forget that the Italians had lots of olives and lots of cheap olive oil, so they used it for everything. When was the last time you saw an olive tree in your backyard?) So for cooking purposes, I use a cheap supermarket olive oil or vegetable oil.

For drizzling or for salad dressings, however, quality does matter. That's when the $30 bottle does make sense. However, price and packaging are deceiving. Some of the nicest-looking (and most expensive) bottles are actually the worst. To test this proposition, I went out and purchased 10 different bottles of expensive extra-virgin olive oil, with prices ranging from $24 to $80 per liter. I then threw in a supermarket oil, Da Vinci, at $8.50 per liter, which had previously won a supermarket olive oil tasting at *Cook's Illustrated*. I then assembled a tasting panel (none of the members were olive oil experts; all were experienced cooks, however) to find out how the oils rated.

The cheap supermarket oil, Da Vinci, took fourth place; a moderately priced Spanish oil (Columela-Hojiblanca, $24/liter) took second place; and the winner was the second-least expensive of the premium brands (Antica Azienda Raineri, $32 per liter). The most expensive oil, Salvatore Mirisola ($80/liter), came in 10th (out of 11).

What to do? Forget about price, forget about packaging, and make up your own mind based on taste. My house brand is now the $24/liter Spanish oil, Columela.

Fine-Tuning Mustard Vinaigrette

Mustard vinaigrettes fall prey to a host of problems, including harsh vinegar, poor-quality olive oil, over-bearing mustards, and proportions that make the dressing too strong, too oily, or just plain insipid. The good news is that mustard is an excellent emulsifier, which makes for a smooth, cohesive dressing, one that holds for hours. The question is, how does one engineer the perfect mustard vinaigrette, varying the formula depending on the assertiveness of the underlying greens? ▶◀

I started off by investigating the basic ingredients: Beginning with the oil, I tested everything in my pantry, including corn oil, walnut oil, canola oil, and even grapeseed oil. Olive oil was the clear winner, although I found the $25-per-bottle brands to be a waste of money for a dressing that is so heavily influenced by mustard. Stick with extra-virgin (never use a "lite" olive oil, which has almost no flavor whatsoever), but don't break the budget.

Most vinegars sold in supermarkets are of relatively poor quality and therefore tend to taste harsh. This, I have found, is all the more true of flavored vinegars, which often start with a cheap, rough product hoping that the rosemary or tarragon will mask its defects. I tried almost 20 different types of vinegar and settled on Alessi white balsamic vinegar, which is widely available in better supermarkets and reasonably priced at about $4.50 for 12.75 ounces. It has a wonderful balance of sweetness and acidity and is neither watery nor overbearing. Stay away from regular balsamic vinegar, which has too much character for greens. A good second choice is rice vinegar, which is relatively low in acidity.

Mustard also comes in many varieties, and I began by eliminating coarse and dry mustards, as they produced truly vile vinaigrettes. Any smooth Dijon mustard works well, but avoid the fancy variations on the theme such as brown, honey, and horseradish. Just keep it simple.

My starting recipe included ¼ teaspoon salt, 1 tablespoon vinegar, 4½ tablespoons olive oil, ½ teaspoon Dijon mustard, and freshly ground black pepper. I dissolved the salt in the vinegar, added all the other ingredients and then whisked until thickened and smooth. (Kosher salt works best here — the crystals dissolve rapidly in the vinegar.) Thinking that the vinegar was a bit subdued, I decreased the olive oil to 4 tablespoons. I then reduced the mustard to ¼ teaspoon, because it was a bit overwhelming. Garlic proved to be too strong, but shallots were just right. A small amount of minced fresh herbs was also called for (parsley, marjoram, and basil were all good), adding flavor without too much personality. Finally, I had a great basic dressing for delicate greens such as Boston lettuce or even romaine.

Next, I wanted a variation that would be good with more assertive greens such as escarole. Starting with my final recipe, I increased the mustard to ½ teaspoon and replaced the shallots with garlic, making the dressing bolder. This variation is great when the underlying greens need a stronger companion. I also tried using a bit of grated Parmesan or Romano cheese, but when used in sufficient quantity to flavor the salad, the emulsion became gummy and the fresh flavor of the cheese was lost.

Although I found that the dressing keeps for two or three days in the refrigerator, the herbs need to be added at the last minute or they turn black and lose their fresh taste. However, I also noted that the garlic mellows after several hours of sitting, so it is not a bad idea to make this dressing ahead of time, adding the herbs at the last second. The emulsion holds for eight hours and can be easily reconstituted with whisking.

Classic Mustard Vinaigrette

MAKES ⅓ CUP, ENOUGH FOR 4 TO 5 SERVINGS OF GREENS

There is no need to slowly drip oil into this dressing while whisking. Once the salt is dissolved, just add the remaining ingredients and whisk away! This dressing — without the herbs — can be refrigerated in an airtight container for 3 days. Rewhisk and add the optional herbs immediately before serving.

¼   teaspoon kosher salt (or ⅛ teaspoon table salt)
1   tablespoon white balsamic vinegar
¼   cup extra-virgin olive oil
¼   teaspoon Dijon mustard
2   teaspoons finely chopped shallot
Freshly ground black pepper

½   teaspoon finely chopped fresh flat-leaf parsley, marjoram, or basil, optional

In a small bowl, combine the salt and vinegar and stir for about 10 seconds to dissolve the salt. Add the oil, mustard, shallot, and pepper to taste and whisk for 15 seconds or until the mixture is smooth, thickened, and evenly colored. If using immediately, whisk in the optional herbs.

VARIATION
Mustard Vinaigrette for Assertive Greens
This version is particularly good on stronger greens such as escarole.

Increase the mustard to ½ teaspoon and substitute ¾ teaspoon very finely minced garlic for the shallot.

Perfecting Blue Cheese Dressing

Blue cheese dressing sounds simple enough, but many cooks turn it into a Frankenstein of a recipe, adding Worcestershire sauce, chopped parsley, lemon juice, red pepper, minced garlic, garlic powder, onion, and even cream cheese. Other recipes seem to forget entirely about the blue cheese, adding so little that one can hardly taste it. The question was, how can one make a relatively simple blue cheese dressing with a creamy consistency, a tangy, slightly sweet flavor, and a big cheese taste without being heavy or overpowering? ▶◀

I started by testing four recipes, one each from *Cook's Illustrated* magazine, *The Victory Garden Cookbook*, *The Fannie Farmer Cookbook*, and *The Joy of Cooking*. I started by eliminating ingredients that seemed unnecessary and unwelcome, including cayenne, Worcestershire, minced garlic, chopped parsley, etc. The next question was consistency. Only one of these recipes used milk to thin out the dressing. The other three simply mashed blue cheese with sour cream. I found that this method produced a heavy dressing, so I tried adding a bit of milk for thinning, finally settling on buttermilk after also testing cream. Two of the recipes also added a whopping amount of mayonnaise — *The Joy of Cooking* dressing used 4 ounces blue cheese to a full cup of mayo — which left one with a dull Miracle Whip of a dressing. I found the same problem with the sour cream: Three of the four recipes used ½ cup sour cream to 2 to 4 ounces cheese, which resulted in the same bland outcome. After much fiddling, I decided that 2½ ounces blue cheese worked well with 3 tablespoons each of buttermilk and sour cream plus 2 tablespoons mayonnaise. Cream cheese, another common ingredient, was voted down because it is the essence of dull, adding none of the sprightly tang evident in sour cream. Yogurt was also tested but came up short in the flavor department and wasn't as smooth in texture as the sour cream. Now I had a recipe that was remarkably similar to the one published in *Cook's Illustrated* in its use of modest quantities of buttermilk, sour cream, and mayonnaise.

Next on the list was the vinegar. Red wine vinegar was out, because it was the wrong color and much too strong. Cider vinegar was not smooth enough in flavor. Lemon juice added off-notes to the dressing. White wine vinegar was good, but I preferred rice vinegar, because it was less acidic. As for the main ingredient, the blue cheese, I tried a variety of brands but preferred domestic blue cheeses, because they are creamier and milder.

I went back to test a bit of chopped herbs — parsley, chives, and maybe even scallion — but they simply complicated the recipe and detracted from the simplicity of the dressing. To even out the taste, both sugar and salt were needed. Although the type of blue cheese will affect the salt level, ¼ teaspoon salt ends up being about right for most cheeses. I also liked a hint of sugar; ¼ teaspoon was just enough to brighten the flavor of the cheese and round out the dressing. A few grinds of pepper were a welcome addition.

For mixing the dressing ingredients, a fork turned out to be the best and simplest method. I liked small chunks of cheese and an evenly mixed dressing. I did note that the type of cheese affects the mixing. A very moist, creamy blue cheese will be harder to mix than a drier variety. If you have a problem mashing the cheese, simply add all of the dressing ingredients at once to a bowl and then mash.

Really Good Blue Cheese Dressing

MAKES ABOUT 1 CUP, ENOUGH FOR
6 SERVINGS OF GREENS

The type of cheese will determine how much salt you will need. I find that creamier, wetter cheeses are harder to mash with a fork. With these sorts of cheeses, add all of the ingredients to the bowl at once, as the additional liquid makes the mashing easier. This sort of rich, creamy dressing is best served over a sturdy, mild green such as romaine or even iceberg. It would also work with endive and escarole.

½   cup crumbled blue cheese
     (2½ ounces)
3   tablespoons buttermilk
3   tablespoons sour cream
2   tablespoons mayonnaise
2   teaspoons rice vinegar or white wine
     vinegar
¼   teaspoon sugar
¼   teaspoon table salt
     Freshly ground black pepper

Mash the blue cheese with a fork until it is the size of small-curd cottage cheese. (If this is difficult, add the balance of the ingredients and continue mashing.) Add the buttermilk and stir to mix. Add the remaining ingredients, including pepper to taste, and stir until well combined. Adjust seasonings and serve immediately or store covered and refrigerated for up to 2 weeks.

THE PROBLEM WITH BLUE CHEESE DRESSING

BLUE CHEESE DRESSING #1
Overspiced with garlic and cayenne pepper.

BLUE CHEESE DRESSING #2
Too much mayonnaise makes this one dull.

BLUE CHEESE DRESSING #3
A mountain of parsley obscures the cheese.

BLUE CHEESE DRESSING #4
Too much cheese means a gloppy consistency.

Everyday Beet and Goat Cheese Salad

I have had more than a few goat cheese and beet salads, most of them a perfect tower of minced beets layered with herbed goat cheese and served on a white plate with a dusting of finely minced herbs. This is fussy work, certainly nothing suited to home cooking. But the pairing of sharp, richly flavored beets with mild, comforting goat cheese, both offset by greens and dressing, is a good idea, one that was worth investigation in an effort to bring it into the home kitchen. ▶◀

There are two ways to roast beets: in their skins (the most common method) or already peeled. Testing both approaches, I found that peeling before roasting allows some of the juices to rise to the surface, where they caramelize and add a lot of flavor. I found that 1-inch chunks were best, small enough to speed up roasting and to maximize the surface area that would be caramelized. When high-roasting vegetables, I always start with the pan covered in order to make sure that the vegetables get cooked through without drying out. Halfway through roasting, the foil is removed to provide direct heat to the surface of the beets, which caramelizes the sugars in the beet juice.

I tried a variety of methods for assembling this salad, including the silly restaurant technique of finely dicing the beets, placing them in ramekins, adding a layer of goat cheese, and then turning out this mini-tower onto a bed of perfectly presented greens. I did that only once and then realized that a quick and rough assembly of ingredients was just fine (and very pretty to boot). This is one case where an "elegant" dish can simply be thrown together.

This recipe does call for two different vinegars (one for the beets and one for the greens). I find that the contrast between the beets dressed with raspberry vinegar and the greens that have a more modest dressing makes for a nice marriage. (Generally speaking, I am no fan of flavored vinegars, as I find them harsh, but the pairing works well here, because the beets are so assertive and absorb much of the vinegar anyway.) This is my one fussy step, but I think that it is worth the trouble.

Chives add some spice, and the goat cheese adds a nice contrast of texture with the acidic, sharp-tasting beets. I prefer a mix of greens with this salad — some sharp, some mild. The choice is yours.

Beet and Goat Cheese Salad with Raspberry Vinegar

SERVES 4

Try to cut the beets into standard-size pieces so that they all end up being cooked to the same degree.

FOR THE BEETS

1   pound beets
1   tablespoon olive oil
1   tablespoon raspberry vinegar
   Salt and freshly ground black pepper

FOR THE SALAD GREENS

10   cups salad greens, washed, dried, and torn into bite-size pieces
4½   tablespoons high-quality olive oil
1   tablespoon white wine vinegar
⅛   teaspoon table salt
1   teaspoon minced chives

5   ounces fresh goat cheese, crumbled
   Minced fresh chives for garnish

1. For the beets: Heat the oven to 425 degrees. Peel the beets, cut them into 1-inch chunks, and toss with the oil. Place the beets in a roasting pan and tightly cover with foil. Roast 20 minutes; remove the foil, toss, and roast, uncovered, an additional 10 to 20 minutes or until tender. Allow the beets to cool to room temperature. Toss with the vinegar and salt and pepper to taste.

2. For the salad greens: Place the greens in a large salad bowl. Whisk together the oil, vinegar, salt, and minced chives. Toss the greens with half the dressing until well mixed. Add more dressing to taste.

3. To serve: Arrange the dressed greens on serving plates, top with the beets, sprinkle with the goat cheese, additional salt and pepper to taste, and the minced chives.

A Culinary Reading List

One way to become a better cook is to read about food, especially books that are histori-
cal in nature. As I read older cookbooks and narratives in bed, my wife hears the occa-
sional "Aha!" as I recognize yet one more silly technique that has survived to modern
times for no good reason at all. Or, I find that some cutting-edge restaurant technique
had already been taught by Fannie Farmer in 1900. Most of all, these books provide
context, so that the modern recipe is understood as part of an evolutionary process. So
the next time one eats a simple omelet, it will provide a link all the way back to Escoffier,
bestowing it with an honorable heritage that makes eating it an event, not just a necessity.

Samuel Chamberlain
Clémentine in the Kitchen
Modern Library, 2001
268 pages, paperback, $13.95

Samuel Chamberlain, a prolific writer and (with his wife, Narcisse) a frequent contributor
to the early *Gourmet* magazine, tells the autobiographical story of the Becks, an American family living in France who had the good fortune to employ Clémentine, a French
cook of unimaginable culinary skill and fortitude. They quit their beloved France just
before the outbreak of World War II and install themselves outside of Boston in Marble-
head. Here, Clémentine searches high and low for ingredients sufficient to continue
the pursuit of her cuisine. Anyone who has even a passing familiarity with French cooking will recognize most of the recipes, and Chamberlain's prose is kinetic, authentic,
and amusing. Why can't most modern food writers slough off their self-absorbed gravity
and just let loose with the word processor? This book explains the enthusiasm for
gourmet cooking that took hold here in America in the 1960s and 1970s and drums up
enthusiasm for all culinary pursuits, including searching the garden for escargots.

Edouard de Pomiane
French Cooking in 10 Minutes: Or Adapting to the Rhythm of Modern Life (1930)
North Point Press, 1994
142 pages, paperback, $10.00

Yes, the recipes in this book are dated — it was written in 1930 — but the idea is still
fresh. Pomiane, a well-respected food writer in his time, deconstructs home cooking in a
chatty, energetic style. The first sentence is a classic: "First of all, let me tell you that this

is a beautiful book." But the joy of this book is how he thinks about preparing food quickly. He simplifies the cook's choices, writing complete recipes in two or three short sentences. (One of my favorite directives, one "adopted" by more than one famous food writer, is, "The first thing you must do when you get home, before you take off your coat, is . . . fill a pot large enough to hold a quart of water. Put it on the fire, cover it, and bring it to a boil.") Pomiane is a cook, not a recipe follower, and anyone serious about the art of cooking would do well to spend an evening reading, or perhaps just skimming, this short book. It speaks volumes about how to *think* like a cook, the first step in becoming a good one.

Robert Clark
The Solace of Food: A Life of James Beard
Steerforth Press, 1996
357 pages, paperback, $16.00

I have enormous affection for James Beard because, not only was he helpful in launching *Cook's* magazine back in 1980, but he was also an unapologetic promoter of American cooking. In *American Cookery,* Beard presented America with the definitive American cookbook as well as a volume that would turn out to be of great anthropological value. Beard's childhood experiences, especially the picnics on the beach, were infused with a purely American magic, one that goes a long way toward explaining what is special about our immigrant cuisine. Clark writes, "The outdoors and indoors unexpectedly mingled and harmonized in sizzle and smoke; the sear of the fire on legs, arms, and cheeks; the granular cool of the sand; the low, incessant simmer of the surf." With a mother who made the best cream biscuits in America and with a large appetite for acting on life's stage, it is no wonder that Beard infused so many of us with a love of American home cooking.

Elizabeth Romer
The Tuscan Year: Life and Food in an Italian Valley
North Point Press, 1996
182 pages, paperback, $13.00

You can't spend 13 bucks more wisely than if you invest it in this terrific story of one year on the Cerotti family's Tuscan farm. It is told through the eyes of Elizabeth Romer,

continues

who moved to Tuscany in the early 1980s and who has a practiced eye for the details of a life lived firmly rooted in one place. One discovers the true origins of bruschetta, which is nothing more than toasted bread rubbed with garlic and topped with warm olive oil and salt. (Forget all the fancy toppings offered in three-star Italian restaurants.) Of course, the key to this dish is wonderful homemade saltless bread that is toasted just enough so that the inside is still soft. Fat, heady cloves of garlic, olive oil that was pressed from one's own grove, and good coarse salt also help. The Cerottis ate bruschetta for lunch, it was that good. Nothing goes to waste, there are no food fads, and there is *always* somebody cooking in that kitchen. If you want to rediscover your passion for cooking, look no further than *The Tuscan Year*. This book is so authentic and honest that most other food writers ought to be ashamed of their pursuit of food as art or social amusement.

David Mas Masumoto
Epitaph for a Peach: Four Seasons on My Family Farm
Harper, 1996
256 pages, paperback, $13.00

This is the story of a California peach farmer, David Mas Masumoto, who decides to give his Sun Crest peaches one more year before they are bulldozed into obscurity. An older variety, these peaches have great flavor but are no longer economical in an age of agribusiness. Masumoto writes about not only his efforts to make these peaches a viable crop but also his effort to find harmony on the farm and in his life. Masumoto finally decides to keep his special crop for yet another season. "The ghosts who dance in the winter fog whisper this to me. They trick me into pruning one tree and then another and another. . . . They understand the power of watching a new generation grow and become established, the young and the old all part of a whole field." If you care about cooking and eating, you care about growing as well, and this tale of one man's relationship to the food he grows will change your view of the supermarket produce section forever.

Baked Goat Cheese Salad at Home?

Virtually everyone who has been to a "fancy" restaurant sometime in the last 10 years has experienced baked goat cheese. It is breaded, baked, and then usually served over a bed of greens. Simple enough in concept, although showy in presentation — I wondered if this ubiquitous recipe would yield its secrets to a home cook. ▶◀

My first step was to investigate the coating. Dried bread crumbs, even when flavored with fresh herbs, tasted stale and uninspired. I tried toasting my own bread crumbs in a skillet with butter, and the results were substantially better. (This takes just a few minutes.) I then wondered if toasted nuts would make a better coating. On their own they were overpowering, but combined with the homemade bread crumbs, the taste and texture were perfect. I finally settled on 1 part nuts to 2 parts bread crumbs. Two teaspoons fresh thyme and just a dash of salt added to the mixture worked well with the flavor of the goat cheese. To make the bread-crumb mixture adhere to the cheese, I dipped each slice (½-inch slices were best) into extra-virgin olive oil before coating. (A 5-ounce log will give you about eight slices — enough to accommodate four salads.) I tried warming the cheese in temperatures from 300 degrees to 400 degrees. At 350 degrees, the cheese warmed through in four minutes, but at higher temperatures, the cheese was apt to become too soft in a matter of seconds. At lower temperatures, the cheese took longer with no apparent benefit.

As for the salad, I found that I preferred greens with lots of flavor, such as arugula, watercress, endive, and radicchio. Most markets sell mesclun and other mixes of baby greens that also worked well in this dish. Lettuces such as Bibb and romaine can be used as part of a mix but do not have enough flavor on their own. For four people you need about 10 cups of greens. I used a traditional vinaigrette based on 1 part vinegar to 4 parts oil along with a bit of mustard to create both flavor and a superior emulsion. I am partial to white balsamic vinegar, but regular balsamic is fine given the strong flavor of the greens. (Regular balsamic vinegar is forbidden with tender greens!)

Baked Goat Cheese Salad

SERVES 4

Make sure that you purchase fresh, soft goat cheese, not aged goat cheese, which is much stronger in flavor and drier in texture. I prefer pecans for this recipe because they have a lot of flavor and are sweet. Walnuts are bitter, and almonds don't add much flavor.

FOR THE GOAT CHEESE

⅓	cup pecan halves
2	teaspoons unsalted butter
⅔	cup fresh bread crumbs from 1–2 slices bakery-style white bread, finely chopped in a food processor
⅛	teaspoon table salt
2	teaspoons chopped fresh thyme
	Freshly ground black pepper
2	tablespoons best-quality olive oil
1	(5-ounce) log goat cheese

FOR THE SALAD

¼	teaspoon table salt
1	tablespoon balsamic vinegar, white preferred
¼	cup best-quality olive oil
¼	teaspoon Dijon mustard
1	teaspoon finely chopped shallot
	Freshly ground black pepper
10	cups mixed greens such as arugula, watercress, radicchio, endive, and/or mesclun mix, washed, dried, and torn into bite-size pieces

1. For the goat cheese: Adjust an oven rack to the center position and heat the oven to 350 degrees. Place the nuts on a baking sheet and bake for 5 minutes or until fragrant. Cool and then finely chop either by hand or in a food processor.

2. Place the butter in a medium skillet over medium heat. When the butter has stopped foaming, add the bread crumbs and cook, stirring often until golden brown. Cool. Combine the chopped nuts, toasted bread crumbs, salt, thyme, and a couple of grinds of black pepper in a small bowl. Place the oil in a small plate. Cut the goat cheese into eight slices (each about ½ inch wide). Dip the slices into the oil to coat on all sides and then coat with the crumb mixture, turning to thickly coat all sides. Place on the cool baking sheet. (The cheese may be prepared up to this point several hours ahead of time.) Bake for about 4 minutes or until the cheese is warmed through and feels soft to the touch but not melted.

3. For the salad: Meanwhile, combine the salt and vinegar in a small bowl and stir for about 10 seconds to dissolve the salt. Add the oil, mustard, shallot, and pepper to taste and whisk for about 15 seconds or until the mixture is smooth, thickened, and evenly colored. Taste for seasoning, adding additional salt and pepper if necessary. Place the greens in a large bowl, drizzle the vinaigrette over the greens, and toss to evenly coat.

4. To serve: Evenly distribute the greens onto 4 plates. Using a spatula, carefully transfer 2 rounds of warm cheese over the mound of greens. Serve immediately.

Rediscovering Greek Salad

There is no definitive recipe for Greek salad, but, as a general rule, it contains lettuce, cucumber, bell pepper, something from the onion family, tomatoes, Kalamata olives, and feta cheese. The dressing is a simple combination of oil and vinegar. At its best, Greek salad is at once crunchy, colorful, and boldly flavored. At its worst, it's a worn-out hodgepodge of poorly matched ingredients. ▶◀

For the lettuce, the backbone of this salad, I tested romaine, Boston, Bibb, red leaf, and even iceberg. It was no surprise that I found that romaine works well, but I was taken aback that I also liked the iceberg. Its sturdiness is a plus in this chunky, crunchy salad-bowl offering. I tried using smaller portions of spicier greens such as watercress, arugula, or escarole, but they were like a skunk at a lawn party — definitely unwelcome. For a salad to serve four to six people, I used 10 cups greens or two medium heads of romaine or one large head of iceberg. Whether you're using romaine or iceberg, it should be sliced into 1-inch pieces (the iceberg should also be separated a bit, because the leaves are so compact) and washed and dried.

Next, I started adding cucumber, bell pepper, onion, and tomato. I found that one half of a large cucumber was ample for the salad. If the skin is bitter, it should be peeled. (I don't think it needs to be seeded, however.) I quartered the cucumber lengthwise and cut it into ¼-inch slices. When adding bell pepper, I also think it needs to be cut into thin slices. I used half of a medium bell pepper that I cut into thirds lengthwise and then into about ⅛-inch slices. I preferred red for both the sweetness and color. I tried red onion, shallots, and scallions, and my favorite was the scallion. It was more flavorful than the shallot and less sharp than the red onion. For this recipe, I used three scallions trimmed and cut into ¼-inch slices. Ripe tomatoes add a bright note to the salad; I preferred two medium or a cup of cherry or grape tomatoes. If you're using large tomatoes, they should be cut into thin wedges or, better yet, bite-size chunks. As for the cherry or grape tomatoes, I sliced each one in half. That also makes them much easier to fork.

Radishes and carrots were nonstarters — the radishes were too sharp and the carrots too hard. I tried mint, dill, oregano, and parsley. The oregano was too strong, even

THE BOWL MATTERS

SMALL BOWL

Too many cooks toss salad greens onto the counter,
even the floor. The culprit is usually a bowl that's too small.

BIG BOWL

If you start with a large bowl that is only half filled,
you will have plenty of room to toss the greens.

finely chopped and in small amounts. The flavor of the dill didn't pair as well with the other ingredients as I had hoped. The parsley was lost and not worth the effort. The mint, however, blended well with the raw ingredients as well as with the olives and cheese and could stand up to the vinaigrette. I used 2 tablespoons thinly sliced leaves, about 10 medium.

Kalamata olives are widely available. They are a product of Greece and, along with the feta, the jewels in the crown of the Greek salad. That being said, they have big flavor, and a little goes a long way. I found that they should be pitted and sliced so that their flavor is incorporated into each bite. I also tried adding capers, but they were voted down by my tasters. As for the feta cheese, fancy versions in specialty stores are good, but the run-of-the-mill grocery-store variety was actually better for this pedestrian application. Some feta is sold already crumbled, but it turned out to be dry and taste-less — purchase feta in a solid block.

I started the dressing with ¼ cup high-quality extra-virgin olive oil and then played around with the acid and finally settled on 1 tablespoon white balsamic vinegar (or white wine vinegar) and 1 tablespoon lemon juice. To this mixture I added ¼ teaspoon salt, black pepper to taste, and ⅛ teaspoon dried oregano (a necessary ingredient in this dish). To finish the salad, I tossed the greens and vegetables gently with the dress-ing and scattered the cheese and olives over the top. The recipe is quick, easy, and a garden-fresh impromptu supper or side dish.

Better Greek Salad

SERVES 4 TO 6

For best flavor and texture, purchase a solid piece of feta cheese and crumble it yourself.

FOR THE DRESSING
- 1 tablespoon white balsamic vinegar (or white wine vinegar)
- 1 tablespoon lemon juice
- ¼ teaspoon table salt
- ¼ cup best-quality olive oil
- ⅛ teaspoon dried oregano
  Freshly ground black pepper

FOR THE SALAD
- 2 medium heads romaine lettuce or 1 medium head iceberg lettuce, cores removed and sliced into 1-inch pieces, washed, and dried (about 10 cups)
- ½ large cucumber, peeled if skin is bitter, quartered lengthwise, and cut into ¼-inch slices
- ½ red or green bell pepper, cored, seeded, cut into thirds lengthwise, and cut into ⅛-inch slices
- 3 scallions, dark green parts removed and cut into ¼-inch slices
- 2 medium tomatoes, cut into bite-size pieces or thin wedges, or 1 cup halved cherry or grape tomatoes
- 2 tablespoons thinly sliced fresh mint leaves
- 12 Kalamata olives, pitted and sliced
- 3 ounces feta cheese, crumbled

1. For the dressing: Whisk together the vinegar, lemon juice, and salt in a small bowl for about 10 seconds to dissolve the salt. Add the oil, oregano, and pepper to taste and whisk until slightly thickened and evenly colored. Set aside.

2. For the salad: Place the first 6 ingredients (the lettuce through the mint leaves) in a large bowl. Remix the dressing and pour it around the perimeter of the bowl. Using your fingers or wooden salad utensils, gently toss to coat the salad evenly with the dressing. Scatter the olives and cheese over the top and serve at once.

Don't Eat on the Run

Americans are suspicious of their food — they think that it is going to kill them. Of course, if you worked for the USDA and your job was to reduce food-borne illness, you would take this subject seriously. But the question is, do you really have to worry about trichinosis, killer eggs, and chicken contaminated with *E. coli*? Well, I made some phone calls and searched the Internet and found out that the risks, at least of death, are less than you might think.

In all of 2000, there were only 105 deaths from food-borne illnesses that were reported to the Centers for Disease Control and included on the death certificates. (The estimates of total deaths from food-borne illnesses are around 1,200 per year, assuming that many more deaths occur than are reported to the CDC.) But let's stick, for the moment, with the CDC-reported cases, as statistics for other types of deaths are also based on reported cases.

For starters, the plague kills 10 to 15 people per year, so eating is indeed a lot riskier than plague. However, contracting leprosy (93 cases per year) has about the same risk as eating — hardly a comforting thought. It turns out, however, that riding a bike is considerably more dangerous than eating, with a whopping 342 deaths by pedaling. If you fancy boating, you are seven times more likely to drown (734 fatalities per year) than to be killed by your dinner. Of course, if you are a serious risk-taker, you might wish to consider becoming a pedestrian, at 2,675 annual fatalities. For those of you who really wish to walk on the wild side, you might consider being a pedestrian *and* crossing the street, which kills 4,739 citizens per year.

So, for all the recent talk of contaminated food, it turns out that cycling, walking, boating, and crossing the street carry much larger risk factors, at least in terms of mortality. And definitely don't even *consider* eating while engaging in any of those activities — that would be really dangerous.

Roasted Pear Salad at Home

In the last few years, roasted pears have become ubiquitous, showing up on restaurant menus as salads, not desserts. They are usually paired with a spicy green, goat cheese, and perhaps a few toasted nuts. I have improvised a few of these at home over the years and found that they range from showstoppers to insipid piles of rabbit food. The secret is in how the pears are roasted as well as in the perfect balance of the remaining ingredients. ▶◀

I started with the pears. First, I peeled, quartered, and coated them with olive oil and then placed them in a 400-degree oven for 30 minutes. They turned out bland and dry and looked like a Vermonter in March (pale and gray). Next, I sliced them, coated them with sugar and melted butter, and roasted them in a 500-degree oven for 15 minutes. I didn't like the added sugar and didn't want to have to turn them, a step that seemed necessary for even coloring. Finally, I quartered the pears, placed them in a buttered baking dish, covered the dish, and placed them in a 450-degree oven. After 15 minutes, I removed the cover and let them cook another 10 minutes, or until done. They were perfect—shiny, spotted golden brown, and very sweet.

My testing was done with Anjou pears, but I also tried red-skinned pears (firm and flavorful), Bartlett (slightly less intense and less firm), and Bosc (dry and grainy). Once the pears have been roasted, they keep fine for three to four hours, so the roasting may be done ahead of time. However, they must not be refrigerated or heated, as their texture will suffer.

For the greens, I tested arugula, Bibb lettuce, mâche, watercress, radicchio, and endive. Arugula was the clear winner—sharp, peppery, and a nice foil for the sweet pears. Watercress would work in a pinch, but Bibb and mâche didn't have enough bite. Radicchio and endive are nice additions to the arugula but are overpowering on their own.

Goat cheese is widely available in small logs that weigh 4 or 5 ounces. Trying to slice it into neat medallions is very difficult. However, the cheese is just as tasty if it is simply crumbled over the top of the salad.

For the dressing, I started with olive oil. I then tried many different types of vinegar and preferred both white wine vinegar and white balsamic. I used a 4:1 ratio of oil to vinegar and also added salt, mustard, and shallot.

To assemble the salad for six people, I started with three bunches of arugula. (Washed, dried, and cut into bite-size pieces, it ended up to be about 9 cups.) I then placed them in a large bowl and added the optional endive and radicchio. Next, the vinaigrette was added and the greens were tossed to coat. This salad is best portioned onto plates and then topped with the crumbled cheese and pear quarters. I tried chopping the pears into bite-size pieces, but they lose their identity and the salad loses some of its style. Topping the finished salad with chopped toasted pecans added crunch and flavor, although they are optional.

Roasted Pear Salad with Arugula and Goat Cheese

SERVES 6

Make sure that you are using fresh, not aged, goat cheese. It should be the texture of cream cheese. Use the largest possible mixing bowl to toss the salad; it makes tossing much easier. To vary this recipe, try dusting the pears with 5-spice powder before baking.

- 3 Anjou, Bartlett, or red-skinned pears, peeled, quartered lengthwise, and cored
  Butter for baking dish
- ¼ teaspoon table salt
- 1 tablespoon white wine vinegar or white balsamic vinegar
- ¼ cup best-quality olive oil
- ¼ teaspoon Dijon mustard
- 2 teaspoons finely chopped shallot
  Freshly ground black pepper
- 3 bunches arugula, washed, dried, stemmed, and cut into bite-size pieces (about 9 cups)
- ½ cup thinly sliced radicchio, optional
- ½ cup thinly sliced endive, optional
- 4–5 ounces goat cheese, crumbled
- ½ cup chopped pecans, toasted in a dry skillet over medium heat until fragrant and lightly browned (about 3 minutes), optional

1. Adjust an oven rack to the center position and heat the oven to 450 degrees. Place the pears in a lightly buttered baking dish and cover with aluminum foil. Bake for 15 minutes. Remove the foil and bake for 10 minutes more or until the pears are just tender and dark golden brown on the bottom. Cool to room temperature.

2. Place the salt and vinegar in a small bowl and whisk until the salt has dissolved, about 10 seconds. Add the olive oil, mustard, shallot, and pepper to taste and whisk until smooth, thickened, and evenly colored. Place the arugula in a large mixing bowl and add the optional radicchio and endive. Add the vinaigrette and toss gently to evenly coat the greens.

3. Distribute the greens onto six plates. Top each with crumbled goat cheese and two pear quarters. Sprinkle the optional pecans over the salads, if using. Serve immediately.

Orange and Onion Salad Perfected

Orange and onion (usually served with oil-cured olives) is a classic Sicilian combination, one that has many variations. At its best, it is an intrepid salad that refreshes with bold strokes of complementary but assertive ingredients: sweet oranges, raw onion, and salty olives. At its worst, the oranges are lackluster and pithy, the onion is overpowering, and the dressing is harsh. ▶◀

I began with the oranges, which are key to this recipe. (Don't make this salad with lousy specimens.) I finally came across some navels and Valencias that were sweet and juicy. They cannot be peeled. Instead, the skin and white pith need to be cut away with a sharp knife. You can serve the oranges in slices or, if you want to be a bit fussier, in segments, which take more preparation time.

The onion quickly becomes overpowering if sliced too thick or if too much of it is used. I preferred red onion and used extremely thin slices. I also tried soaking it in water, as one recipe suggested, but this did not ameliorate its bite and just made the salad watery. So one half of a medium red onion was sufficient for five oranges. Shallots and green onions were tried and voted down.

I tested both brined and oil-cured olives and preferred the latter—Italian, Greek, and French oil-cured olives were all great. Some are more pungent than others, so you may vary the quantity accordingly. I used anywhere from eight to 10 olives that had been pitted and roughly chopped. I do think you want to taste some olive in every bite.

I fell in love with fennel as an ingredient in this recipe. It offers lots of crunch, and its sweet-spicy flavor is subtle but strong enough to stand up to the orange and onion. One medium bulb cut into very thin slices was just right.

I felt the salad was crying out for something green, even if it were just a garnish. I tried adding several herbs (chives, mint, thyme, parsley, tarragon), as well as tips from the fennel bulb. The herb that worked best was basil; I used about a quarter cup of thinly sliced leaves. The basil fortifies the fennel and adds yet one more bold flavor.

The salad tastes best when dressed with ¼ cup first-rate extra-virgin olive oil. In terms of vinegar, I found that less was best. (Some recipes don't even include vinegar.) My favorite vinegar was white balsamic, and I only used 1 teaspoon, enough to lend a bit of bright flavor but not overtake the oranges. (Try rice vinegar if you can't find white balsamic.) Along with the oil and vinegar, I used ¼ teaspoon salt and freshly ground black pepper to taste.

The salad goes together easily. Instead of arranging the oranges, I simply toss the ingredients together with the dressing. Once the salad is dressed, it should be eaten fairly soon, as the onion and fennel begin to wilt and lose crunch.

Orange, Onion, and Fennel Salad

SERVES 4 TO 6

For this recipe, the peel and pith must be sliced off the orange. This is done most easily by first cutting off a small section from the top and bottom of the orange. Stand the orange on one flat end and slice off the rind and white pith, following the contour. Once all of the skin has been removed, the segments can be cut away by holding the orange in the palm of your hand and making V-shaped cuts along the membranes to free each section. For a less elegant but easier method, you may cut the skinned orange in half pole to pole and then cut each half into half-inch slices through the segments. A small, inexpensive mandoline (under $20) is a good tool for thinly slicing vegetables.

5	medium or 6 small sweet ripe oranges, such as navels or Valencias, prepared using one of the methods at left
1	small or ½ medium red onion, halved and very thinly sliced
1	medium bulb fennel, trimmed, halved, and very thinly sliced
8–10	oil-cured black olives, pitted and coarsely chopped
¼	cup best-quality olive oil
1	teaspoon white balsamic vinegar
¼	teaspoon table salt
	Freshly ground black pepper
¼	cup loosely packed thinly sliced fresh basil leaves (about 8 medium)

Place the oranges, onion, fennel, and olives in a large bowl. Add the olive oil, vinegar, salt, and pepper to taste and gently toss to combine the ingredients and coat evenly with the dressing. Taste for seasoning, adding more salt or pepper if needed. Sprinkle with sliced basil and serve immediately.

Real German Potato Salad

German potato salad is, contrary to what I expected, a real dish in Germany — a simple combination of warm potatoes, bacon, vinegar, and onion. In America, this dish is often served cold, gussied up with chopped pickles or celery, and is often greasy and unappealing. I wanted to go back to the original to find out how to make German potato salad the right way. ▶◀

The first issue was the potatoes themselves. Small red potatoes were the clear winner, as they held their shape nicely in the salad. I decided to cut them before cooking (they should be bite-size) to reduce cooking time and to avoid shredded skins, which often happens when slicing into a hot potato. Starting them in cold water, it took only seven minutes of boiling until they were ready. Plenty of salt in the cooking water (1 tablespoon salt to 4 quarts water) adds flavor, and by splashing the warm potatoes with 3 tablespoons vinegar, the flavor is also enhanced.

As for the vinegar, red wine won the taste test when compared with white wine, cider, and balsamic vinegars. White wine vinegar was a close second. An additional tablespoon was used in the dressing, bringing the total to ¼ cup. For the bacon, I used ¼ pound cut into ¼-inch pieces and cooked it until well browned and crispy. I found that thick-cut held up better, because it has a meatier texture. If you are not serving the salad immediately after it is prepared, the bacon should be held and tossed in at the last minute. Every recipe I found included chopped onion or shallot sautéed in bacon fat, which I tested and found to be dull-tasting. To brighten the flavor and texture, I tried using raw onion and shallot, but the flavor was too sharp. The solution was to cut paper-thin slices of shallot and toss them in with the hot potato; the shallot lost its crispness and bite but still had lots of bright, raw flavor. (Red onion also works well if you cannot find shallots.)

As for the other ingredients, I tried pickles, which had an odd texture. Celery offered little but unwanted crunch. Toasted mustard seeds work well, but I have listed them as an optional ingredient, as they are assertive. (The seeds add heat and crunch along with mustard flavor.) Ground mustard or prepared mustard seemed overbearing and less interesting than lightly toasted seeds. The salad also benefits from chopped parsley and/or chives. A few tablespoons of either adds fresh flavor and needed color.

The dressing for this salad turned out to be quite simple. Once the bacon was fried, some of the fat was reserved in the pan. A tablespoon of vinegar was added, and then I needed some liquid to add moisture. Chicken stock seemed to be the liquid of choice, but the easy solution was to use some of the potato cooking liquid. You don't have to open a can, and it adds both flavor and a touch of saltiness. I tried adding vermouth or sherry to the dressing, and it was not improved, but a pinch of sugar was a nice addition. These few ingredients were swirled around in the bacon-cooking skillet, and after one minute, the warm dressing was ready to be poured onto the potatoes. As mentioned above, the salad is best served immediately.

Warm German Potato Salad

SERVES 6 AS A SIDE DISH

Please serve this salad immediately. It can be held for up to a half hour but, in that case, add the bacon at the last minute.

- 2 pounds small red potatoes, scrubbed and halved or quartered into bite-size pieces
- 1 tablespoon table salt
- ¼ cup red wine vinegar
- 3 medium shallots, sliced paper thin (about ½ cup) or ½ red onion, sliced paper thin
- 1 tablespoon mustard seeds, optional
- ¼ pound thick-cut bacon (about 4 slices), cut into ¼-inch strips
  Pinch sugar
  Freshly ground black pepper
- 3 tablespoons finely chopped fresh flat-leaf parsley or chives or a combination of both

1. Place the potatoes and 4 quarts cold water in a large pot and bring to a boil over high heat. Add the salt and cook until the potatoes are tender but firm when poked with a paring knife or skewer, 6 to 8 minutes. Drain the potatoes, reserving ⅓ cup cooking liquid. Transfer the potatoes to a bowl, add 3 tablespoons of the vinegar, stir gently, and let stand for 1 minute. Add the sliced shallots or red onion and stir to combine.

2. Heat a large skillet over medium-high heat. Toast the optional mustard seeds until very lightly browned, 1 to 2 minutes. Remove and set aside. Cook the bacon in the skillet until well browned and crispy. Remove to paper towels to drain and pour off all but 2 tablespoons bacon fat. Add the remaining 1 tablespoon vinegar, the reserved potato-cooking water, and sugar. Swirl the ingredients together and cook for about 1 minute. Pour over the potato mixture. Add the optional mustard seeds, bacon, pepper to taste, and parsley and/or chives. Toss gently to combine. Taste for seasonings, adding salt if necessary. Turn into a serving bowl or onto a platter and serve immediately.

Pasta 101

When I was growing up, Thursday night was spaghetti night, and it was always the same dish: spaghetti topped with sautéed ground beef infused with tablespoons of old dried oregano topped with Aunt Millie's Spaghetti Sauce. To test the spaghetti for doneness, we threw it at the brick wall behind the stove to see if it would stay put. Most nights, the pasta stuck together in the colander; the sauce, the meat, and the pasta never "married"; and we all loved it.

My view of pasta began to change in the early 1960s at a small Italian restaurant in San Francisco. I still remember that the waiter brought out a large skillet filled with pasta and sauce that he heated over a small burner. The sauce and the pasta were one, the former actually being absorbed into the latter. This notion of marrying the two components was revelatory and was the beginning of my pasta education.

Since then, I have learned a lot about making pasta, mostly through trial and error and head-to-head kitchen testing. Here is what I have learned:

- You need 4 quarts of water for 1 pound of pasta.
- Add 1 tablespoon of table salt per gallon of pasta water.
- Make sure that the water comes up to a boil as quickly as possible after adding the pasta — putting the lid back on is usually necessary. (Watch the pot very carefully at this point, as it can boil over quickly.)
- Briskly boiling water and lots of stirring prevent pasta from sticking together during cooking.
- Never add oil to the pasta water. It does nothing (except float on top of the water).
- Always reserve 2 cups of the pasta cooking water before draining the pasta. This is used to either thin the sauce or keep the pasta moist if it needs to be held a few minutes before serving.

- For most sauces, it is best to cook the pasta and sauce together for a minute or two before serving. This means that the pasta should be slightly undercooked.
- Pasta and sauce can be cooked together either in the pasta pot or in a large skillet, the one that was used to cook the sauce.
- Never trust the directions on the back of the pasta box. They almost always produce overcooked pasta. (Start checking the pasta two minutes before it is supposed to be done.)
- To determine when pasta is cooked, taste a piece — don't throw it against a wall.
- Never rinse pasta. You want the sauce to adhere to the pasta, and rinsing will remove a lot of the starch on the outside of the pasta. (The one exception to this rule is Chinese noodles; they often require rinsing, as they have a remarkable tendency to clump together.)
- For most applications, simply let the pasta sit in the colander for 15 seconds with no shaking. You want the pasta to be slightly wet, so it does not stick together.
- Chunky, hollow pasta shapes are best for chunky sauces. (They trap the bits of meat or vegetable in the sauce.) Straight, flat pastas are best for smoother sauces.
- Fresh pasta is best with a creamy sauce such as Alfredo. However, supermarket brands of fresh pasta are universally second-rate, not even close to the real thing.
- Italians use dried pasta for most applications. Don't feel embarrassed to buy the stuff in the boxes.
- Ronzoni is a high-quality pasta and often wins taste tests at *Cook's Illustrated,* even when compared with many higher-priced Italian imports.

Pasta with Bread Crumbs Done Right

Garlicky pasta tossed with pan-toasted bread crumbs can be heaven on earth, or it can be a soggy, lifeless mess of a dish. The difference? Well, as with most cooking, it's all in the details. The garlic must be prepared and cooked just right, the bread crumbs need to have crunch, and one or two additional flavorings help to round out the dish. The most important issue, however, was going to be how to prepare the bread crumbs. ▶◀

I found that a rustic bread—not too doughy or tough—is best. A country white loaf works well, but any sort of coarsely textured white bread, or even a day-old baguette, will do. The bread should be trimmed of most of the crust, especially the bottom crust, which is often dark and thick. I found that the best way to prepare the bread is to use a food processor fitted with the metal blade (cut the bread into 1-inch cubes before processing, for best results). I tested various crumb sizes and found that pieces no larger than a small pea worked best. Depending on the type and freshness of the bread, you may need to process the bread cubes for up to 30 seconds. This recipe calls for 1½ cups crumbs, which works out to two 1-inch slices from a large, rustic loaf or about five 1-inch slices from a baguette.

The next step was to toast the crumbs. I usually do this in an oven, but to simplify things I tried using the same skillet I intended to use for the rest of the recipe. This worked well, especially when the crumbs were first tossed with salt and then toasted with 2 tablespoons butter. The crumbs need moderate heat and frequent stirring for even browning.

The next issue was the garlic. For a story in the March/April 2001 issue of *Cook's Illustrated,* our test kitchen director discovered that a combination of fresh and cooked garlic was best for the classic dish *pasta aglio e olio* (pasta with garlic and oil). I played with various amounts and ended up with 2 tablespoons cooked garlic paired with 2 teaspoons raw per pound of spaghetti. I then tested the best method for preparing the garlic, trying sliced garlic, crushed whole cloves, and garlic that was minced or passed through a garlic press. The whole cloves, if removed from the oil before serving, did not contribute enough flavor; if left in the dish, they did not allow for even distribution—either you got a large hunk of garlic on your fork or you didn't. The sliced garlic had the same problem of uneven distribution. The minced or pressed garlic provided tiny pieces of garlic in each bite — just what I wanted. I found that the garlic was best cooked over low heat just until it became straw colored. But if you make the mistake of cooking the garlic over medium heat, it will likely burn and taste harsh in the pasta sauce.

As for other ingredients, a high-quality, fruity, extra-virgin olive oil is a must. I used 3 tablespoons for cooking the garlic and an additional 3 tablespoons to toss with the pasta before serving. A quarter teaspoon of red pepper flakes added flavor, as did a few anchovy fillets (these are optional), which dissolve in the oil during cooking. A trick I picked up from the *Cook's* test kitchen is adding a bit of hot pasta water along with the raw garlic to help distribute it evenly. The dish is finished with the bread crumbs and chopped parsley. Some folks also like a bit of grated cheese on top, but I pass on the grated cheese for this dish, because I find that it muddies the flavors. This dish couldn't be easier, and it couldn't be better.

Garlic Pasta with Butter-Toasted Bread Crumbs

SERVES 4 TO 6

For best results with the bread crumbs, use two 1-inch slices cut from a rustic white loaf of bread. After removing the crusts, cut the bread into 1-inch cubes and process, using the metal blade of a food processor, for 20 to 30 seconds. The largest crumb should be no larger than a small pea.

FOR THE BREAD CRUMBS

- 1½ cups fresh bread crumbs (see above)
- ¼ teaspoon table salt
- 2 tablespoons unsalted butter

FOR THE PASTA

- Salt
- 6 tablespoons extra-virgin olive oil
- 10 medium garlic cloves, finely minced (about 2 tablespoons plus 2 teaspoons)
- ¼ teaspoon red pepper flakes

- 5 anchovy fillets, coarsely chopped, optional
- 1 pound spaghetti
- 3 tablespoons chopped fresh flat-leaf parsley

1. For the bread crumbs: Toss the bread crumbs with the salt in a bowl. Place the butter in a large (12-inch) skillet set over medium heat. After the butter foams, turn the heat to low, add the bread crumbs, and toss to coat evenly. Toast the crumbs, stirring frequently, until golden brown, 5 to 6 minutes. Remove the pan from the heat and set aside, uncovered, to cool. Transfer the toasted crumbs to the bowl. Wipe out the skillet with a paper towel.

2. For the pasta: Bring 4 quarts of salted water to a rolling boil in a large pot over high heat.

3. Add 3 tablespoons of the olive oil, ½ teaspoon salt (omit if using anchovies),

2 tablespoons garlic, the red pepper flakes, and optional anchovies to the 12-inch skillet. Cook over low heat until the mixture is very fragrant and the garlic is straw colored, about 10 minutes.

4. Meanwhile, add the pasta to the boiling water and cook until al dente. Drain the pasta, reserving ⅓ cup of the cooking water. (The pasta should not sit for more than a minute before finishing the dish.)

5. When the garlic is cooked, remove the skillet from the heat and add the remaining raw garlic, 2 tablespoons of the reserved water, and the parsley; stir to combine. Add the drained pasta, the remaining 3 tablespoons olive oil, and the remaining pasta cooking water and toss to evenly coat the pasta. Serve immediately with a liberal sprinkling of bread crumbs.

The Raw Deal

One simple way of adding flavor to a dish is to add raw ingredients just before serving. Good candidates include minced ginger, garlic, onion, or just about any fresh herb. The flavor of raw garlic, for example, is quite different from that of cooked garlic and will brighten and expand the flavor profile of the dish. And I find that fresh herbs are almost always best added at the last minute or so of cooking. A test performed in the *Cook's Illustrated* test kitchen compared simmering chicken stock for half an hour with dried rosemary versus fresh. The dried version was significantly better, indicating that fresh herbs don't always take well to long cooking. In any case, fresh herbs taste entirely different from the cooked variety. (I wonder if many recipes that call for adding herbs at the beginning were based on dried herbs, and then when America started using the fresh variety, we forgot to change our technique?)

Another trick is to use an ingredient twice: Include it at the beginning of the recipe and then add just a small amount — raw — at the end. This is particularly effective with garlic.

Canned Tuna as Pasta Sauce?

The most useful recipes for weeknight dinners use pantry staples with pasta. They are quick, they are easy, and they are satisfying. A common Italian approach to this sort of recipe is to pair canned tuna with tomatoes, olives, capers, and anchovies. Having tested a handful of these recipes, however, I found that they are still tomato sauces, using either chunks of tomatoes or tomato paste. This requires a bit more cooking time, but, more to the point, tomatoes mute the bold flavors of the ingredients. I wanted a recipe that was fast, bold, and easy. ▶◀

I cobbled together a working recipe using olive oil, garlic, anchovies, olives, capers, tuna, pine nuts, and chopped parsley. I started with olive oil in a large heated skillet, followed by the garlic and anchovies. Next; I added olives, capers, tuna, and a bit of pine nuts and stirred just long enough to heat through. Finally, I tossed in 1 pound cooked pasta, the chopped parsley, additional olive oil, salt, and pepper.

The first problem was the garlic. Onion made a better pairing, and, after some testing, I settled on thin slices of red onion that retain some of their punch. The anchovies were keepers; they provided a nice briny undercurrent to the sauce. I settled on two large or three medium anchovies — any more and the tuna was overpowered. For the olives, oil-cured black olives were best. (Brine-cured olives were too salty.) Two tablespoons capers were a nice addition, although I quickly dumped the pine nuts, which were too sweet and therefore out of place. For the tuna, I tested the Italian variety soaked in olive oil, which was too soft. I also tried chunk light tuna soaked in water and found that it was just as mushy. However, solid white albacore tuna was just right. It was best when it was drained and flaked before using. I tested a variety of herbs, but the fresh, grassy flavor of chopped parsley was both the simplest and the best.

In terms of cooking, I found that it was best to heat the anchovies in the olive oil before adding other ingredients. They start to dissolve and their flavor is slightly muted. Next, the sliced onions are added — they're cooked just until they lose their crunch — and then the tuna, olives, capers and ¼ teaspoon salt are added. When the ingredients are mixed together and heated through, about 1 minute more, they are ready for the pasta, parsley, and raw olive oil. For this recipe, I liked using penne, because it offers crevices in which this chunky sauce can lodge. (You can also use rotini, fusilli, or farfalle.) Cheese was unnecessary and unwelcome, but a few grinds of black pepper were a nice finishing touch. Total cooking time: 5 minutes (not including the pasta). Total experience: bold and satisfying.

Pantry Pasta Sauce with Tuna, Olives, and Capers

SERVES 4

This sauce is best made quickly, so that the bold flavors of the ingredients maintain their personality — other than the anchovies and onion, you are simply heating them through.

	Salt and freshly ground black pepper
1	pound pasta, penne or some other shape that will trap bits of the sauce preferred
¼	cup best-quality olive oil
2	large or 3 medium anchovies, chopped
½	cup very thinly sliced red onion
1	(6-ounce) can solid white tuna packed in water, drained and slightly flaked with a fork
⅓	cup pitted and coarsely chopped oil-cured black olives
2	tablespoons capers
2	tablespoons chopped fresh flat-leaf parsley

1. Bring 4 quarts of salted water to a rolling boil in a large pot over high heat. Add the pasta and cook until al dente. Drain, reserving 1 cup cooking water.
2. Meanwhile, heat a large skillet or sauté pan over medium heat. Add 2 tablespoons of the oil and the anchovies and cook, stirring, until the anchovies dissolve, about 1 minute. Add the onion and cook until just softened, about 1 minute more. Add the tuna, olives, capers, and ¼ teaspoon salt and cook, stirring, until heated through, 1 to 2 minutes.
3. Add the cooked pasta, parsley, and the remaining 2 tablespoons olive oil and mix well, evenly coating the pasta with sauce. Moisten with the reserved cooking water as needed. Season with pepper to taste and serve immediately.

Perfecting Pasta with Cheese Sauce

Deceptively simple in concept, pasta with cheese sauce is in reality an exercise in subtlety. Who hasn't watched this cheese congeal into a stringy mass within a few minutes after serving or, even worse, been served a gluey, lifeless sauce, reminiscent of a third-rate hollandaise? Although by no means a light offering, the flavor of the different cheeses should stand out clearly, and the sauce should complement the pasta rather than overwhelm it. ▶◀

For starters, I reviewed a variety of other recipes and found that most started with either a béchamel (a basic French white sauce made with butter, flour, and milk) or a variety of simpler liquids including milk, half-and-half, light cream, heavy cream, and condensed milk. Cheese is then melted into these liquids to produce a cheese sauce. The béchamel sauce tasted pasty and not as clean as sauces made with milk or light cream. The condensed-milk version displayed its distinctive and, to my mind, unwelcome flavor. The plain milk-and-cheese combination was good, the half-and-half was better, and the light-cream version was best, because the taste was richer and the consistency was smoother. The heavy-cream sauce was too heavy.

Up to this point, I had been using cheddar and Jack cheeses, but now I wanted to perform tests to determine which combination of cheeses would work best as well as the best method of adding them to the liquid. I quickly discovered that the type of liquid made a huge difference in how well the cheese melted. When I tried milk or half-and-half as a medium, the mixture became grainy and separated, whereas the light cream produced a consistently smooth sauce. I also discovered that some cheeses melted well and others didn't, so this narrowed the field.

Next, I had to decide the proper ratio of cheese to light cream. For 1 cup light cream, it seemed 1½ to 2 cups cheese (cut into ½-inch dice) was ideal. This amount also proved the proper amount to dress 1 pound of pasta. I wanted enough sauce to properly coat the pasta but also wished to demonstrate some degree of culinary restraint so as not to overwhelm the pasta with sauce. I also tried a variety of pasta shapes and settled on penne, because the sauce clung to it nicely.

Now I had to find just the right combination of cheeses. Using my collection of smooth melting cheeses, I divided them into three categories: mildly flavored, medium

The Sad Story of Mac and Cheese

Do you remember the story of the frog? He was put in cold water that was slowly heated, and by the time he figured out it was boiling, it was too late. That reminds me of the story of convenience foods in the 20th century. Somehow, very slowly, a great deal of home cooking got derailed and replaced by inferior supermarket products. The question is, how did this happen?

To answer this question, I researched Kraft Mac & Cheese to see how the real thing ended up a cultural castoff to be replaced by that blue box. James Kraft got the patent in 1916 for a processed cheese formula that would not spoil. It was not a hit with consumers, so he sold 6 million pounds of it to the Army. When the boys returned, some of them had developed a taste for it, but the dried, grated cheese was still not a hit with the American public at large. (It was sold as a complement to soups and baked dishes.) It wasn't until the Depression, in 1936, that Kraft introduced the Macaroni & Cheese Dinner. The slogan was "Make a Meal for Four in Nine Minutes," the selling point being cost as well as convenience. Meat rationing during the war led to "meatless Tuesday," and the Kraft Mac & Cheese dinner became the meal of choice that night in many households. The thought was that, after the war, mothers would once again make the real thing, but there was a catch: Kids loved the boxed version, so the brand became a cultural icon. By 1960, real macaroni and cheese had just about disappeared from the American table.

In 2000, the company went one step further and introduced Easy Mac. Now kids could make this ubiquitous dinner in less than five minutes, shaving four minutes off of the original time. (It is microwavable.) Kraft now sells *more than one million boxes of Mac & Cheese dinners every day!* In addition, the product line has been expanded to include Extreme Cheese, Nacho Cheese, White Cheddar, Cheesy Alfredo, and, of course, SpongeBob and Scooby-Doo! pasta shapes.

The conclusion? Like the frog in the story, the American palate acclimates itself to new food products with a preference for the familiar. This is especially true of children, who develop lifetime taste preferences at an early age. (Hence Happy Meals and Ronald McDonald.) This is why many folks prefer ersatz maple syrup over the real thing, Baker's chocolate to Callebaut or Scharffen Berger, and margarine to butter. The antidote is to go back and taste the original to see what you are missing. Trust me. The childhood memory of Campbell's tomato soup, for example, is a lot better than the real thing, as countless tastings at *Cook's Illustrated* have proven over the years.

flavored, and bold flavored. I found through experimenting that it was best to create a base with a mild cheese, layering in more strongly flavored cheeses in smaller quantities. I discovered that this recipe can be made with as little as two cheeses or as many as four, based on what you have on hand. In terms of specific cheeses, both Parmesan and Romano cheese were omitted from the sauce, as they are grainy in texture, but either (choose one or the other) is very good when sprinkled on top of the finished dish in small quantities. Other commonly used cheeses that I decided not to include in this recipe are ricotta (unpleasant texture), mozzarella (too stringy), and cream cheese (too bland). Because the cheeses all differ in salt content, I had a hard time putting a definitive amount of salt in the recipe. I settled on ½ teaspoon, but that may need to be adjusted based on your cheese selection. I would add the salt ¼ teaspoon at a time.

In terms of preparation and serving, I found that if the sauce is finished several minutes before the pasta, it can easily become too thick. This is remedied by adding more light cream 1 tablespoon at a time. As for texture, I liked the sauce when it was the texture of crème anglaise but not as thick as a pastry cream or mayonnaise. Most Americans boil their pasta and then put the sauce on top. I prefer the Italian method of placing the cooked pasta directly into the skillet containing the sauce. This way, the pasta can be very briefly warmed in the sauce to coat evenly and served from the skillet without dirtying a platter. I think freshly ground pepper is a must.

By using light cream instead of milk, selecting a mild cheese that melts well, and avoiding Parmesan- and Romano-style cheeses, I was successful in creating a sauce that maintains a pleasant consistency longer than other such sauces I have tasted. It can also be reheated, if necessary, but it is much better when served hot right out of the skillet.

Four-Cheese Pasta

SERVES 6 AS AN APPETIZER
AND 4 AS A MAIN COURSE

I like to use 4 cheeses for this recipe, although 2 will do nicely in a pinch. The sauce is made with 1 cup mild cheese (use American, Monterey Jack, or mild or sharp cheddar), and then one also adds ¼ cup of medium-flavored cheese (Swiss, Gruyère, extra-sharp cheddar, fontina, Brie, Camembert, Saint André, Morbier) plus just 2 tablespoons sharper, bolder cheese (use Gorgonzola, blue cheese, Stilton, or Roquefort). My preferred mix of cheeses is American, fontina, and Gorgonzola. Be sure that the cheese is in ½-inch dice, as larger pieces will take a lot longer to melt.

Salt and freshly ground black pepper
1 **pound tubular pasta such as penne or ziti**
1 **cup light cream, or more as needed**
1 **cup mild cheese, cut into ½-inch dice**

¼ cup medium-flavored cheese, cut into ½-inch dice

2 tablespoons crumbled bold cheese, optional

2–4 tablespoons grated Parmesan or Romano for sprinkling, optional

1. Bring 4 quarts of salted water to a rolling boil in a large pot over high heat. Add the pasta and cook until just al dente.

2. Once the pasta has gone into the boiling water, place the cream in a large skillet over low heat. (The skillet should be large enough to hold the sauce and the cooked pasta; if you do not have one large enough, you will need a large bowl or platter to finish the dish.) When the cream begins to steam, add the mild cheese and stir occasionally until fully melted and smooth, 3 to 4 minutes. Add the medium-flavored cheese and stir occasionally until melted and smooth, 2 to 3 minutes. Add the optional bold cheese and stir until melted and smooth, another 1 to 2 minutes. Add ¼ teaspoon salt, taste, and add more if necessary. This sauce may come up to a slow simmer (small bubbles around the outside) but should never boil. It should be smooth and leave a thick coating on the back of a spoon. If it seems too thick, add a bit more light cream 1 tablespoon at a time.

3. Once the pasta is cooked, drain and add it to the skillet. Mix to combine; I found tongs to be the best utensil for this step. Serve at once with the optional grated cheese and pepper to taste. (If the pasta is ready before the sauce, reserve 1 cup of the cooking water. Lightly drain the pasta — it should still be wet — and put it back into the cooking pot with the top on until the sauce is ready. Use the reserved water, if necessary, to keep the pasta from sticking. Drain thoroughly before adding to the sauce.)

Simpler Pasta Primavera

Pasta primavera has its origins in the restaurant business, and therefore its preparation is laborious and finicky — just the sort of thing to serve at New York's Le Cirque but hardly suitable for those of us who cook midweek dinners for four. Yet the notion of pasta paired with fresh vegetables is compelling, especially during warm weather, so I set out to make pasta primavera light, fresh, and relatively simple. ▷◁

What first struck me about the recipes I found was the sheer complexity of their preparation. Four or more pots are called for, a tomato sauce must be made, and a battalion of fresh vegetables must be individually prepared. The total time invested was well over two hours. In addition, this is no light meal. It has plenty of cream, which is necessary when one wishes to charge $20 a plate but, to my palate, incongruous with the essential thrust of the recipe: fresh vegetables matched with pasta.

The first question was how to avoid preparing a tomato sauce. I tried fresh and canned tomatoes and finally settled on chopped ripe Roma (plum) tomatoes, adding them to the sauce to be heated through but not cooked. (I found that varieties other than plum tend to be too watery for this dish.) This not only contributed to the fresh, spring flavor but also eliminated the need to peel the tomatoes; because they do not actually cook, the skins did not separate into those red rolled-up bits. Note, however, that dull plum tomatoes with no aroma will add little to this dish, and therefore I would opt to eliminate tomatoes altogether unless they are truly ripe and flavorful.

The next issue was which vegetables were worthy additions and which were mere baggage. Asparagus was a clear winner; it is quick to cook and flavorful. I tested broccoli, cauliflower, and red, yellow, and green peppers and found that their taste and/or texture were not a good match with the other selections. Surprisingly, I found the same to be true of onions, scallions, and leeks. I liked fava beans in the recipe, but their preparation is exhausting (they must be shelled and steamed, and then each bean must be stripped of its tough outer skin) and their availability scarce. Green beans didn't add anything as far as texture or flavor. Carrots also seemed out of place; the texture more than the taste bothered me. I also tried the addition of pine nuts, and, while the taste was nice, the nuts ended up at the bottom of the sauté pan. I tried toasting them and serving them as a garnish, but this violated my oath of simplicity. After further testing, I settled on zucchini or summer squash, mushrooms, asparagus, and peas. To streamline the recipe, I cooked the first two ingredients in a sauté pan (with the plum tomatoes added at the end) and the asparagus and peas right along with the pasta.

To make this dish a success, however, it is crucial to have ripe, flavorful vegetables. Dull or bitter zucchini and large, woody asparagus aren't going to produce a light, tasty dinner. (I found that the asparagus was best when only the first few inches from each stalk were used.) This dish derives all of its flavor from the vegetables plus a good dose of garlic, which, by the way, also needs to be fresh and pungent. (Lots of stores sell old, flavorless garlic bulbs.) I eliminated the cream from this recipe, as it seemed anathema to the notion of a garden-fresh dinner. I finished the recipe with thinly sliced basil and plenty of freshly ground Parmesan cheese. This is one dish where freshly ground black pepper is a serious ingredient, one that is key to success. Also, pay attention to the salt level—taste a bit before serving and make adjustments accordingly.

I tried both fresh and dried pastas and preferred the latter. Fresh pasta is best with creamy sauces, which need to be absorbed, and dried pasta is preferred for cleaner, simpler sauces. Both fettuccine and fusilli are good choices, while shapes such as shells, ears, or tubes were less well suited to this recipe.

Pasta Primavera

SERVES 6

This dish is about fresh, flavorful vegetables. If your ingredients are second-rate, don't bother making it, as it has little else to fall back on for flavor. Check the salt level once the pasta has been tossed with the sauce and add plenty of freshly ground black pepper and freshly grated Parmesan before serving.

Salt and freshly ground black pepper
3 tablespoons best-quality olive oil
3 tablespoons unsalted butter
2 medium zucchini or summer squash, cut into ½-inch pieces (about 3 cups)
12 ounces medium white mushrooms, stemmed, wiped clean, and quartered (about 3 cups)
3 medium garlic cloves, finely minced
3 firm but ripe plum tomatoes (about ½ pound), cut into ½-inch pieces
1 pound dry pasta, fettuccine preferred
1½ pounds asparagus, tips cut diagonally into 1-inch pieces (use only the first 3–4 inches from each spear; you should have about 2 cups)
1 cup fresh or frozen peas
⅓ cup thinly sliced fresh basil
Freshly grated Parmesan cheese

1. Bring 4 quarts of salted water to a rolling boil in a large pot over high heat.
2. Set a large (at least 12 inches in diameter) sauté pan with a lid over medium heat. When hot, add the oil and butter, and when the butter stops foaming, add the zucchini and mushrooms. Stir to coat

with the oil-butter mixture, cover, and cook for 5 minutes. Remove the lid and add the garlic; stir, and cook, uncovered, for 1 minute longer. The zucchini and mushrooms will be softened some but not fully cooked. Add the tomatoes and salt to taste, turn off the heat, and stir to combine. Allow to sit uncovered while the pasta and remaining vegetables are prepared.

3. When the water is at a rolling boil, add the pasta and cook until al dente. Five minutes before the pasta is finished cooking, add the asparagus. Two minutes before the pasta is finished cooking, add the peas. (The water should not stop boiling with either addition.) Turn the burner under the sauté pan to medium.

4. Drain the pasta for 15 seconds in a colander without shaking and empty the contents into the sauté pan. Using two large spoons or a pair of tongs, combine the contents while sautéing for 2 minutes. Remove from the heat and stir in the basil. Adjust the seasonings, adding salt to taste. Serve immediately topped with pepper to taste and lots of cheese.

The Problem with Cooking Science

I once gave a cooking demonstration that included a chocolate tasting. Each of the 75 attendees was to taste two different chocolate cookies: One was made with Baker's and the other with Callebaut. As Baker's had come in last in most of our chocolate tastings and Callebaut had either won or come in close to the top, I thought that this would be an easy but informative exercise. As it turned out, I learned more than the tasters did.

That afternoon, before the demonstration was to begin, my test kitchen director showed me the two cookies. The Baker's cookie was smooth and glossy, but the Callebaut cookie was rough and ugly—so ugly that one would be hard-pressed to serve it. But serve them we did, and most folks picked the Callebaut (for flavor only) over the Baker's cookie.

So what went wrong? Why did the same exact recipe perform so differently with different brands of chocolate? My first thought was that the pH of the chocolates differed. A local scientific laboratory put that one to rest: All of the chocolates in a recent tasting were about the same. They were also tested for fat content, and there was little difference there either.

After speaking to *Cook's* consulting food scientist, Robert Wolke, the answer became apparent. The most likely explanation is that some of the Callebaut chocolate had not fully melted (or had seized up when added to the butter and eggs), and that is why the outside of the cookie was rough. It wasn't the brand of chocolate at all.

Other tests have proved equally mysterious. When Doritos won a tortilla chip tasting, beating out more authentic "stone-ground" brands, we were at a loss for an explanation. It turns out that tasters preferred thinner, less coarse chips. But the real surprise was the packaging: Our top three brands were packaged in "metallized" bags that kept the chips fresher longer.

Brewed coffee involves as many as 800 different flavor compounds and is dependent on the type of bean, how fresh it is, the country of origin, how it was grown, etc. Yet, a simple measurement of how dark the bean was roasted turned out to be the primary factor in determining the preferences of tasters.

The conclusion? Food is complicated, and the cooking process makes it even more so, as hundreds of chemical reactions take place. So, quick and easy science explanations are often wrong or, at best, incomplete, given the exact circumstances of any particular situation. I can, for example, easily explain the difference between baking powder and baking soda, but exactly how each of them reacts in different batters is a complex subject indeed. (Did you know that using brown sugar rather than white sugar affects the pH of a chocolate chip cookie batter, and therefore it can affect the rise and texture?)

Even Einstein must have taken food science with a grain of salt.

In the summer, I often serve pasta with a raw tomato sauce, as I find the flavors of the cool tomatoes and extra-virgin olive oil combined with the hot pasta a compelling marriage. The heat of the pasta brings out the flavor of the tomatoes and the olive oil, yet there are plenty of raw, fresh-from-the-garden flavors to give this dish some guts. But bad raw tomato sauce can be watery and bland with an overpowering garlic flavor, so I set out to improve both the texture and the taste. ▶◀

After years of making this sauce, I finally came to the conclusion that the tomatoes do need to be seeded, a step that is completed in just a minute by slicing them through the equator and then shaking the seeds loose from each half (do this over the sink or a bowl). Seeding reduces the liquid content of the sauce, making it meatier and more flavorful. The bigger issue, however, was the garlic. Simply mincing or pressing the garlic results in a raw flavor that can be overpowering. Instead, I found that if I heated the oil, added the garlic, cooked it gently for a few minutes, and then let it steep, I had better luck. Finally, I strained out the garlic and poured the garlic-flavored oil over the seeded and chopped tomatoes.

Over time, I added one last trick to this recipe. I wanted more of the raw olive flavor, but heating the oil had made it less complex. The obvious solution was to reserve some of the oil (2 tablespoons) before the cooking process and add it later. This preserved the fruitiness and bite of the olive oil, an important part of the recipe.

Pasta with Raw Tomatoes, Basil, and Mint

SERVES 4

If the tomatoes are earthy and aromatic, and the basil and mint are fresh-picked, you can't go wrong with this recipe. Do not make this recipe with supermarket or canned tomatoes. Serve it with hot pasta, tubular or corkscrew shapes preferred.

2   pounds locally grown tomatoes, seeded and cut into ½-inch dice
½   cup extra-virgin olive oil

4   garlic cloves, crushed and peeled
2   tablespoons minced fresh basil
2   tablespoons minced fresh mint
     Salt and freshly ground black pepper
¼   teaspoon sugar
1   pound pasta

1. Place the tomatoes in a large bowl. Heat 6 tablespoons of the oil in a small saucepan. When hot, add the garlic and cook for 4 minutes or until the garlic is lightly browned. Remove the pan from the heat and let the oil steep for 10 minutes; pour the hot oil through a strainer onto the tomatoes. Add the remaining 2 tablespoons oil. Add the basil, mint, ½ teaspoon salt, the sugar, and pepper to taste and let marinate for at least 1 hour. Taste and add more salt if necessary.
2. Bring 4 quarts of salted water to a rolling boil in a large pot over high heat. Add the pasta and cook until al dente. Drain the pasta and toss in the bowl with the sauce. Serve immediately.

Secret Ingredients

There are a few ingredients that most cooks have on hand that do wonders for a wide range of recipes. Very often, they are difficult or impossible to detect but add a depth of flavor that makes the recipe substantially better. Here is my shortlist of favorite additions.

Anchovies: Two to four chopped anchovies sautéed in olive oil are a great way to add depth of flavor to stews, braises, and hearty soups. They dissolve quickly, and there will be no fishy flavor if used sparingly. I add them right at the beginning of the recipe when the onions, garlic, or shallots are being sautéed.

Black peppercorns: Unfortunately, ground black pepper is used on everything and in insufficient quantity to make itself known. Have you ever noticed that waiters try to put pepper on everything, even delicate dishes that would be much worse off with a burst of heat? If you think of black pepper as a spice, however, it assumes a totally different character. Try crushed black peppercorns with poached pears or grind peppercorns over strawberries dressed with balsamic vinegar (a classic Italian combination). Use crushed peppercorns in a stew or braise. Even add pepper to spice cookies or gingerbread. I also like a good grinding of black pepper over a winter orange salad.

Coarse salt: Although taste tests run in the test kitchens of *Cook's Illustrated* determined that, under most conditions, it was impossible to tell gourmet salts from regular table salt, there are some exceptions to this rule. When sprinkled on a steak, for example, coarse salt adds a unique taste experience, because each grain provides a burst of flavor. Try sprinkling a coarse salt on grilled or roasted meats just before serving.

Cocoa powder: This can be added to a beef stew or chili. Just one or two tablespoons will do. It's subtle — you won't taste the chocolate — but it does lend an extra dimension to the background flavor notes.

Crystallized ginger: You can create variations on a wide variety of baked goods by simply adding some finely chopped crystallized ginger. It is also a lot easier than dealing with fresh ginger, which must be peeled and then grated or minced. I use crystallized ginger with fruit pies (peach and apple are both good), biscuits, scones, muffins (e.g., corn), etc.

Parmesan rind: This ingredient is no secret — lots of cookbook authors suggest using a leftover rind when making soups. (You can freeze the rinds for long-term storage.) Just add one to the soup along with the liquid.

Peanut butter: A little dab will do you when making a beef or pork stew. Just dissolve it in the stock for added richness.

Vinegar: I often add just a teaspoon or so of vinegar to many dishes to perk up the flavor, including soups (lentil soup, for example), stews, and braises. It also works if used sparingly with quick pan sauces; it pairs well with sweet or spicy flavors. Add the vinegar right at the end, just before serving. By the way, white balsamic vinegar is now my "house" vinegar. It is less acidic than white wine vinegar but less syrupy and overpowering than real balsamic vinegar. Use it for salad dressings or in any situation in which white wine vinegar is called for. Rice vinegar is also a milder tasting, sweeter vinegar that is good with very delicate salad greens.

Cherry Tomatoes as Pasta Sauce

There are plenty of fresh tomato sauce recipes, but I find that cherry tomatoes (I grow the Sungold variety, which are yellow) mature more quickly and have better flavor than most globe tomatoes, especially for those of us who live in colder climates. I was looking for an uncooked tomato sauce here, something that could go from garden to pasta in a matter of minutes. ▶◀

My first test included throwing the tomatoes into a food processor with olive oil, salt, and two cloves of garlic. This produced a runny mess of a sauce that was not properly balanced. Next, I halved 1 cup of the tomatoes and then threw the rest into the machine, a step that provided some textural contrast. Then, I added 1 cup fresh basil to make the sauce more interesting and, finally, added a bit of vinegar to give the tomatoes an extra flavor dimension. The last element was the addition of thinly sliced raw onion that added both crunch and bite.

Ripe Cherry Tomatoes with Pasta

SERVES 4

I am partial to penne, farfalle, or similar shapes that will trap the sauce. The sauce improves as it sits, but if you are in a hurry, make the pasta and sauce at the same time. If you cannot find a mild onion, mince it so the pieces are not so overpowering.

4	cups ripe cherry tomatoes
1	cup lightly packed fresh basil leaves
¼	cup extra-virgin olive oil
½	teaspoon minced or pressed garlic
1	teaspoon white wine vinegar
½	medium red onion, thinly sliced
	Salt and freshly ground black pepper
1	pound pasta

1. Halve 1 cup of the tomatoes and place them in a large bowl. Place the remaining 3 cups tomatoes in a food processor along with the basil, oil, garlic, and vinegar and pulse until well mixed. Transfer the contents of the food processor to the bowl with the halved tomatoes and stir in the onion. Add salt and pepper to taste.

2. Bring 4 quarts of salted water to a rolling boil in a large pot over high heat. Add the pasta and cook until al dente. Drain the pasta for 15 seconds in a large colander without shaking and toss it with the sauce. Taste for seasoning, adding salt and pepper if needed, and serve immediately.

Quick tomato-based summer pasta dishes are the modern equivalent of the Victorian standby pease porridge ("some like it in the pot nine days old"), because they are what a lot of folks eat for dinner when they are out of time and ideas and the weather is warm. The problem with these last-minute, made-up recipes is that they are usually not very good. Since the ingredient list is short, small mistakes in quantities or preparation methods often result in watery, garlicky, dull, or unbalanced dishes. The question I set out to answer was how to take a few ingredients — I wanted to stick with greens, cheese, and tomatoes — and toss them with hot pasta to make a quick but inspiring dinner. ▶◀

I began with the greens, testing arugula, Swiss chard, spinach, and escarole. Cooked, the latter three greens had more flavor than arugula. However, raw arugula was my favorite, because it required no cooking and has a wonderful peppery flavor that complements cheese. (I found it best to cut the arugula into 1-inch strips.) For the cheese, I found that fresh, not aged, goat cheese melts nicely into a creamy sauce over the cooked pasta. Although ricotta and mascarpone were also creamy, they were quite bland, and mozzarella turned into a stringy mess when paired with hot pasta. About one cup of crumbled goat cheese was the right amount.

I then set out to test the addition of tomatoes. I began by cooking fresh tomatoes until they were quite soft (about 10 minutes), just barely soft (about two minutes), and then using them raw. The cooked versions were less flavorful than the uncooked tomatoes, making this recipe that much easier to prepare. I found it best to seed the raw tomatoes, although they do not have to be peeled.

Other ingredients tested were onions, garlic, capers, and basil. Onions were too strong tasting, as was garlic. I liked the addition of capers, but they were strictly optional. It turned out that fresh basil was a nice addition, balancing the arugula and tomatoes; ½ cup of leaves cut into ¼-inch strips was just right. All that was left to round things out was 2 tablespoons of fruity extra-virgin olive oil, about a half teaspoon of salt, and lots of freshly ground pepper. As for the pasta, I liked penne or fusilli because the chunky texture trapped the cheesy sauce and the small size allowed for pieces of tomato and greens in each bite.

Pasta with Arugula, Goat Cheese, and Raw Tomatoes

SERVES 4

Other than boiling pasta, this recipe requires no cooking and little preparation.

	Salt and freshly ground black pepper
1	pound pasta, penne or fusilli preferred
2	cups chopped (½-inch pieces) and seeded good-quality fresh tomatoes
2	cups well-rinsed arugula, cut into 1-inch strips
½	cup fresh basil, cut into ¼-inch strips
5	ounces fresh goat cheese, crumbled
2	teaspoons capers, optional
2	tablespoons extra-virgin olive oil

Bring 4 quarts of salted water to a rolling boil in a large pot over high heat. Add the pasta and cook until al dente. Reserve ½ cup cooking water. Once the pasta is cooked and well drained, place it in a large serving or mixing bowl. Add the remaining ingredients, including ½ teaspoon salt and pepper to taste; mix (I found large tongs to be easiest for this step) until the cheese is melted and the other ingredients are well distributed. Add the reserved hot cooking water as necessary to make a creamy sauce. Serve immediately.

Nothing sounds simpler than a quick, fresh tomato sauce with cream. What could go wrong? Well, the tomatoes might be flavorless, the skins can quickly become unappetizing when cooked, garlic can be an odd partner with cream, and tomato seeds floating in sauce are not ideal. And of course, a heavy hand with the butter or cream can turn a fresh summer supper into a heavy, tasteless mess. ▶◀

The first issue was the tomatoes. Do not make this recipe with anything but truly flavorful local tomatoes. Next, I found that peeling and seeding were, in fact, necessary — but there is some good news: A quick bath in boiling water (only 30 seconds) was all that was needed to loosen the skins. A subsequent dunk in ice water turned out not to be necessary. As for coring and seeding, the easiest method is to cut away the core and then halve the tomato through the equator. The seeds are then quickly removed by shaking the halved tomato over the sink or a bowl.

Butter turned out to be better than olive oil for cooking, because butter marries well with cream. Garlic, no matter how little I used and how I cooked it, was out of place. One half of an onion, finely diced and then lightly sautéed, made for a better combination with the other ingredients. As for the cream, heavy cream beat out half-and-half or light cream for standing up to the tomatoes. However, a mere ¼ cup was sufficient; larger quantities subdued the garden-fresh taste of the tomatoes. Salt and black pepper were a must, and ¼ teaspoon nutmeg also worked well.

Pasta with Fresh Tomato Sauce, Cream, and Nutmeg

SERVES 4

To peel the tomatoes, score each bottom with an X and plunge into boiling water for 30 seconds. Once cool enough to handle, the skin will peel away easily. To seed the tomatoes, cut them in half through the equator and shake the seeds into the sink or a bowl.

Salt and freshly ground black pepper

2 tablespoons unsalted butter

½ large onion, finely diced (about 1 cup)

2 pounds fresh, ripe tomatoes (6–8 medium), peeled, cored, seeded, and cut into ½-inch dice

¼ cup heavy cream

¼ teaspoon freshly grated nutmeg

1 pound pasta

1. Bring 4 quarts of salted water to a rolling boil in a large pot over high heat.
2. Melt the butter in a large skillet over medium-low heat. When the foam has subsided, add the onion and cook until very soft and just starting to turn blond, about 7 minutes. Add the tomatoes, increase the heat to medium, and cook until the tomatoes have reduced to a chunky sauce, about 10 minutes. Add the cream and nutmeg and cook until the sauce has thickened and the cream has lost its raw flavor, 1 to 2 minutes. Add ½ teaspoon salt and pepper to taste.
3. Meanwhile, cook the pasta until almost al dente. Reserve 1 cup of the cooking water. Drain the pasta and add to the skillet (or, if your skillet is not large enough, add back to the pot and then add the sauce to the pasta). Combine gently and simmer until the pasta is al dente. Add a bit of the reserved cooking water if necessary to thin the sauce. Serve immediately.

Pasta with Tomatoes and Arugula

In a small mountain village north of Rome, I was once served a simple dish of pasta with a sauce that had penetrated the pasta itself, flavoring it and bathing it with a silky salve of fruity olive oil, garlic, and herbs. This was a far cry from the usual American spaghetti dinner — a watery mound of pasta onto which is dumped an oily flow of tomato sauce. As we all know, oil and water don't mix. ▶◀

I was also bothered by the comments of Italian friends who reprimanded me on the subject of the ratio of sauce to pasta. Although they insisted that a small amount of sauce goes a long way, I found that my attempts at lightly sauced pasta simply yielded underdressed, bland plates of spaghetti.

My first thought was to cook the pasta in the sauce itself, not in boiling water. Using a simple, 10-minute tomato sauce, I added angel hair pasta with horrific results. By the time the center of the pasta was cooked, the outside had turned slimy. In addition, the sauce was starchy from the pasta, and it became very dry (dried pasta absorbs a lot of liquid during cooking). When I then added vast amounts of liquid to the pan to thin the sauce, the flavor of the sauce was compromised.

Next, I tried starting the pasta in water and finishing it in the sauce. This method proved superior, because the water rinsed off excess starch, the texture of the finished pasta was good, and the cooking water made the perfect liquid for thinning the sauce. Using fettuccine, I reduced the cooking time in water by one, three, five, and seven minutes, finishing the cooking in the sauce itself. When the pasta spent just a few minutes in the sauce, the results were disappointing: The noodles had not absorbed much flavor. When I precooked the pasta for only a couple of minutes, however, I ended up with the same situation I had started with — slimy pasta. Finally, I settled on cooking the pasta about half the time in boiling water and half in the sauce. This was perfection — the sauce penetrated the pasta and clung to it like suntan lotion. A little bit of sauce went a long way.

Now that I had tested fettuccine, I wanted to test other shapes. Surprisingly, from angel hair to fusilli, it ended up to be the same: Half the cooking time in water and half in sauce produced an amazingly flavorful piece of pasta, although the amount of cooking liquid that had to be added to the sauce varied. I also wanted to try this with other types of tomato-based sauces. Meat sauces were wonderful, as were an amatriciana (tomato sauce with pancetta or bacon) and a ragu, although a puttanesca was less successful. My favorite, however, is still a quick tomato sauce with a handful of arugula thrown in near the end. It's fast, it's easy, and it marries perfectly with the pasta.

Pasta with Quick Tomato Sauce and Arugula

SERVES 4

The amount of pasta water you add to the sauce is variable—just be sure to reserve 2 cups cooking liquid before the pasta is drained. This approach is also very good with any meat sauce.

1   (28-ounce) can diced or whole tomatoes packed in juice (not puree), Muir Glen preferred
2   medium garlic cloves, peeled
3   tablespoons extra-virgin olive oil
¼   teaspoon sugar
     Salt and freshly ground black pepper
1   pound pasta
2   tablespoons coarsely chopped fresh basil leaves
2   cups arugula leaves, washed and dried
     Freshly grated Parmesan cheese

1. If using diced tomatoes, go to step 2. If using whole tomatoes, drain them and reserve the liquid. Dice the tomatoes into about ¼-inch pieces either by hand or with a food processor. Add enough juice to yield 2 cups.

2. Process the garlic through a press (or mince with a knife) into a small bowl; stir in 1 teaspoon water. Heat 2 tablespoons of the oil and the garlic mixture in a very large skillet or sauté pan (at least 12 inches) over medium heat until fragrant but not browned, about 2 minutes. Stir in the tomatoes and simmer until slightly thickened, about 10 minutes. Stir in the sugar and ½ teaspoon salt.

3. Meanwhile, bring 4 quarts of salted water to a rolling boil in a large pot over high heat. Add the pasta and cook for half of the time indicated on the package. Reserve 2 cups of the cooking water and drain the pasta. At this point the pasta has started to soften but still appears quite raw in the middle. Add the pasta to the skillet (or, in the absence of a large enough skillet, add the pasta and sauce back to the pasta pot) and complete cooking the pasta in the sauce, adding the reserved cooking water as needed to keep the sauce moist, stirring frequently. With 2 minutes cooking time remaining, add the remaining 1 tablespoon oil and ½ teaspoon salt as well as the basil and arugula, and stir to combine. The pasta and sauce will likely look drier than normal but will be moist and flavorful upon tasting. Taste and adjust the salt level if necessary. Serve immediately with cheese and pepper to taste.

CANNED TOMATOES 101

WHOLE TOMATOES IN PUREE

Puree gives the tomatoes an unwelcome cooked flavor. Avoid this product.

WHOLE TOMATOES IN JUICE

Juice ensures that the tomatoes taste fresh. A good choice, but be prepared to chop the tomatoes yourself.

DICED TOMATOES

My favorite choice because the tomatoes are packed in juice (so they are fresh tasting) and ready to use straight from the can. Note the large size of the tomato chunks, which is not ideal.

WHOLE TOMATOES CHOPPED BY HAND

If you chop canned whole tomatoes yourself, you can cut the tomatoes very finely — either by hand or in a food processor. As a result, they will cook very quickly in a pasta sauce.

CHOOSING THE RIGHT MEAT

FOR PASTA SAUCE

BEEF SHORT RIBS
Rich and robust. My favorite choice.

SPARERIBS
Meaty and flavorful. A good choice.

COUNTRY-STYLE PORK RIBS
Meatier than spareribs but not as flavorful.

LOIN PORK CHOPS
Too dry and not appropriate for tomato sauce.

LAMB SHANK
Rich but gamy. For lamb lovers only.

Four-Star Meaty Tomato Sauce

Most tomato sauces are best prepared quickly, so that the fresh, acidic flavor of the tomatoes doesn't become dull and flat. This goes for sauces made with both canned and fresh tomatoes. However, there is an exception to every rule, and when preparing a tomato sauce with meat, long cooking serves two purposes: It provides a method for cooking the meat while giving the sauce time to absorb its flavors. This is one time when long, slow cooking makes a superior tomato sauce. ▶◀

The first question was which type of meat was best. Oxtail was rich but not very meaty, pork spareribs were good, country-style pork ribs were meatier than spareribs but not as flavorful, pork loin chops were dry, and lamb shanks were rich but only for lamb lovers. Although the pork-rib versions were excellent, I finally settled on beef short ribs, which were fabulous — rich, beefy, and robust, just the thing for a hearty tomato sauce. The flavor of the pork tended to fade over the long cooking time, and I also found that the pork tended to be a bit on the dry side. The beef short ribs, however, always tasted moist and rich, even after a full two hours in the pan. They are also widely available and inexpensive. I found that 1½ pounds of short ribs was just right for one 28-ounce can of tomatoes. In terms of preparation, the ribs need to be trimmed of fat, otherwise the resulting sauce is too oily. Browning is also crucial, because adding raw meat to a tomato sauce produces a flat taste compared with the richer flavor of browned meat.

The tomatoes themselves were an issue. I was using canned tomatoes, which are vastly superior to most fresh tomatoes, at least in New England 11 months out of the year. Diced tomatoes (Muir Glen is my top choice) were very good, as were whole tomatoes packed in their own juices, which I finely minced to produce a smooth texture. In terms of vegetables, onions and garlic were essential (no surprise), but I also tested carrot and celery. The celery added an unwelcome flavor to the sauce, but the carrot rounded it out and added a hint of sweetness. I also tried adding herbs during the simmering process. Rosemary and bay leaf were added at the beginning of the cooking but turned out to be overpowering. Basil tasted out of place. Oregano was too strong.

Chopped parsley added at the end of the cooking process contributed a burst of fresh flavor and color.

Although I do not use wine in my standard 10-minute tomato sauce recipe, it seemed to make a lot of sense in a meaty sauce. I found that ½ cup red wine was about right, and I used it to deglaze (scrape up) the pan after browning the onions. I tried reducing the wine before adding the tomatoes, but the long cooking time made this step unnecessary. In terms of wine varieties, I tested Cabernet, Shiraz, Chianti Classico, Merlot, and Barbera—all were fine. Any good robust red wine seemed to fit the bill. Of course, the rest of the bottle tastes great with this dish, so you won't have any half-empty bottles after dinner.

Pasta with Short-Rib Tomato Sauce

SERVES 4

This is a simple recipe, though it does require about 2 hours of cooking time to soften the ribs and enrich the sauce. Note that the cooking time may vary considerably depending on the meat, pan, and heat level. This is one recipe that can be made well ahead of time, even the day before, with no loss of flavor. Just add the parsley for the last 5 minutes of cooking time.

1   tablespoon olive oil
1½   pounds beef short ribs (2–3 ribs),
     trimmed of fat
     Salt and freshly ground black pepper
1   medium onion, minced
1   medium carrot, minced
1   large or 2 medium garlic cloves,
     minced
½   cup dry, robust red wine
1   (28-ounce) can diced tomatoes packed
     in juice (not puree), Muir Glen brand
     preferred, or 1 (28-ounce) can whole
     tomatoes packed in juice (not puree),
     drained, juice reserved, tomatoes
     finely minced
½   cup chopped fresh flat-leaf parsley
1   pound fusilli, rigatoni, ziti, or farfalle
     Freshly ground Parmesan cheese

1. Heat the oil in a deep, 10- to 12-inch sauté pan or Dutch oven over high heat. (Don't use nonstick.) Season the ribs with salt and pepper and brown them well on all sides, about 10 minutes. Remove the ribs from the pan and set aside. Reduce the heat to medium. Add the onion and carrot and sauté for 5 minutes or until softened but not browned. Add the garlic and sauté for an additional 1 minute. Add the wine and scrape the bottom of the pan to loosen any browned bits.

2. Add the tomatoes and their juices, ribs, and any accumulated juices back to the pan and bring to a boil. Reduce the heat to maintain a gentle simmer, cover the pan, and cook, stirring occasionally, for about 2 hours or until the meat is very tender and falling off of the bones. (The cooking time may vary considerably. Just cook the ribs long enough so that they are fork-tender and fall off the bones.)

3. Remove the ribs from the pan and set them on a plate to cool. Once they're cool enough to handle, remove the meat from the bones and shred with a fork or your fingers. (The recipe can be made well ahead up to this point. Refrigerate the meat and sauce separately and then remove the layer of solid fat from the top of the sauce before reheating.) Add the shredded meat and the parsley to the sauce and bring to a simmer. Cook, uncovered, for about 5 minutes or until the sauce has slightly thickened. Taste for seasoning, adding salt and pepper if necessary.

4. Meanwhile, bring 4 quarts of salted water to a rolling boil in a large pot over high heat. Add the pasta and cook until al dente. Drain without shaking for 15 seconds and return the cooked pasta to the cooking pot along with the sauce and stir gently to mix. Serve with grated cheese and freshly ground pepper.

When More Is Less

Other than our Vermont neighbors, who are intrepid about inviting my wife and me over to dinner, very few people invite us to their home for dinner. It may be that our dinner table conversation is lacking or that we are perceived to be overly critical of home cooking. (Or, perhaps, we are lacking in some other form of social intercourse that others are too kind to reveal.) In any case, I have had the good fortune to be entertained by some of the best in the business (Child, Beard, and the like) and have discovered something quite remarkable about their menu planning: They cook simply, preparing a very short list of items but, of course, cooking them well.

My first meal with Julia Child back in the early 1980s was an oyster stew with freshly heated baguettes from a local Cambridge bakery. That was it, and it was one of the best meals of my life — the briny oysters married perfectly with the dairy, and the bread added the needed hint of chew. Other meals have included a pan-seared steak with homemade bread, a roasted leg of lamb with braised endive, and freshly boiled Maine new potatoes with caviar.

The other extreme is the cooking enthusiast's Sunday brunch "smorgasbord" with a dozen different dishes, including smoked salmon, scalloped potatoes, sticky buns, a green salad, a fruit salad — you get the picture. So I have taken a page from the masters and now plan very simple meals when entertaining. A large pot of chowder, some good bread, and some fresh fruit and cheese make a wonderful meal. This is one case where more is less. (Now everyone can relax and have me over for dinner.)

Pesto on the Cheap

I say "pesto" and you immediately think of basil, right? Yes, basil is the most common herb used in pesto, but you can make this simple combination of fresh herbs, nuts, olive oil, cheese, garlic, and salt with almost any like ingredients, including chives, mint, parsley, pistachios, almonds, etc. I was particularly interested in a chive pesto because, unlike basil, this herb grows like a weed. It comes up early and keeps growing well into the fall, and if chives are store-bought, they are relatively cheap. ▶◀

I started by using a standard basil pesto recipe and simply substituted chives, but the mixture tasted too much like onions. I felt that by adding a small amount of another herb I could balance the flavors, so I tested basil, parsley, and arugula. The basil made an odd partner for chives, arugula was peppery and fresh but overpowering, and the parsley was just right. Parsley is plentiful year-round and inexpensive as well. After much fiddling, I ended up with 2½ cups chives and only ½ cup parsley.

I settled on only one garlic clove — the chives already add an onion flavor — and pine nuts tasted better than other varieties including almonds, which were a bit sweet. Some recipes recommend toasting the nuts, but I found raw pine nuts to be just fine. (Note that pine nuts go stale quickly, imparting a sour, stale flavor. Taste one before buying.) For the cheese, I tried both Parmesan and Romano, but the former was the clear winner; the Romano was simply too harsh for this recipe. Be sure to purchase the best-quality Parmesan — Parmigiano-Reggiano — which has a sharp, nutty flavor and will cost you about $12 per pound. It is worth every penny. Oh, and be sure to use a high-quality extra-virgin olive oil, as it is a major ingredient. "Pure" olive oil has virtually no flavor and is only good for frying or other cooking situations in which the oil is heated.

Chive Pesto

MAKES ENOUGH SAUCE FOR
1 POUND OF PASTA

In addition to making a great pasta sauce, this pesto is wonderful over steamed red potatoes.

2½ cups coarsely chopped fresh chives
½ cup coarsely chopped fresh flat-leaf parsley
1 medium garlic clove, crushed
¼ cup pine nuts
½ teaspoon table salt
½ cup best-quality extra-virgin olive oil
½ cup freshly grated Parmigiano-Reggiano, plus more for serving
Freshly ground black pepper

Place all of the ingredients except the cheese in a food processor. Process until very finely chopped (sort of like a grainy paste) but not pureed. Scrape the mixture into a bowl and stir in the cheese. Serve over hot pasta with freshly ground pepper and additional Parmesan.

Introducing Sichuan Noodles

We are besotted with the notion of Italian pasta, yet
we know little, if anything, about Asian noodle dishes,
which are, dare I say, more interesting and more sharply
flavored than the rather bland spaghetti and tomato sauce
served up in most American home kitchens. (Of course,
authentic pasta dishes served in Italy are another matter
altogether.) The Asian approach to noodles is, to a large
extent, based on strong flavors such as ginger, soy sauce,
chili oil, and garlic, which marry nicely with rather
bland but nicely textured Chinese noodles. In China, many
of these dishes are considered snack foods and served
in small portions in tiny, hole-in-the-wall restaurants.
For us, they can easily be translated into a quick but
appealing dinner. ▶◀

I began with a recipe called *Dan Dan Mian* (Spicy Sichuan Noodles) from Ken Hom's *The Taste of China*, which consists of minced pork with soy sauce, garlic, ginger, peanut butter, chili oil, etc. married with Chinese noodles. The recipe was wonderful, but there were two problems: First, a few of the ingredients were not easily found in the supermarket, and, second, the flavors were a bit over the top for my palate — raw, garlicky, and spicy. Although anyone who has grown up with this type of food would violently disagree, I felt that the recipe needed to be taken down a notch or two for the American kitchen.

First, I decided to substitute ground pork for the minced variety and then, instead of frying the pork in peanut oil, as Hom suggests, I decided to use less oil and sauté it instead. The result was less greasy and, to my American palate, tasted better. Next, I found the sauce to be a bit garlicky, so I reduced the minced garlic to 2 tablespoons from 3. The original recipe calls for cooking the garlic and ginger for only 30 seconds, but a full two minutes of cooking produced a less raw, more subtle flavor.

The next question was whether sesame butter was better than peanut butter. I actually liked the peanut butter version better, and since it is a staple in almost every home kitchen, it also made the recipe easier. The original sauce, made with 2 tablespoons chili oil, was too spicy, so I reduced the amount to 1 tablespoon — or less, if you are not fond of spicy foods. I found that a touch of sweetness complemented the spicy chili oil, so I tested honey and sugar, and the latter was better. (It seems odd to add a tablespoon of sugar to a pasta sauce, but this is not uncommon in Chinese cooking.) Hom also uses 1 teaspoon salt in addition to the soy, which seems a bit much, so I reduced it by half.

As for the noodles, I tested fresh noodles versus dried and preferred the latter. Chinese noodles come in 10-ounce packages and cook in just three minutes. The package directions suggest rinsing the noodles after cooking — something I would never do with Italian pasta. But I found that these noodles do have a tendency to stick together, so rinsing is recommended.

Skillet Sichuan Noodles

SERVES 2 TO 3
(BUT CAN BE EASILY DOUBLED)

I make no claims for authenticity here — this is an Americanized version of a classic Chinese dish. However, it is well suited to a quick midweek supper, and all of the ingredients can be found in any decent supermarket. I prefer ground pork, but chicken can be used in a pinch. If you do not like spicy food, cut the chili oil back to either 1 or 2 teaspoons. You can also use spaghetti instead of Chinese noodles.

　　Salt and freshly ground black pepper
8　ounces ground pork or chicken
3　tablespoons soy sauce
¼　cup peanut oil
2　tablespoons finely chopped garlic
2　tablespoons finely chopped fresh ginger
2　scallions, half of the green stalks removed, thinly sliced (about ¼ cup)
2　tablespoons smooth peanut butter
1　tablespoon chili oil

1　tablespoon light brown or granulated sugar
1　cup chicken stock
1　(10-ounce) package dried Chinese noodles (lo mein noodles) or
12　ounces spaghetti

1. Bring 4 quarts of salted water to a rolling boil in a large pot over high heat.
2. Set a large skillet over medium-high heat. In a small bowl mix the ground pork or chicken, 1 tablespoon soy sauce, and a few grinds of pepper to combine well. Add 2 tablespoons peanut oil and the pork to the hot pan. Cook the meat for 5 to 7 minutes or until it is well browned, breaking it apart with a spatula as it cooks. Remove the meat to a paper towel to drain.
3. Wipe out the skillet and set over medium heat. Add the remaining 2 tablespoons peanut oil to the skillet. Add the garlic, ginger, and scallions and cook for 2 minutes. Add the peanut butter, the remaining 2 tablespoons soy sauce, chili

oil, sugar, ½ teaspoon salt, and the chicken stock to the skillet and stir or whisk to combine. Cook for about 5 minutes or until the sauce is thickened and shiny.

4. Meanwhile, when the water comes to a boil, cook the noodles until al dente (as little as 3 minutes for lo mein), separating them as they cook. Drain and rinse with hot water. (If using Italian pasta, partially drain and place the wet pasta back in the cooking pot until needed.) Place the noodles on individual plates, ladle the sauce over them, and garnish with the pork and ground pepper.

Happy Meals Are Made at Home

Here are some depressing facts: Hamburger Helper's annual sales are $400 million and growing nicely. Teenage boys get 9 percent of their daily caloric intake from soda. The average amount of time Americans want to spend making dinner is 15 minutes. The total number of pots and pans Americans want to use to make dinner is — you guessed it — one.

Yet, I find that serious foodies spend a great deal of time and money traveling to conventions, writing books, and reading magazine articles about the latest hot food item (pomegranate molasses, anyone?), the history of food in the Dark Ages, and how long it took to get through dinner at the French Laundry. Wake up and smell the french fries. McDonald's has won. Ronald has slam-dunked Escoffier — it was no contest. The war is over, and we just lost.

But one thing is for sure. We have not only lost our culinary heritage, we have lost the joy of cooking. Cooking is never really about just the food; it's about the process. It's about having someone in the kitchen when the kids come home from school. It's about making buttermilk pancakes at 6:30 A.M. before the school bus shows up. It's about baking a loaf of bread for a neighbor who is ill. It's about investing the time to do something for others. It's about learning a new skill. It's about being productive as a human being.

I have a proposal: Let's start at the very beginning. Let's initiate a program in public schools to teach cooking (remember Home Economics?). Nothing fancy, mind you. We'll start with how to boil an egg, how to make pancakes, and how to refrigerate butter properly. Then we can move on to steaming a vegetable, sautéing a filet, or pot-roasting a tough cut of meat.

As I have said a million times, happy meals are made at home. Let's get into the kitchen and get busy. If you go into the kitchen a little more often, I'll even get off my soap box.

Risotto in Half the Time

Pasta, not risotto, has the distinction of being America's number one dish, because it takes less than 10 minutes to boil. Risotto, on the other hand, has always seemed to be a bit of a bother, with constant stirring and small amounts of stock or water added over a long period of time. The question is, can one make good risotto quickly and without a lot of stirring? ▶◀

The first issue was what sort of rice to use. I tested Arborio, the fat grains used in Italy for risotto, as well as medium- and short-grain rices. What is the difference between different rice lengths? Well, the most obvious difference is shape. Long-grain rice is three to five times longer than it is wide; a kernel of short-grain rice is less than twice as long as its width. Short-grain rice is the type served in Chinese restaurants; it has a lot of starch, which makes it sticky. Medium-grain rice is more similar to short-grain than long-grain in terms of cooking properties and may be used as a substitute. In my tests, the Arborio was the clear winner, although one can certainly make risotto using either medium- or short-grain rice.

The next issue was cooking method. I tried the microwave, the oven, and the stovetop. I found the microwave to be problematic because, in order to release enough starch to create the thick sauce that is typical of a good risotto, the rice needs to be stirred. This meant that the dish had to be moved in and out of the microwave a number of times, which was too much work. The oven method had the same problem. It is easier to stir risotto on the stovetop.

With that settled, I moved on to the basic stovetop method. Most traditional recipes suggest adding a half cup or so of water or stock at a time, stirring constantly. This reminded me of making polenta, for which there is a mystique about the long, arduous preparation time. Instead, I decided to dump a few cups of the liquid into the rice at the beginning and simply walk away. After a few minutes, when the liquid started to cook down, I stirred occasionally. Then I added additional liquid in 3/4-cup increments but only stirred when the liquid started to become absorbed. This method was quite good but needed some refinements. I decided to heat the broth/water first in a separate saucepan to decrease the cooking time. This speeded up the recipe considerably.

I then turned my attention to the liquid. I found that water made a bland risotto;

I preferred a good chicken stock. But it still needed some punch, so I used 1 cup white wine with 4 to 5 cups stock. If you use a relatively salty canned chicken broth, I suggest diluting it with water. However, the best choice is to use a homemade stock or buy decent low-sodium canned broth, such as Campbell's Healthy Request Chicken Broth, which will not have to be diluted. For added flavor, I started the recipe by sautéing some onion in olive oil and then adding the rice and stirring to coat with the mixture. I finished off the dish with some grated Parmesan and just 1 tablespoon butter for added flavor.

I have included plenty of variations, because, like pasta, risotto is endlessly adaptable. Other than simple spices or other flavorings, there are two types of ingredients that can be added to risotto: One type can stand a good deal of cooking; firm vegetables, for example. For these ingredients, sauté them for a few minutes in the pan after the onion has been cooked in the oil. Then proceed with the recipe. For ingredients that cannot stand a half hour or so of cooking, add them at the end. However, these should be precooked separately before adding. Seafood — shrimp, for example — should be added just before serving.

Master Recipe for Risotto

MAKES 4 MAIN-COURSE SERVINGS
OR 8 FIRST-COURSE SERVINGS

Arborio rice makes the best risotto, but medium- or short-grain rice also works well. You do not have to dilute canned chicken broth if it is a low-sodium variety.

- 5 cups homemade chicken stock (or 3 cups canned broth mixed with 2 cups water)
- 3 tablespoons olive oil
- 1 small onion, minced
- 2 cups Arborio rice
- 1 cup dry white wine
- 1 cup high-quality freshly grated Parmesan cheese
- 1 tablespoon unsalted butter
  Salt and freshly ground black pepper

1. Place the stock in a saucepan and heat to a simmer.

2. In a large saucepan or deep-sided skillet, heat the oil and onion over medium-high heat. Sauté for 5 minutes or until lightly browned, stirring frequently. Add the rice and stir for 3 minutes to coat.

3. Add 3 cups of the hot stock to the rice and bring the mixture to a boil. Reduce the heat until the liquid simmers slowly; stir occasionally. When almost all of the liquid has been absorbed, add the wine. Adjust the heat to maintain an even simmer and stir occasionally. When almost all of the wine has been absorbed, continue cooking, adding stock in ¾-cup increments once each batch has been absorbed, and stirring occasionally. When the last of the stock has been added, test the rice. It should be tender but still firm in the center, and the sauce should be creamy. You may end up adding more liquid than called for (just use water). The total cooking time will be around 20 minutes.

4. Stir in the cheese, butter, and salt and pepper to taste. Serve.

VARIATIONS
Risotto with Aromatic Spices
Add ½ teaspoon ground cinnamon, ½ teaspoon ground coriander, ¼ teaspoon ground cloves, and ¼ teaspoon ground cardamom along with the onion.

Risotto with Hot Pepper
Add ¼ cup finely chopped celery, ¼ cup finely chopped red bell pepper, and 1 small jalapeño pepper (cored, seeded, and finely chopped) along with the onion.

Risotto with Asparagus
Steam, sauté, or stir-fry ½ pound asparagus cut into bite-size pieces and add to the risotto just before serving.

Risotto with Tender Greens
Add 1 teaspoon minced garlic to the cooked onion and sauté for 1 minute before adding the rice. Just before serving, add ½ pound spinach or other tender spring greens (arugula or dandelion greens), which have been torn into bite-size pieces. The heat from the rice will wilt the leaves.

POLENTA IN 7 MINUTES

1 MINUTE

Watery and loose. Looks like it has a long way to go,
but things will start to happen quickly.

3 MINUTES

As the cornmeal swells, the polenta thickens quickly.
Still a bit loose, so keep stirring.

7 MINUTES

Thick enough to leave a clear path in the bottom of the pan.
The polenta is ready to serve.

Seven-Minute Polenta

Polenta is both a name for coarsely ground cornmeal as well as the Italian equivalent of cornmeal mush. (Polenta can be loose and creamy, thick, or subsequently baked into dense blocks.) The great mystery of polenta (the cooked variety) is that Italian cookbooks tell you that it takes at least 30 to 90 minutes to make. Refusing to stand by the stove for half an hour stirring anything, much less cornmeal mush, I set out to make polenta in 10 minutes or less. Nuts to the traditionalists. ▶◀

The first thing I noticed about polenta recipes is that they have little in common. Starting with 1½ cups coarsely ground cornmeal, one recipe uses 4 cups water, another 7 cups, and a third 8 cups. The cooking times range from 30 minutes to 90 minutes (in a double boiler), yet the quicker-cooking recipes use twice as much water as the slow-cooked version, a culinary anomaly if there ever was one.

I began testing with 1½ cups coarsely ground cornmeal and 4 cups water. Many recipes warn about adding the cornmeal too quickly — some even suggest that this process should take five minutes. In fact, the cornmeal can be added in about 30 seconds, as long as one keeps stirring. As for cooking time, I just don't know how one could possibly cook the mixture for 45 minutes. It was creamy and thick in five to seven minutes, had a nice corn flavor, and had a bit of texture from the cornmeal. Italian cooking experts warn that quick-cooked polenta is harsh and bitter, which is simply not true. In fact, I prefer seven-minute polenta, because the texture is more interesting. (I suspect that the coarse cornmeal traditionally used in Italy may, in fact, take longer to cook. Nobody has bothered to adjust the cooking times to reflect the American product.)

Next, I investigated the varieties of cornmeal available at retail stores. The first is coarsely ground, which is often referred to as polenta. In natural food stores, it is also called corn grits. This is the type of cornmeal I was using in the testing, and it worked well. Next, I tried fine cornmeals sold by Quaker and Arrowhead Mills. (Quaker lists other ingredients on the package; Arrowhead is made just from corn.) Both brands produced polenta that was tasteless, slimy, mushy, and lumpy, no matter how carefully I added the cornmeal. Instant polenta, which is precooked cornmeal, is available in 500-gram packages and sold under a variety of different labels. It cooked in two to three minutes and made decent polenta, although the coarsely ground variety is better. Use instant in a pinch.

As for other ingredients, many recipes suggest that half of the water may be replaced with milk or chicken stock. I tried milk, half-and-half, and light cream and preferred the batch made with half-and-half as a variation. It was creamy without being overpowering. The stock added an unwelcome flavor that detracted from the pure corn taste I was looking for. Of course, the polenta needs salt; I added 1½ teaspoons to the boiling water. Two other common ingredients are butter and cheese. I added 4 tablespoons butter and ½ cup grated cheese off the heat. I also added a few grinds of black pepper. My favorite cheese was Parmesan, although I liked fontina as well. Ingredients tested and rejected include garlic, onion, bay leaf, cloves, cinnamon stick, olive oil, and bits of chopped herbs. This is one dish for which simplicity is key — don't muck it up with four-star-chef ingredients.

This dish can be served with just about any tomato sauce — Bolognese is especially good. It is also good with oven-roasted sausages, any kind of braised meat or poultry, or a sauté of mushrooms. And it can be used instead of rice or noodles as a side dish to a stew. Like cornmeal mush, it can be served for breakfast with honey, cinnamon sugar, or hot maple syrup.

Seven-Minute Polenta

SERVES 4 TO 6 AS A SIDE DISH

It is important to use coarsely ground cornmeal, which is also sold as polenta or corn grits. Do NOT use finely ground cornmeal.

1½   teaspoons table salt
1½   cups coarse cornmeal
4   tablespoons (½ stick) unsalted butter
½   cup freshly grated Parmesan or fontina cheese
    Freshly ground black pepper

Bring 4 cups water to a boil in a medium saucepan. Add the salt and then gradually add the cornmeal while stirring with a wooden spoon. Reduce the heat to maintain a simmer, stirring constantly. The polenta should be smooth, and large bubbles will pop on the surface. Cook until very thick but not stiff, 5 to 7 minutes. This will vary slightly depending on the grind of the polenta and the freshness of the grain. Off heat, add the butter, cheese, and pepper to taste. Serve immediately.

VARIATIONS
Rich and Creamy Polenta
Substitute 2 cups half-and-half for 2 cups of the water.

Instant Polenta
Using the precooked version of the grain, called instant polenta, follow the above recipe, reducing the cooking time to 2 to 3 minutes.

CHICKEN

file opened ___3/9___

file closed ___6/21___

POUNDING GENTLY

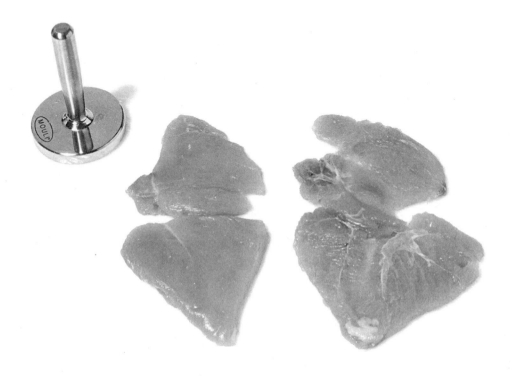

Cooking is about paying attention to details. A cutlet has a smooth side (which was right under the skin) and a rough side (made by cutting the meat away from the bone). Pounding the cutlet between sheets of plastic wrap helps ensure good results, but you need to orient the cutlet properly, too. If you pound the cutlet with the smooth side facing up, the finished cutlet will be nicely shaped and even (left). If you pound the cutlet with the rough side facing up, the finished cutlet will be ragged and uneven (right).

The Fastest Chicken in the West

The term *paillard* is familiar to anyone who eats out at expense-account restaurants. It refers to an extremely thin cut of meat or fish that is cooked quickly. (The name comes from a 19th-century Parisian restaurant, Paillard's.) I set my sights on Chicken Paillard and wanted to find a technique for making it juicy and tender and serving it with a simple pan sauce. ▶•◀

After some testing, I decided that a paillard of chicken should be ¼-inch thick and that boneless, skinless breasts were the cut of choice. Starting with four breasts, I found it best to cut each piece in half. Otherwise, the pieces are hard to arrange in the skillet, plus the pounding process easily reduces larger pieces to mush. I found that it was best to layer the chicken in plastic wrap and use a meat pounder, although a small heavy skillet works fine as well. One other trick: It is best to pound the chicken pieces with the smooth side up (the side that was in contact with the skin). This prevents them from falling apart during the pounding process.

Before investigating cooking, I wondered if brining would help keep the meat moist. This proved to be a dead end, as these super-thin chicken pieces soaked up brine like a sponge, rendering them salty and artificial tasting. The unbrined chicken had much better flavor.

I cooked the pounded paillards in a combination of butter and olive oil after seasoning them with salt and pepper. The thin pieces of chicken cooked in about two minutes per side over medium-high heat. This temperature was hot enough to achieve a spotty brown color and still maintain a juicy, tender interior. When I cooked the chicken more slowly, it became tough. Higher temperatures simply burned the butter and created a bitter flavor. The chicken needs to be cooked in batches with a bit of oil and butter added as needed. Even so, the first batch is still hot by the time the last batch is finished.

As for serving suggestions, a simple drizzle of high-quality olive oil and a squeeze of lemon juice do the trick. (During summer months, pesto is another nice choice.) Of course, the chicken may also be popped into a sandwich.

For a quick pan sauce, I found that white wine was the liquid of choice, followed by some chicken stock. Then I tried adding a variety of herbs, preferring thyme and/or parsley. I tried adding many of the usual players, like anchovies, mustard, garlic, and shallots to the sauce. The anchovy, mustard, and garlic were too pungent, but one finely chopped shallot was a pleasant, though not essential, addition. I thickened the sauce with 3 tablespoons cold butter that I stirred in off the heat. As with any sauce mounted with butter, this one finished with velvety consistency and was not at all heavy. In the end, this quick pan sauce gave the paillards an elegant, flavorful cloak.

Chicken Paillard

SERVES 4

The chicken may also be grilled over high heat for 1 minute per side. If grilling, omit the butter and brush the pounded chicken lightly with olive oil before seasoning with salt and pepper. No matter how you cook the chicken, you can also pound the tenders (see step 1) and cook them along with the rest of the breast meat. Be careful not to overcook the chicken. I also recommend serving this dish with the Salsa Verde on page 169.

FOR THE CHICKEN

4   boneless, skinless chicken breasts, rinsed and patted dry with paper towels
     Salt and freshly ground black pepper
2   tablespoons best-quality olive oil
2   tablespoons unsalted butter

FOR THE OPTIONAL HERB-BUTTER SAUCE

¼   cup dry white wine
1   medium shallot, finely chopped, optional
⅓   cup chicken stock
1   teaspoon finely chopped fresh thyme or flat-leaf parsley or a combination of both
3   tablespoons cold unsalted butter, cut into ½-inch pieces

1. For the chicken: Remove the tender (the small piece under the breast) and cut the individual breasts in half to yield a total of 8 pieces. Using a flat meat pounder or small skillet, pound the chicken (smooth-side up) between two pieces of clear plastic wrap to a thickness of ¼ inch. Season the chicken with salt and pepper to taste.

2. Place a heavy-duty 12-inch skillet over medium-high heat until hot, about 3 minutes. Add 1 tablespoon each of olive oil and butter. Once the butter stops foaming, swirl the skillet to evenly coat the surface with the butter and oil. Add as many chicken pieces as will fit in one layer without crowding and cook until spotted deep golden brown, about 2 minutes. Turn the chicken pieces and cook for an additional 2 minutes, or until colored similarly to the first side. Note that the cooking time will vary a great deal depending on your skillet and your stovetop! Remove to a warm plate and cover with aluminum foil. Repeat with the additional pieces in batches, adding a bit of olive oil and butter as needed. Serve with Salsa Verde (page 169), a scant drizzle of best-quality olive oil, and a squeeze of lemon juice or prepare the herb-butter sauce as directed in step 3.

3. For the sauce: Once all the chicken is cooked, add the wine and optional shallot to the skillet. Using a spatula, scrape up any browned bits that may be stuck to the bottom of the pan. Cook until the wine is almost completely reduced, 1 to 2 minutes. Add the stock and the chopped herb(s) and cook until the liquid is reduced by about two thirds and has thickened slightly, about 3 minutes longer. Off heat, stir in the cold butter pieces. Adjust the seasoning with salt and pepper if needed. Spoon the sauce over the chicken paillards and serve immediately.

A Sprig of Thyme

Give me a break. When has a sprig of anything lent much flavor to a dish? The French are always adding sprigs to everything, but I find that the flavor is muted at best. (Maybe French thyme has more flavor.) Most of the time, I prefer to add fresh herbs near the end of cooking and add plenty of them so you can really taste them. One sprig of thyme in a beef stew is like adding a can of Coke to a swimming pool—you won't notice it. So if you do feel like adding a sprig early on in a recipe, add a lot more than one—at least you'll be able to taste it.

Chicken Cutlets in Four Minutes?

I am appalled at the lengths to which some folks will go
to get dinner on the table fast, gulping down frozen dinners, jarred spaghetti sauce, bad take-out Chinese food,
and the ubiquitous Domino's Pizza. I am no food snob —
I love a burger as much as the next carnivore — but I am
wedded to from-scratch home cooking for reasons of taste,
health, and, well, philosophy. So, in order to compete
with Lean Cuisine, I set out with a near-impossible task.
Could I create a recipe for a homemade chicken dinner
that would take 20 minutes or less, including all preparation and cooking? ▶◀

My first thought was that skin and bones would have to go in order to speed up
cooking time. That left me with boneless, skinless cutlets. But chicken breasts can be
quite thick, and as such they would never cook in just a few minutes. So after a bit of
testing, I decided to slice them in half horizontally to make them thinner and quicker
cooking. The next barrier to quick and easy cooking was the unevenness of the chicken
breast. I found it necessary to quickly pound the thicker parts of the breast so that the
sliced cutlets were an even ¼ inch thick.

A hot sauté pan is fast and easier to manage than a broiler or hot oven. But thin,
naked cutlets would dry out quickly in a hot pan. My solution was to devise a simple
coating for the cutlets to keep them juicy and add some textural contrast as well. The
first choice was dried bread crumbs, but they were a bit dull. A combination of grated
Parmesan cheese and bread crumbs was better, providing both flavor and a crispy coating. I then tested egg whites, whole eggs, and then no eggs at all as a coating before
adding the bread crumb–cheese mixture. The whites were the winner; the whole eggs
made the coating too thick and heavy, and without any egg, the cutlets were bland.

Because of the large amount of cheese, I found a nonstick skillet to be essential.
Hot oil is crucial to developing a nice crispy crust. To determine whether the pan is hot
enough to add the chicken, heat the pan over medium-high and wait until the oil starts
to smoke. Now you know the pan is ready. The cooking time was fast — three to four
minutes total — and I could handle four cutlets at a time if I used a 12-inch skillet.

Now that I had a lightning-fast chicken recipe, I wanted to make a whole meal of it. A bed of arugula arranged on the plate with one sliced tomato worked nicely. These are drizzled with extra-virgin olive oil and balsamic vinegar and sprinkled with fresh tarragon leaves. The hot chicken cutlets are then placed on top. Serve this quick dinner with a fresh baguette and a fruity wine, and you have a quick, from-scratch dinner — a whole lot better than any frozen pizza.

Four-Minute Chicken Cutlets

SERVES 4

Use very fine textured store-bought bread crumbs for this recipe instead of fussing with homemade. You can skip the bed of greens if you like, although peppery arugula adds a lot to this dish. The idea for this recipe was inspired by New Food Fast *by Donna Hay.*

- 4 boneless, skinless chicken breasts, rinsed and patted dry with paper towels
- 3 large egg whites
- ¾ cup freshly grated Parmesan cheese
- ½ cup fine dried bread crumbs
- 3 cups arugula or tender greens of your choice
- 4 small or medium tomatoes
   Extra-virgin olive oil for drizzling
   Balsamic vinegar for drizzling
   Salt and freshly ground black pepper
- 1 bunch fresh tarragon or basil
- 4 tablespoons olive oil, or more as needed

1. Cut each individual breast in half horizontally to yield a total of 8 pieces. Using a flat meat pounder or small skillet, pound the chicken (smooth-side up) between 2 pieces of clear plastic wrap to a thickness of ¼ inch. In a small bowl, lightly whisk the egg whites with a fork. Combine the grated cheese and bread crumbs in a shallow dish or pie plate. Make a bed of ¾ cup arugula on each of 4 dinner plates. Slice the tomatoes and place on top of the greens. Drizzle with the extra-virgin olive oil and balsamic vinegar and season with salt to taste. Scatter tarragon leaves over the tomato.

2. Heat 4 tablespoons olive oil in a 12-inch nonstick skillet over medium-high heat until just starting to smoke. Meanwhile, season 4 pieces of chicken on both sides with salt and pepper. Dip each piece into the egg whites and then into the cheese-crumb mixture, pressing on the chicken to collect a thick coating on both sides. Place the chicken in the heated pan and cook 1½ to 2 minutes on each side, or until deep golden brown. (Only 3 very large pieces of chicken may fit into a 12-inch pan, so you will have to cook 3 batches, not 2.) You can cut into a piece of chicken to check for doneness — it should be just cooked through and juicy. Remove to paper towels to drain. Repeat with the remaining pieces of chicken, adding more olive oil when necessary. On each of the 4 dinner plates, arrange 2 pieces of hot chicken over the tomatoes and arugula. Serve immediately.

How to Pan-Roast Chicken Breasts

The major problem with roast chicken breasts is the skin — it is often pallid, rubbery, and tasteless. In addition, the meat of the chicken breast is usually lacking in flavor. One solution is to sauté the breast skin-side down in a very hot pan on the stovetop, followed by a short stay in the oven to finish the cooking. This delivers great skin and the opportunity to make a quick pan sauce to finish the dish. I set out to test the details of this approach, hoping to find a superior recipe for this common Tuesday-night dinner. ▶◀

I began by testing whether the chicken would benefit from a quick brine. (Brine is simply a solution of cold water, sugar, and salt, in which the chicken pieces are immersed.) I found that a quick one-hour brine made a substantial difference in both flavor and juiciness. In addition, the skin of the brined breasts turned a much deeper color, due to the sugar. Although this step does require a bit of advance planning, the results are clearly worth it.

I wanted this recipe to serve four and found that I needed a 12-inch skillet to handle four split breasts. In addition, the skillet had to be extremely hot; otherwise it cooled down quickly once the breasts were added. Covering the pan to avoid splattering only made the skin soggy, so a large splatter screen was helpful. The breasts are cooked skin-side down for about eight minutes; the skin should be very dark brown and crispy. The cooking time will vary depending on the type of pan you use and the heat output of your burners.

Next, I put the skillet with the chicken breasts into a low oven, 250 degrees. Unfortunately, the breasts took 40 minutes to finish. I tested a variety of temperatures and finally settled on 350 degrees, which required only 20 minutes of oven time. This higher temperature did not dry out the meat, because the chicken had been brined and was therefore juicy. I also found that a few slashes in the skin made it even crispier.

The last element was the sauce. I assembled many of the standard pan-sauce ingredients: wine, stock, sherry, vermouth, garlic, shallots, anchovies, mustard, parsley, thyme, tarragon, oregano, olives, capers, lemon, bay leaves, cloves, and butter.

Anchovies, garlic, and cloves were too strong for this simple dish. I liked a combination of shallots and sherry, but it needed lightening with a bit of chicken stock. I found that the addition of mustard, lemon juice, thyme, and parsley rounded out the flavors nicely. I also developed a quick sauce of dry vermouth, stock, bay leaf, capers, olives, lemon juice, and parsley or oregano. The second sauce, which has a bit of a raw quality (the capers, olives, and herbs are all thrown in at the end), seemed lighter, and the sherry-and-shallot sauce was richer. Both recipes are offered below.

Pan-Roasted Chicken with Mustard and Sherry

SERVES 4

If you purchase kosher chicken breasts, you should skip the brine, as these chickens are already salted. If using canned chicken broth, choose a low-sodium brand, or the sauce will be too salty.

FOR THE CHICKEN

- ½ cup table salt
- ½ cup sugar
- 4 split bone-in, skin-on chicken breasts, 12–14 ounces each
  Freshly ground black pepper
- 2 tablespoons olive oil

FOR THE SAUCE

- 1 tablespoon finely chopped shallot
- ½ cup sherry
- ¾ cup chicken stock
- 1 teaspoon Dijon mustard
- ½ teaspoon finely chopped fresh thyme
- 1 tablespoon lemon juice
- 1 teaspoon finely chopped fresh flat-leaf parsley

1. For the chicken: Dissolve the salt and sugar in 2 quarts cold water in a large bowl. (You can also use a large freezer bag.) Immerse the chicken in the brine and refrigerate until fully seasoned, about 1 hour. Remove the chicken from the brine and rinse well under cold running water. Dry thoroughly inside and out with paper towels. Adjust an oven rack to the center position and heat the oven to 350 degrees.

2. Using a sharp knife, make three diagonal slashes in the skin of each piece of chicken, being careful not to cut into the meat. Season both sides with pepper. Meanwhile, add the olive oil to a heavy-duty 12-inch skillet over medium-high heat, and when the oil just starts to smoke, add the chicken breasts, skin-side down, and stand back — they will splatter. Cook for 7 to 8 minutes or until dark brown. Turn the breasts skin-side up and place the skillet in the heated oven. Cook for 15 to 25 minutes or until an instant-read thermometer reads 165 degrees at the thickest part of each breast. Carefully remove the pan from the oven (the handle will be VERY hot). Transfer the chicken to a warm platter and cover with aluminum foil to retain heat.

3. For the sauce: Pour off all but 1 tablespoon of fat from the skillet and place the skillet over high heat. Add the shallot, sherry, and chicken stock and scrape the browned bits from the bottom of the pan. Cook at a vigorous boil until the liquid has thickened slightly and has reduced by about two thirds, about 5 minutes. Add the mustard and thyme and cook 1 minute. Add the lemon juice and parsley and cook 30 seconds more. Serve immediately spooned over the chicken breasts.

Pan-Roasted Chicken with Olives, Capers, and Vermouth
Omit the shallots. Use dry vermouth in place of the sherry and add 1 bay leaf along with the liquid. Omit the mustard and thyme and add 2 tablespoons capers and ¼ cup pitted and chopped oil-cured or Kalamata olives in their place. Freshly chopped oregano may be substituted for the parsley.

Hot Stuff

Cooking is a poorly named activity. After all, much "cooking" involves no actual cooking at all. Do you cook when you make a salad? This brings us to the most basic question of all: Why do we cook? Why not simply eat raw ingredients? Well, some foods, such as poultry, cannot be eaten raw for reasons of both taste and safety. Yet, the Japanese have elevated eating raw fish to an art (to say nothing of sea urchins and monkey brains), and we readily eat raw fruit and vegetables out of hand. What is there, then, about cooking? Well, one might begin by saying that cooking transforms foods — a cooked roast is entirely different from a raw one. A cake batter bears no resemblance to a cake. Whipped egg whites and yolks beaten with sugar and flavorings don't give us a hint of their transformation to a soufflé. Scrambled eggs and raw eggs cannot be confused.

Other than the transformation of ingredients, which occurs most often during baking, cooking does two things: It adds and/or changes flavors, and it changes texture. Scrambled eggs are improved dramatically over raw on both counts. A beef tenderloin tastes a whole lot better high-roasted than simply ground up. (At least, most of us think so.) Yet, a perfectly ripe summer peach cannot be improved upon in a pie or cobbler or when poached. It just doesn't get any better.

All of this seems simple enough — you might comment that you have learned nothing new so far. Yet, if you approach cooking with the notion of developing and balancing flavors, you are ahead of 98 percent of all home cooks. Most people think that cooking is about "cooking," that is, turning raw foods into cooked foods. Not really. At the most basic level, it is about developing, juxtaposing, and balancing flavors. If one were to take an anthropological tour of world cuisine, one would note that the cooking that is considered ideal by different cultures varies tremendously. Even in the United States, that standard has changed dramatically in the last 10 years. Try ordering your steak or tuna well done at an expense-account restaurant, and see what happens. Some chefs will actually refuse your order.

Okay, so how does cooking enhance flavor? The first, most obvious, method is that food changes chemically when it is heated. Hundreds of chemical reactions occur on the outside of a roast or in a pie crust that create a variety of flavor compounds. Here is a simple rule: The more heat you use, the more flavor you create. That's why a vegetable stir-fry made in a pan that is too small over a burner that is too weak will produce lackluster results. You want a lot of heat to turn those simple vegetables into big flavors. That's why recipes tell you not to crowd a pan when sautéing and why they tell you to preheat the pan. The biggest mistake a home cook makes is succumbing to the fear of using extreme heat. Remember, heat equals flavor.

Let's take a good example of heat and flavor. A roux is a simple combination of butter and flour that is whisked over heat until it creates a thickened mixture. If one adds milk, it is called a béchamel, the basis for countless sauces. If one adds chicken stock, it is called a velouté, another all-purpose sauce that is used in traditional French and American cuisine. But these white sauces don't have a lot of flavor. The flavor is added through other ingredients: onions, shallots, garlic, wine, liquor, spices, herbs, etc. Now take Cajun cooking, which is famous for gumbos. Gumbos are based on the notion of a dark roux, an oil-flour combination that is stirred over low heat for up to an hour until it becomes the color of mahogany. It has a distinctive and completely different taste than the classic white roux. It is as if the two compounds have nothing in common.

Onions are another good example. Taste them raw versus diced and cooked until soft, or sliced and cooked over low heat in a covered skillet until they caramelize, up to half an hour. The same could be said for a pan-cooked steak, a grilled hamburger, or a few cloves of garlic that are cooked instead of eaten raw. And any Indian cook worth his or her salt knows that many spices, especially cumin, are better toasted. Why? Because cooking enhances flavors.

So cooking isn't really about heating raw foods; it's about producing complex flavor compounds that occur only through the application of heat. Think of heat as a flavor enhancer, and don't be afraid to use lots of it when sautéing, stir-frying, or grilling.

HOW BROWN IS BROWN?

MUCH TOO PALE

Most chicken stews or braises start
by browning skin-on parts. Some cooks are
much too timid, and, as a result, they
don't render enough fat from the chicken.

GETTING CLOSE

Most cooks stop when the chicken
is golden brown. Although this will render a fair
amount of fat, I take this process further.

JUST RIGHT

I brown chicken parts until the skin is
dark brown. Almost all of the fat has been rendered,
so the cooking medium for the stew
is especially flavorful.

There is nothing new about combining balsamic vinegar with chicken. Italian experts Lidia Bastianich and Lynne Rossetto Kasper offer recipes in their cookbooks with this simple marriage of flavors. My goal was a basic chicken dinner based on this modest culinary pairing. ▶◀

Chicken thighs are the best bet for this type of recipe, because they are juicier and more flavorful than breasts. By sautéing them with the skin on and then removing the skin before braising, I was able to protect the meat from drying out, while adding a bit of flavor to the fond (browned bits) on the bottom of the pan as well.

Next, I removed the browned chicken and sautéed one large sliced onion. Its sweetness would prove a nice counterpoint to the vinegar. As for the vinegar itself, I started with ¼ cup of balsamic but also tested red wine and white balsamic vinegars, both of which were too acidic. I now wanted to balance the vinegar with sugar; I preferred 2 tablespoons light brown sugar. Now I had a sweet-sour combination that made the dish a lot more interesting.

Next up was the addition of some tomato; Muir Glen diced tomato was best. (You can use any brand, as long as it is packed in juice, not puree, although, based on a taste test, Muir Glen is my favorite.) Two tablespoons capers added an extra dimension, and some fresh basil added just before serving rounded out the dish. Other herbs fought with the main ingredients.

The dish itself is simple enough. The chicken thighs are browned and removed, the onion is softened, and then the pan is deglazed with chicken stock. After about a minute, the tomatoes, vinegar, sugar, capers, and chicken are added. Once the ingredients are brought to a boil, the pan is covered and left to simmer for 10 minutes. The chicken is flipped over and cooked for 10 minutes longer. To finish, I stir in the chopped basil. This dish is simple and quick but bold enough even to satisfy company.

Chicken with Balsamic Vinegar, Tomatoes, and Capers

SERVES 4

Use only canned diced tomatoes packed in juice, not tomatoes packed in puree. If you cannot find canned diced tomatoes, use whole tomatoes packed in juice and dice them yourself. Be sure to drain off and use some of the juice along with the tomatoes. You can serve this dish with rice, mashed potatoes, or polenta.

8   bone-in, skin-on chicken thighs, rinsed and patted dry with paper towels
    Salt and freshly ground black pepper
1   tablespoon plus 1 teaspoon olive oil
1   tablespoon plus 1 teaspoon unsalted butter
1   large onion, halved and cut into ¼-inch slices
½   cup chicken stock
1   cup canned diced tomatoes along with their juice, Muir Glen preferred
¼   cup balsamic vinegar
2   tablespoons light brown sugar
2   tablespoons drained capers
2   tablespoons thinly sliced fresh basil

1. Liberally season the chicken thighs with salt and pepper on both sides. Heat a large heavy-duty skillet with a lid over medium-high heat. When hot, add 1 tablespoon each of the olive oil and butter. Once the butter has stopped foaming, swirl the pan to evenly coat the bottom with olive oil–butter mixture. Add the chicken and brown well on both sides, 10 to 15 minutes total. Remove the chicken pieces and set aside. Pour off any accumulated fat from the skillet and reduce the heat to medium. Remove the chicken skin after the thighs have cooled slightly.

2. Add the remaining 1 teaspoon each olive oil and butter to the skillet. Once the butter has stopped foaming, swirl to evenly coat the bottom of the pan. Add the onion and cook, stirring frequently, until softened and translucent, about 5 minutes. Add the chicken stock and scrape up any browned bits stuck to the bottom of the pan using a wooden spoon or spatula. Add the tomatoes and their juices, vinegar, sugar, and capers and stir to combine. Arrange the chicken pieces in the pan in one layer. Bring the liquid to a boil and reduce the heat to maintain a simmer. Cover and cook for 10 minutes. Turn the chicken pieces over, cover, and cook for an additional 10 minutes or until the chicken is firm to the touch, the juices run clear, and an instant-read thermometer reads 165 degrees at the thickest part of each thigh. If the sauce is very thin, you may increase the heat and boil to thicken for 1 to 2 minutes. Stir in the basil. Taste for seasonings and adjust with salt and pepper. Serve immediately.

On the Trail of Hunter's Chicken

In a continuing search for yet one more way to prepare chicken, I came across a classic French dish, Chicken Chasseur — otherwise known as Hunter's Chicken. Sautéed chicken pieces are simmered in a wine-tomato sauce with plenty of onions and mushrooms, and sometimes other ingredients such as leeks. The problem with this recipe is that it is either too fatty due to the chicken skin or too lean, having been stripped of its flavor by the health crowd. I was looking for a reasonably quick recipe, something appropriate for a midweek dinner, with a robust, clean flavor. ▶◀

The first issue was the chicken itself, the skin being a particular problem. Although I could remove some of the fat through browning, chicken skin is unappealing when simmered in a liquid — it turns rubbery. So skinless chicken pieces seemed the best way to go. Next was the problem of overcooking. White meat is always a bit dodgy, as it often ends up dry, so I tested chicken thighs. These worked well, delivering a moist, rich taste and texture, and, because I removed the skin after sautéing, there was no soggy skin to contend with.

Although some cooks use a nonstick skillet and almost no oil or butter for sautéing, I did not want this dish to taste like homemade Lean Cuisine. A decent amount of olive oil was necessary to add flavor to the dish and to ensure even cooking of the chicken. I have also found that a "stick" skillet, rather than a nonstick one, is important, because you want dark bits sticking to the pan that can later be deglazed (scraped off and dissolved) with the wine. I tested flouring the chicken thighs before sautéing but was not happy with the results, as the dish took on an odd pinkish color and became too thick. (I had to use too much flour to coat all of the pieces.) Instead, I simply added a tablespoon of flour to the vegetables as they were cooking. Larger amounts of flour muddied the flavor and were not needed for thickening.

In terms of the other ingredients, onions were a must, and I sliced rather than chopped them. I tested various types of peppers and preferred either red or yellow —

green peppers tasted a bit too bitter for this recipe. Big bite-size pieces were fine, as this is a rustic preparation. Garlic or shallots work well here, and mushrooms are not only an important part of this recipe but also add some variation in texture.

For the tomatoes, I tried fresh and canned but preferred the latter, as they have more flavor than fresh tomatoes during most of the year. I found that canned diced tomatoes are particularly well suited to this recipe, because they taste great and there is no preparation necessary.

Hunter's Chicken

SERVES 4 TO 6

If you can only find whole canned tomatoes, make sure that they are packed in juice and not a sauce or puree. Muir Glen, Progresso, and Redpack are good brands. (Tomatoes packed in sauces or purees are very dull in flavor, because the sauce must be cooked, which makes it bland and less acidic.)

8   bone-in, skin-on chicken thighs, rinsed and patted dry with paper towels
    Salt and freshly ground black pepper
3   tablespoons olive oil
2   red or yellow bell peppers or a combination of both, cut into 1-inch chunks
1   large onion, halved and cut into ¼-inch slices
3   medium garlic cloves, finely minced or pressed (about 1 tablespoon), or 3 tablespoons minced shallots
1   tablespoon flour
1   cup white wine
1   (28-ounce) can diced tomatoes, or whole peeled tomatoes packed in juice, Muir Glen preferred, coarsely chopped
1   pound white mushrooms, wiped clean and trimmed
2   teaspoons chopped fresh rosemary
2   teaspoons chopped fresh thyme
2   tablespoons chopped fresh flat-leaf parsley, optional

When Is the Skillet Hot?

This is one of those perennial culinary queries that never get answered satisfactorily. Some cooks place their hand a couple of inches off the surface of the pan. Others test the skillet by placing a small bit of food in it. Others time the preheating period.

My solution is simpler: First of all, put the oil (most recipes that use a skillet start by adding oil) in the skillet before it is heated. Heat the pan and watch the oil. It will start to shimmer in the pan, and then it will start to smoke. At the point at which small curls of smoke start to rise from the pan, it is hot enough for sautéing.

1. Season the chicken thighs liberally with salt and pepper. In a large sauté pan or skillet with a tight-fitting lid, heat 2 tablespoons of the oil over medium-high heat. Add the chicken and brown well on both sides, 10 to 15 minutes total. Remove the chicken and set aside. When cool enough to handle, remove the skin.

2. Reduce the heat to medium and add the remaining 1 tablespoon oil. Add the peppers and cook, stirring occasionally, for 5 minutes, being careful to not let them brown. Add the onion and stir to combine. Cover and cook for 5 minutes. Add the garlic and cook for 1 minute.

3. Add the flour to the vegetable mixture and combine well. Add the wine and scrape any browned bits stuck to the bottom of the pan. Add the tomatoes, mushrooms, rosemary, and thyme. Add the chicken and stir to combine, bringing the mixture to a boil. Reduce to a simmer, cover, and cook for 25 minutes or until the chicken is tender. (Check after 15 minutes.) Adjust the seasonings, add the optional parsley, and serve at once.

Cassoulet, the traditional French dish of beans and meat — usually pork, duck confit, and sausage — is cooked very slowly to allow the flavors to meld. It can be dry, heavy, and salty, but when prepared properly, it is juicy and succulent without being overbearing. The problem, of course, is that this dish is inordinately time-consuming, making it unsuitable for anyone other than an intrepid retiree. ▶◀

The first step was to simplify the ingredient list and shorten the cooking time. Gone was the duck or goose confit and the long, slow simmering. Instead, I opted for quicker-cooking chicken thighs (they stay moist even when slightly overcooked) and either bacon or sausage. The next issue to resolve was how to prepare the beans. After some testing, I decided to precook them and then build the finished dish. (Overnight soaking produces only marginally plumper beans.) I wanted to infuse flavor into the beans during cooking, so I added a small onion studded with whole cloves, a bay leaf, and salt to the cooking water. The cooking takes 45 to 60 minutes (or a bit longer if the beans are old), but you can leave the kitchen while the beans cook.

For the chicken, bone-in, skin-on chicken thighs worked best. I found that the skin becomes gummy during braising, so I simply removed it after sautéing. I found that brining (soaking in salted water to add flavor and moisture) did not make much difference in this dish, because the thighs are braised, which infuses them with flavor.

I thought that the dish needed one more type of meat, so I opted for pork. At first, I rendered fat from a few slices of bacon and then used the fat to brown the chicken and the bacon to garnish the finished dish. I then tried using sweet Italian sausage removed from its casing in place of the bacon; this was a major improvement, as it added depth of flavor and texture and made the dish hearty and rustic.

The liquid I preferred was ½ cup white wine and 3 cups chicken stock. The water used to cook the beans had an overpowering flavor, and plain water didn't add enough taste or body. Additions that made the cut were onion, carrot, and a couple of tablespoons of tomato paste for flavor and color; actual chopped tomato seemed out of place. Finally, I added a bit of fresh rosemary during the last 10 minutes of cooking, although you could try either fresh sage or thyme. The dish is garnished with chopped parsley.

Quick Cassoulet

SERVES 4 TO 6

A word of caution about the beans: Do not undercook them; they will not soften much when cooked with the meat, so they should be just shy of soft after precooking. There is nothing worse than half-cooked beans in this sort of dish.

1 pound dried great Northern or navy beans, rinsed and picked over
1 small onion, peeled and studded with 8 whole cloves
1 bay leaf
   Salt
½ pound sweet Italian sausage, removed from casing and crumbled
8 bone-in, skin-on chicken thighs, rinsed and patted dry with paper towels
   Freshly ground black pepper
1 tablespoon olive oil
1 medium onion, cut into ½-inch dice
1 medium carrot, cut into ½-inch dice
2 garlic cloves, finely minced or pressed
½ cup white wine
2 tablespoons tomato paste
3 cups chicken stock
1 tablespoon chopped fresh rosemary
¼ cup chopped fresh flat-leaf parsley

1. Combine the beans, onion studded with cloves, bay leaf, and ¾ teaspoon salt with 10 cups water in a large saucepan. Bring to a boil over medium-high heat; reduce the heat to maintain a simmer, partially cover, and cook for 45 to 60 minutes or until just tender. Discard the clove-studded onion and bay leaf.

2. Place a large Dutch oven over medium-high heat. Add the sausage and brown well on all sides, breaking apart any large pieces with a spatula. Remove with a slotted spoon and set on paper towels to drain. Pour off all but 1 tablespoon of the fat. (Some sausage is very lean and may not render much fat.) Season the chicken with salt and pepper and brown it well on both sides, in batches if necessary. Remove the thighs and reserve, pouring off all but 1 tablespoon of the fat. When cool enough to handle, remove the skin.

3. Adjust the heat to medium and add the olive oil. Add the chopped onion and carrot and cook, stirring occasionally, until soft, 5 to 7 minutes. Add the garlic and cook for an additional 2 minutes. Add the white wine and scrape the browned bits from the bottom of the pan with a wooden spoon or spatula. Add the tomato paste and stir to combine. Drain the beans and add them to the Dutch oven along with the chicken, sausage, and chicken stock. Bring to a boil, reduce the heat to maintain a simmer, and cook, covered, for 20 to 30 minutes or until an instant-read thermometer reads 165 degrees at the thickest part of each thigh. Add the rosemary and cook for 10 minutes more or until the beans and chicken are very tender. At this point, if the braising liquid is very thin, simmer, uncovered, for a few minutes more. Season to taste with salt and pepper. (Add liberal amounts of both.) Serve immediately, garnished with the chopped parsley.

Chicken in a pot is, from a culinary point of view, braised meat. It is usually cooked with carrots, onions, and potatoes, or some combination. It is a very good dish and simple enough, but I wanted to pair the chicken with sweet potatoes, a richer, more interesting proposition. ▶◀

The first issue was the chicken skin. If left on, it becomes quite unpalatable when served, due to the moist cooking environment. If removed before cooking, the chicken tends to toughen and dry out during sautéing. The solution was to sauté the chicken parts with the skin on, thus rendering delicious chicken fat and also protecting the meat of the bird. Before adding the chicken to the pot for the braising, the skin was quickly removed using paper towels and discarded. Now I had the best of both worlds.

As for the sweet potatoes, I found that two large were about right, yielding about 4 cups. Cutting them into 1-inch pieces helped them cook in the same amount of time as the chicken. As for the onions, I found that large pieces were best to lend this dish some texture, so I peeled and quartered two medium onions, yielding eight large pieces. A 250-degree oven cooked the meat, onions, and potatoes slowly and gently. As for flavorings, 1 tablespoon each of maple syrup and grated ginger added just enough interest to an otherwise pedestrian dish.

Note that just about everything in a supermarket that is labeled a "yam" is actually a sweet potato. (Yams are large, brown tubers that look nothing like a sweet potato.) My favorite sweet potato is actually labeled "sweet potato" and has white flesh, although any sweet potato or yam will do for this dish.

Braised Chicken with Sweet Potatoes, Ginger, and Maple Syrup

SERVES 4

Use a 6-quart Dutch oven for this recipe, as the chicken pieces will all fit nicely in one layer. Place the breasts in the pot bone-side up to make sure that the meat is thoroughly cooked. Note that the cooking time can vary depending on the type of pot you use and how well calibrated your oven is.

¼ cup olive oil, approximately
1 tablespoon unsalted butter
3½ pounds bone-in, skin-on chicken parts (breasts, thighs, and legs only), rinsed and patted dry with paper towels
2 medium onions, peeled and quartered
2 large sweet potatoes, peeled and cut into 1-inch pieces (about 4 cups)
½ cup white wine
2 tablespoons vermouth
1 cup chicken stock

¼ teaspoon table salt

½ teaspoon dried thyme or
   1½ teaspoons fresh

1 tablespoon minced or finely grated
   ginger

1 tablespoon maple syrup

2 tablespoons minced fresh flat-leaf
   parsley
   Freshly ground black pepper

1. Heat the oven to 250 degrees. Heat 2 tablespoons of the olive oil and the butter in a Dutch oven over medium-high heat and brown the chicken on both sides in 2 separate batches. (Each batch will take about 10 minutes.) Add more oil if necessary for the second batch. Do not overcrowd the pan. Reserve the browned chicken in a bowl. When cool, remove and discard the skin.

2. Add the onion to the fat in the empty pan and sauté over medium heat for 3 minutes, stirring occasionally. Add the sweet potatoes, turn the heat to medium-high, and sauté for 3 additional minutes. Remove the onions and sweet potatoes to the bowl with the chicken. Add the white wine and vermouth to the pan with the heat still on medium-high, scraping up the browned bits from the bottom of the pan, about 1 minute. Add the chicken, sweet potatoes, and onion back to the pan along with the chicken stock, salt, and thyme (if using dried). Bring the stock to a simmer, place a large sheet of aluminum foil over the top of the pan, cover with the lid, and place in the heated oven. After 30 minutes, add the ginger, thyme (if using fresh), and maple syrup. (Check the internal temperature of the chicken at this point. It is done when the thigh pieces are 165 degrees.) Cook for about another 15 minutes or until done. Sprinkle with parsley and adjust the seasonings, adding salt and pepper to taste. Serve with a small amount of the liquid.

Although there is no specific American tradition for a dish called chicken and rice, this combination is neither surprising nor innovative. Perhaps closest to a jambalaya or paella, this dish is nothing more than chicken pieces sautéed until well browned and then cooked on top of the stove in casserole fashion with sautéed onions and garlic, a liquid (chicken stock, water, or wine), and rice. Its appeal is obvious. It's a one-dish supper, it's easy, and it's eminently variable. Yet, after having made a dozen attempts at perfecting this recipe, I found two major problems: The white meat tends to dry out before the dark meat is cooked, and the rice is often heavy and greasy. I also wanted to devise a master recipe that lends itself to variations, perhaps a blend of Indian spices or a version with Latin overtones. ▶◀

First, I tackled the problem of overcooked breast meat. It turned out that the solution was rather simple. By adding the breast meat to the dish 15 minutes after the thighs and legs, all cooked perfectly. Of course, one could make this dish with just dark or light meat, but, like most cooks, I am most likely to have a whole chicken on hand rather than just thighs or breasts. In addition, our family of six has distinct and different taste preferences encompassing both kinds of meat.

The texture of the rice, however, was a more vexing issue. My first thought was to reduce the amount of olive oil used to sauté the chicken and onion from 2 tablespoons to 1. This simply was not enough fat to get the job done, and the resulting rice was only fractionally less greasy. I thought that perhaps the chicken skin was the culprit, but after making this dish with skinless chicken pieces, I was surprised to find that the rice was still heavy and the chicken, as I suspected it would be, was tough and chewy. The skin is effective at maintaining succulent meat, especially during heavy sautéing.

I then thought that reducing the amount of liquid in the recipe would produce less-sodden rice. I was using 1½ cups long-grain white rice to 1½ cups chicken stock plus

2 cups water. By reducing the stock to a mere half cup, I had better results. The rice was indeed lighter, but the layer of rice on top was undercooked and dried out. I solved this by stirring the dish once when adding the breast meat, so that the rice on top was stirred into the bottom, producing more even cooking. I then made four different batches using four different liquids: chicken stock (heavy, greasy rice), water (bland, flat tasting), a combination of wine and water (the acidity of the wine cuts through the fat producing clean, clear flavors), and a combination of water, chopped canned tomatoes, and tomato liquid (the acid in the tomatoes punches up and enriches the flavor). I then used a combination of white wine, water, chopped tomatoes, and tomato liquid with excellent results.

Finally, I tested different varieties of rice to see which held up best to this sort of cooking. A basic long-grain white rice was fine, with good flavor and decent texture; a medium-grain rice was creamy with a risotto-like texture and excellent flavor (I found this version too heavy for my taste, but others on the tasting panel overlooked the dense texture for the improved flavor); basmati rice was nutty with separate, light grains (this was by far the lightest version, but the basmati rice seemed somewhat out of place in such a pedestrian dish); and converted rice was absolutely tasteless although virtually indestructible. So basic long-grain white rice is a fine solution, although both medium-grain and basmati rices can also be used with different but good results.

Better Chicken and Rice

SERVES 4 TO 6

You can make this dish with either all breast meat or just chicken thighs. I prefer to cut each breast in half, which yields 10 pieces from a whole chicken (4 breast halves, 2 legs, 2 thighs, and 2 wings). Be sure to use canned tomatoes that are packed in their own juices rather than in a puree or sauce. Medium-grain rice or basmati rice may be used in place of long-grain rice, if desired. Basmati is an especially good choice in the variation with Indian spices.

1   **whole chicken cut into 10 pieces (see above) or 2 pounds chicken pieces, rinsed and patted dried with paper towels (breast pieces cut in half)**

   Salt and freshly ground black pepper

2   **tablespoons olive oil**

1   **medium onion, chopped**

3   **garlic cloves, pureed or minced**

1½   **cups long-grain white rice or basmati rice**

1   **cup chopped canned tomatoes plus ½ cup of the juice**

½   **cup white wine**

1. Season the chicken liberally with salt and pepper. Heat the oil in a heavy, nonreactive Dutch oven over medium-high heat. When hot, brown the chicken parts (skin-side down first) on both sides, about 12 minutes. The chicken should be very dark. Remove the chicken to a bowl. Pour off all but 2 tablespoons of the fat. Remove the chicken skin when cool enough to handle.

2. Lower the heat to medium and add the onion; cook for 3 to 4 minutes to soften, stirring frequently. Add the garlic and continue to cook for 1 minute. Stir in the rice and cook, stirring, for 1 minute. Add the remaining ingredients plus 1 teaspoon salt and 2 cups water, scraping up the browned bits on the bottom of the pot with a wooden spoon. Add back the chicken thighs and legs (the breasts will be added later) and bring to a boil. Cover and simmer gently for 15 minutes. Add the chicken breasts and stir the ingredients gently so that the rice is thoroughly mixed. Cover and continue to cook for 10 to 15 minutes or until the rice is done. Serve.

VARIATION
Chicken and Rice with Indian Spices
This variation has many spices traditionally used in Indian cooking, including turmeric, cumin, and coriander.

Follow the master recipe through step 1. At the beginning of step 2, add a 3-inch piece of cinnamon stick and stir with a wooden spoon over medium-high heat until it unfurls (about 10 seconds). Add the onion and garlic along with 1 teaspoon ground turmeric, 1 teaspoon ground coriander, 1 teaspoon ground cumin, and 2 green bell peppers, cored and chopped. Sauté until the onion and peppers are just soft, 5 to 6 minutes. Add the basmati rice, stirring for 1 minute, then add the remaining ingredients. Follow the master recipe instructions.

The Problem with Chicken Skin

Unless roasted using high heat, chicken skin is a problem. It is flabby, soggy, tough, and, well, rather disagreeable. Who in their right mind would want to eat it? Yet, when chicken pieces are sautéed, the skin serves two purposes: It shelters the meat from the searing heat (thus leaving it juicier and more tender), and the skin also renders some of its fat, which adds flavor to the dish. Because skinless chicken is not a good solution, I prefer to leave the skin on for the sautéing and then remove it before the chicken is added back into the dish. (Most chicken stews or braises start by sautéing the chicken; it is then removed from the pan, onions and other ingredients are cooked, and then the chicken pieces are put back in.) This way, you get the best of both worlds: tender, juicy chicken and all the flavor of the rendered chicken fat.

Faster, Easier Fried Chicken

Although I am a great fan of authentic fried chicken, it does have its drawbacks: It requires a lot of cooking oil, and it leaves a big mess. The question was, how could I get a crunchy outer coating and a moist interior and do it all quickly and easily? ▶◀

My first thought was to investigate oven-fried chicken. I admit some skepticism toward this approach, as I had never tasted oven-fried chicken that could hold a candle to the real thing. I tested a variety of oven-fried recipes with only mediocre results. The basic approach is to dip the chicken pieces in an egg-milk mixture and then coat them with seasoned bread crumbs. The chicken pieces are then baked in a 425-degree oven for about 35 minutes. In all cases, the chicken was on the dry side and the coating wasn't particularly crispy. Some recipes suggested using skinless pieces; others used coarsely chopped Melba toast instead of bread crumbs, which provided a hard crunch but not the flavorful crispness of true fried chicken. So, I still had dry chicken and a rather dull outer coating.

To solve the dry-chicken problem, I decided to soak the chicken pieces in a quick brine made from 1 quart cold water, ½ cup kosher salt, and 1 tablespoon sugar. After further testing, I reduced the salt to ¼ cup, because the chicken was a bit too salty for my taste. Next, I wanted to test the egg mixture. In an effort to achieve maximum crispness and flavor, I tried chicken dipped in all buttermilk, all egg, egg and buttermilk, egg and a bit of oil, and a combination of the three. The best combination of flavor and crispness turned out to be two eggs, ½ cup buttermilk, and 2 tablespoons olive oil. The recipe worked with both skinless and regular pieces, but neither was truly satisfactory: The skin was rubbery and unappealing, and the skinless pieces were drab and tasteless.

Faced with yet another lackluster oven-fried dinner, I had an epiphany. I turned off the oven, grabbed my bottle of peanut oil, and decided that I was going to fry the chicken pieces in just ⅜ inch of oil. I wanted real fried chicken flavor and the crispness that only frying can produce. This shallow-fry technique was only going to work with thin pieces, so I purchased chicken cutlets (boneless, skinless chicken breasts that have been pounded to an even thickness), brined them for only 30 minutes (thinner pieces without skin need less time), used my coating recipe without the oil (the oil was only helpful when the chicken was baked in a dry, hot oven), and went to work. Finally,

I had chicken worth eating, not a half-hearted compromise — a crisp, flavorful coating with juicy meat. Best of all, it took only five minutes of cooking!

There was still one problem: When developing my traditional fried chicken recipe, I found it helpful to let the coated chicken chill in the refrigerator before frying. The coating sticks better to the chicken, and it becomes thicker and crispier. A one-hour chilling period is recommended, but if you don't have the time, try 15 minutes in the freezer. I also found that it was important to have the cutlets pounded to a uniform thickness (a quarter inch is good), although you do not want them to be too thin, because the meat will easily overcook. So, even with a half-hour brine and 15 minutes in the freezer, this recipe can be made, start to finish, in an hour, and you can produce real fried chicken with a minimum of fuss and bother.

Quick Skillet-Fried Chicken

SERVES 4

It is important to use chicken cutlets for this recipe for quick, even cooking. If you cannot find them at the supermarket, purchase boneless, skinless chicken breasts, place them between 2 sheets of plastic wrap, and pound them with the bottom of a heavy saucepan until they are about double in size. Use peanut oil here, not canola or corn oil. Also, be sure to get the oil nice and hot, about 375 degrees, before frying. If you do not have a thermometer, simply place a bit of the coating into the oil — it should bubble vigorously. Note that the cooking time will vary depending on the size and thickness of the cutlets. For draining the chicken, I prefer to use a clean cooling rack placed over a jelly-roll pan rather than paper bags. (Never use the same cooling rack used to hold the raw chicken pieces, unless it is properly cleaned first.) You can also serve this for lunch in a sandwich.

4   boneless, skinless chicken cutlets
    Salt
1   tablespoon sugar
2   cups unseasoned bread crumbs, homemade preferred
6   tablespoons cornmeal
1   tablespoon dried thyme or oregano
    Pinch cayenne pepper
½   teaspoon freshly ground black pepper
2   large eggs
½   cup buttermilk
2   cups peanut oil, approximately

1. Rinse the chicken pieces and place them in a gallon zipper-lock bag or into a medium bowl. In a large measuring cup or pitcher, dissolve ¼ cup salt and the sugar in 1 quart cold water. Add the water mixture to the chicken and refrigerate for 30 minutes. Remove the chicken pieces and rinse under cool water; pat dry and set aside. (The chicken must be completely dry.)

2. Mix the bread crumbs, cornmeal, thyme, cayenne, black pepper, and 1 teaspoon salt together in a shallow bowl. In a medium bowl, whisk together the eggs and buttermilk. One at a time, dip each of the chicken pieces into the egg mixture and then into the bowl of bread crumbs. Turn the chicken over and press the crumbs onto the surface of the chicken, being careful to give a generous coating to each piece. After coating each piece, place on a large piece of waxed paper or onto a cooling rack set over a baking sheet or jelly-roll pan. Refrigerate for 1 hour or freeze for 15 minutes.

3. Heat the peanut oil (the oil should be ⅜ inch deep) in a large skillet until it reaches 375 degrees. Add two pieces of chicken at a time and fry for approximately 3 minutes on one side; turn and fry for an additional 2 minutes. The coating should be nicely browned, and the meat should register 160 to 165 degrees when measured with an instant-read thermometer. (If you do not have a thermometer, cut into the chicken at the thickest part to see if it is cooked through.) Place the cooked chicken on a clean cooling rack set over a jelly-roll pan or a sheet of waxed paper, cook the remaining pieces, and serve hot.

High-Roast Chicken without the Smoke

The allure of a high-roast chicken is akin to that of cold fusion: The results are spectacular, but the technique is elusive. Roasting chicken in a 500-degree oven takes no more than 45 minutes for a 3- to 4-pound bird, and the skin is second to none. The problem is that the breast meat dries out in the hot oven, and the smoke is so bad that you think you are on the set of *Backdraft*. So, how does one get moist meat, great skin, short roasting times, and no smoke? ▶◀

In the past, I have brined the chicken briefly to solve the dry breast-meat problem. This works just fine. (The chicken is submersed in a solution of water, sugar, and salt for one hour before roasting.) But I was still stymied by the problem of the smoke. My original solution was to start the oven at 425 degrees, raising the temperature to 500 degrees halfway through cooking. This produced quite a good bird, but I wanted dark, crispy skin — the holy grail of the high-roast chicken set. For that, I needed a constant 500 degrees.

Adding water to the pan just made the skin soggy, although it did solve the smoke problem. Adding thinly sliced potatoes — the approach favored by my test kitchen at *Cook's Illustrated* — works fine (although the potatoes, as a side dish, are a bit on the greasy side), but you need potatoes and a mandoline or great knife skills to slice them. I was looking for an easier, everyday solution. I tried bread cubes and slices, which simply burned to a crisp. Cooked rice meant extra work, and it ended up a burnt mess, although it did prevent smoking. A dry kitchen towel started to brown around the edges — this was a walk on the wild side, as it might actually burst into flames. (A damp towel did not fare much better, and the skin was less crispy.) Damp cheesecloth and paper towels were no better than the kitchen towel. My last test was sliced onions, which prevented smoking and also cooked down to a pleasing garnish. Voilà! This was the solution I was looking for, as almost everyone has onions on hand, and the onions could, in fact, be eaten along with the roast chicken.

To perfect this approach, I roasted the onions with some balsamic vinegar. I also added salt and a touch of sugar. As expected, lots of fat dripped down onto the onions during roasting, so when the pan came out of the oven, I moved the cooked onions to a mesh strainer while the chicken rested. (They can also be drained on several layers of paper towels.)

Because this is a recipe for high-roast chicken, I knew the oven had to be hot. I tried the chicken at 450 degrees and found that it did not brown as well or as evenly and needed 10 minutes longer to cook. So I decided to stick with the 500 degrees for 40 to 45 minutes. In terms of basting, butter burned, a naked bird lacked flavor, and olive oil added a nice even color without burning. The *Cook's* test kitchen suggested tucking the legs up to sit between the thigh and breast, a technique that helps to speed the cooking of the thighs, which means that the breast meat does not overcook. I also tested letting the brined chicken sit in the refrigerator uncovered for eight to 24 hours. Air-drying (this technique is used to make Peking duck) does produce extra-crispy skin, but it doesn't seem practical, as the chicken roasted without a long refrigerator stay was fine.

Crispy, Moist High-Roast Chicken

SERVES 4

Don't forget to brine the bird, as the breast meat will dry out in the high oven if you don't. This recipe is designed for a 3½-pound bird. Adjust the roasting time accordingly for different sizes.

FOR THE CHICKEN

½   cup table salt
½   cup sugar
1   whole high-quality chicken (about 3½ pounds), giblets and fat around the cavity removed
1   teaspoon olive oil
    Freshly ground black pepper

FOR THE ONIONS

2   medium onions, cut pole to pole and into ¼-inch slices (about 3 cups)
2   tablespoons balsamic vinegar
½   teaspoon sugar
¼   teaspoon table salt

1. For the chicken: Dissolve the salt and sugar in 2 quarts cold water in a large bowl or container. Immerse the chicken in the brine and refrigerate for 1 hour. Meanwhile, adjust an oven rack to the lower-middle position and heat the oven to 500 degrees.

2. For the onions: Place the onions in the bottom of a broiler pan and add the vinegar, sugar, and salt and toss to coat evenly.

3. Remove the chicken from the brine and rinse thoroughly under cold water. Remove the backbone of the chicken by cutting through the bones on either side (this can best be done with kitchen or poultry shears); discard. Flip the chicken over and use the heel of your hand to flatten the breastbone. Transfer the chicken to the broiler-pan rack and dry thoroughly with paper towels. Rub the chicken with the olive oil and sprinkle with pepper. Push the chicken legs up to rest between the breast and thighs. Place the broiler rack in the pan.

4. Roast the chicken for 20 minutes, after which time the skin will be spotty brown. Rotate the pan 180 degrees and continue to roast until the skin has crisped and turned a deep brown and an instant-read thermometer registers 160 degrees in the thickest part of the breast, 20 to 25 minutes longer. Transfer the chicken to a cutting board and let it rest for 5 to 10 minutes before carving. Using a slotted spoon, remove the onions to a mesh strainer or allow them to drain on paper towels until the chicken is ready to be served. Serve the onions with the chicken.

The Dull Blade

I have made this speech a thousand times, but each time I make it, I find that the content is new information for most home cooks. So, let me cast this message one more time upon the waters.

Virtually every knife in your kitchen is dull. It is so dull that a few minutes with a sharpening steel will not fix it. It is so dull that the edge of the knife has turned over in a "U" shape so that the only way to sharpen it is to regrind the blade. How do you know if a knife is sharp? Hold an 8½-by-11-inch piece of paper and slice down through the paper with the knife. (You should start the cut close to the point where you are holding the paper.) If you cannot make a clean slice, the knife edge is dull.

There are three ways to remedy the situation: by sending the knife out to a knife-sharpening service (see "Knife Sharpening" in the Yellow Pages); by using a whetstone or wheel; or by using the electric three-slot Chef's Choice Diamond Hone Professional Sharpener electric knife sharpener, which will run you about $90. (The two-slot model does not include a regrinding slot — it just has medium and fine sharpening blades.)

Which option is best? Sending knives out is a nonstarter for me, as they can get dull in a matter of minutes, especially if you are cutting through chicken bones. The whetstone does work, but it requires skill, practice, and a good 10 minutes to do one knife. The Chef's Choice three-slot model is the best choice. It takes just a few minutes to sharpen a knife, the magnetic slots ensure that the knife is held at the correct angle to the spinning wheel, and it takes no skill. A sharpening steel is fine for tuning up a knife but, as mentioned above, cannot remedy a truly dull blade.

If you don't have a sharp knife in the house, don't even bother trying to cook. Mincing an onion with a dull blade is akin to driving on black ice with bald tires. You just aren't going to get anywhere fast.

IS YOUR KNIFE SHARP?

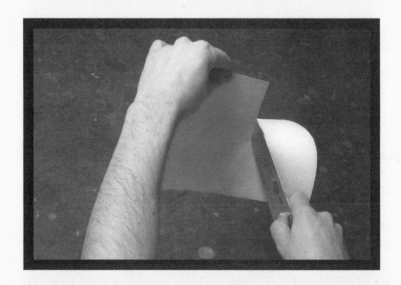

Most cooks use knives that are too dull. To test your knives, hold a piece of 8½-by-11-inch paper in one hand. With the knife in your hand, slice through the paper. If the cut is ragged (bottom), your knife is dull. If the cut is smooth and straight (top), your knife is good to go.

Bad grilled chicken is the culinary equivalent of divorce — it's messy, it's unpleasant, and the person responsible for it is none too popular. Of course, great grilled chicken is one of life's great pleasures, but the design of the chicken itself stands in the way of success. The white and dark meat do not cook at the same rate, and therefore the breast meat turns out overcooked and dry. ▶◀

To solve this problem, I decided to butterfly (remove the backbone and flatten) the chicken before grilling. For my first test, I seasoned the butterflied bird with salt and pepper and set it on the grill skin-side down over a medium-hot fire. After 12 minutes, the skin was brown and crispy with signature grill marks. The bad news was that the chicken had contracted into a lump. I flipped the chicken and found it necessary to apply downward pressure with a spatula to press the underside of the breast closer to the hot coals. The total cooking time for a 3½-pound chicken was about 40 minutes on a covered grill. The chicken had a well-browned and crispy skin, but the breast was overcooked.

Next, I tried using a weighted baking sheet to flatten the chicken as it cooked. With this method, the chicken cooked more evenly and in less time, about 30 minutes for a 3½-pound bird — 15 minutes per side. The baking sheet also helped to maintain the flattened butterfly shape I started out with. I then tried a technique in which the bird is grilled skin-side down for two minutes and then finished over indirect heat (there are no coals directly under the bird) on a covered grill. The result was good but not quite as juicy as I would have liked, so I decided that the direct-heat method was best.

To solve the dry breast meat issue, I decided to use a quick brine (the butterflied chicken is immersed in cold salted water), and I got the result I wanted: flavorful, juicy meat. I then wondered if a marinade wouldn't add additional flavor, so after brining, I combined the chicken with olive oil, lemon juice, garlic, and fresh rosemary. I tested various marinating times and found that 12 hours was necessary to impart flavor, although a full 24 hours was even better. (If you do not have time to marinate, brush the bird with olive oil and freshly ground pepper before grilling.)

Garlic-Lemon Grilled Butterflied Chicken

SERVES 4

Brining is easy and quick and should not be overlooked if you want juicy, flavorful meat.

½   cup table salt

½   cup sugar

1   whole high-quality chicken (3½–4 pounds), giblets and fat around the cavity removed

½   cup olive oil

4   garlic cloves, minced or pressed

¼   cup lemon juice

1   tablespoon finely chopped fresh rosemary or thyme or a combination
    Freshly ground black pepper

1. Dissolve the salt and sugar in 2 quarts cold water in a large bowl or container. Immerse the chicken in the brine and refrigerate for 1 hour. Remove the chicken from the brine and rinse thoroughly under cold running water. Remove the backbone of the chicken by cutting through the bones on either side (this can best be done with kitchen or poultry shears); discard. Flip the chicken over and use the heel of your hand to flatten the breastbone. Combine the remaining ingredients in a small bowl and then add them, with the chicken, to a large, heavy-duty, zipper-lock bag. Press out as much air as possible; seal the bag and turn to coat the chicken evenly with the marinade. Place in the refrigerator for 12 to 24 hours.

2. Ignite the grill. Remove the chicken from the marinade and brush or wipe off the excess marinade. When the fire is medium-hot (you can hold your hand 5 inches from the flame for no longer than 4 seconds), place the chicken skin-side down onto the grill. Set a jelly-roll or other flat pan on top of the chicken and place 2 bricks or heavy cans in the pan. Cover and grill for 15 minutes; the chicken will be deep brown and have grill marks. Turn the chicken and replace the weighted jelly-roll pan. Grill about 15 minutes more or until an instant-read thermometer inserted into the inside of the thigh registers 170 degrees. Transfer to a platter and let rest for 10 to 15 minutes. Cut into individual portions and serve.

Hold the Cheeseburger,
Pass the Ice Cream

Diet experts have come to the conclusion that the only way to lose weight is to consume fewer calories per day than one expends. It's simple arithmetic. For a weight-neutral diet, women should consume an average of about 2,200 calories per day; men can eat 2,500. Yet, the startling statistic is that the food industry is producing 3,800 calories per day per person, up from 3,300 in the 1970s.

However, it turns out that most of us don't really understand where our calories come from. Let's say that one wanted to lose weight by consuming only 2,000 calories per day. Here is a little test. Which of the following meal plans do you think has the fewest number of calories and the least amount of fat?

MEAL ONE	MEAL TWO
Breakfast	**Breakfast**
Cappuccino with One Cup Whole Milk	One Cup Strawberries
Blueberry Muffin	One Cup Orange Juice
	One Bagel
Lunch	Cappuccino with One Cup Skim Milk
Cheeseburger	
Medium French Fries	**Morning Snack**
Medium Coke	One Apple
Dinner	**Lunch**
Boston Market Quarter of a Roasted	Turkey Sandwich on Rye with Two Slices
Chicken, White Meat with Skin	Swiss Cheese, Tomato, and Mustard
	One Oatmeal Cookie
	Five Pretzel Sticks
	Afternoon Snack
	One Cup Grapes
	Dinner
	One Half Salmon Fillet
	One Cup Boiled Broccoli
	One Cup Wild Rice
	One Cup Vanilla Ice Cream

The answer, as you probably guessed, is that the second menu has slightly fewer calories *and about half the fat*. (Meal One includes 2,029 calories and 84 grams of fat; Meal Two has 1,995 calories and 48 grams of fat.) The other obvious difference between the two menus is that the first one is all take-out food and the second one is home-prepared. In fact, these simple examples mirror the trend in food consumption started in the 20th century: Processed foods, prepared outside of the home, are delivering a larger, and increasingly unhealthy, share of the American diet. In 1977, for example, home-prepared food accounted for 84 percent of food expenses; in 1995, that number had decreased to 73 percent.

So, is this really a problem? Is there anything wrong with foods prepared outside of the home? Let's take some examples. *Added fats* is a term that describes fats added directly by consumers (butter on bread), as well as those added in commercially pre-pared foods such as cookies and fried foods. (This term excludes natural fats in foods such as milk and meat.) Around 1900, the total per capita consumption of added fats was just over 30 pounds a year; today, it is close to 70 pounds.

Consumption of milk as a beverage (not an ingredient) has dropped from 45 gallons per capita in 1945 to 25 gallons today, whereas soft-drink consumption has risen from 10 gallons in 1945 to more than 50 gallons today. In 1919, Americans consumed 150 pounds of fresh fruit per capita. Today, that figure has dropped to 130 pounds, but we eat 165 pounds of processed fruit each year. Home-cooked vegetable consumption has dropped from 131 pounds per capita in 1919 to just 11 pounds in 1998. Consumption of cane and beet sugars (which the body can digest properly) has dropped from about 85 pounds per capita in the mid-1970s (this amount remained consistent throughout most of the 20th century) to about 60 pounds today, while corn sweeteners (hard to digest and used extensively in processed foods) rose precipitously from about 20 pounds in the mid 1970s to more than 80 pounds today.

More and more of our food is processed, not natural, and we are paying for it in obesity and poor health. Today, 14 percent of children and more than half of all Ameri-cans are considered overweight. Although 62 percent of heads of household between the ages of 18 and 34 recently indicated that they are "too tired" at the end of the day to engage in meal preparation, maybe they ought to think twice. Processed foods are a serious danger to our health and (in my opinion) well-being.

Coca-Cola Chicken: The Real Thing?

Everybody in the continental United States has probably heard of beer-can chicken. You know the recipe: A chicken is impaled on an open can of beer and then grill-roasted. The steam from the beer gives the chicken an especially good flavor and helps to keep the chicken moist. I wanted to revisit the technique, get it down pat, and then see if Coca-Cola, the darling of many Southern cooks, wouldn't make a better flavoring liquid than beer. ▶◀

The first issue was whether I needed to brine the chicken or not. A simple test — one bird brined and one not — quickly convinced me that the brined bird was juicier and more flavorful. I used a mixture of 1 cup kosher (or ½ cup table) salt and ¼ cup sugar to 2 quarts water. The small amount of sugar gives a more balanced flavor and also produces a more deeply colored skin.

Next, I wondered if the type of liquid mattered. I knew that beer worked well, but I also tried Coke, Dr Pepper, root beer, and ginger ale. All except the ginger ale added deep flavor and a sweetness that worked well with the smoky fire. I also tried lemonade, white wine, and iced tea, but none were as good as Coca-Cola. For fun, I added a tablespoon of rum to the Coke and came up with Cuba Libre Chicken. (The difference is marginal, but you can actually notice a slightly deeper, warmer taste with the rum.) For best results, the can should be two-thirds to three-quarters full, and extra holes need to be punched in the top to allow more steam to escape.

I then wondered if the can itself was doing the chicken any favors and made an interesting discovery: The can acts like a vertical roaster. The skin doesn't stick to the grill, and it browns evenly. Of course, the Coca-Cola also adds a lot of flavor and produces juicier meat.

The last step was to come up with a simple recipe for a rub. Wet rubs were hard to work with, and using olive oil or butter on the skin made it less crispy. The simple remedy was a dry rub applied both on top of and under the skin before roasting. I came up with a simple combination of cumin, chili powder, coriander, pepper, sugar, cinnamon, and allspice, which is both sweet and peppery — the classic barbecue combination.

As for the cooking itself, you need to use indirect heat and a covered grill to avoid drying out the breast meat before the rest of the bird is cooked. The method you choose depends on your grill. If you can place the chicken on one side of the grill and the cover still fits, then build the fire on the other side. (The chicken will need to be rotated 180 degrees halfway through cooking.) If, however, you need to put the chicken in the center of the grill for the top to fit, then build a pile of coals on either side. A 3½-pound bird seemed to work best (larger birds will overcook on the outside) and fit easily on my grill.

Coca-Cola Grill-Roasted Chicken

SERVES 4

You can use any similar soda you like, such as root beer, Dr Pepper, or Pepsi. Lighter sodas such as ginger ale are less flavorful. You can also use beer as a substitute. If the cover of your grill will not fit with the chicken to one side, place the chicken in the middle of the grill and place equal piles of lit coals on either side.

FOR THE DRY SPICE RUB

1 tablespoon ground cumin
1 tablespoon chili powder
1 teaspoon freshly ground black pepper
1 teaspoon ground coriander
1 teaspoon sugar
½ teaspoon ground cinnamon
½ teaspoon ground allspice

FOR THE CHICKEN

½ cup table salt
¼ cup sugar
1 whole high-quality chicken (about 3½ pounds), giblets and fat around cavity removed
1 (12-ounce) can Coca-Cola

1. For the spice rub: Combine all the ingredients in a small bowl.

2. For the chicken: Dissolve the salt and sugar in 2 quarts cold water in a large bowl or container. Immerse the chicken in the brine and refrigerate for 1 hour. Remove the chicken from the brine and rinse inside and out with cool running water. Pat the chicken dry with paper towels. Apply the spice rub all over the chicken, inside and out. Lift up the skin over the breast and thighs and rub the spices directly onto the meat. Pour out or drink about ½ cup Coke. Poke 2 extra holes into the top of the can. Slide the chicken over the can so the drumsticks reach the bottom of the can.

3. While the chicken is brining, light the grill. Prepare the fire for indirect cooking by placing all of the coals (about 50 briquettes) to one side. (See recipe note above.) Place the prepared chicken on the cool side of the grill using the drumsticks and can to form a tripod. Place the lid on the grill, making sure the vents are partially open and positioned directly above the coals. Cook for about 30 minutes. Rotate the chicken 180 degrees, cover, and cook 25 to 35 minutes more or until an instant-read thermometer inserted into the thigh registers 170 degrees. Transfer the chicken to a platter and let rest for 10 minutes, being careful to keep the can upright. Carefully lift the chicken off the can (using a kitchen towel or wad of paper towels). Carve the chicken and serve immediately.

VARIATION
Cuba Libre Grill-Roasted Chicken
Add 1 tablespoon rum to the Coke can before slipping on the chicken.

All You Really Need — Is Love and 25 Good Recipes

Most cooks I know are constantly looking for new recipes the way some folks are constantly on the lookout for antiques, clothes, computer software, or specials down at Price Chopper. There is nothing wrong with living life vicariously through recipes — we all do it to some extent — but the problem with most home cooks is that they have *too many* recipes rather than too few.

Two hundred years ago, good cooks generally had a relatively limited repertoire, extending to perhaps 50 key recipes. They could make a roast, a cake, a loaf of bread, a few casseroles, etc. As a result, they became experts at what they cooked — they could make buttermilk biscuits, a pot roast, wax beans, or chocolate cake from memory, even with their eyes closed. The point? Well, they soon realized that details mattered, that small variations in preparation yielded different results, and that baking a pie in July was quite different from doing so in February, because the dough was more likely to heat up and become unworkable. They also learned that different cuts of meat behave differently in a pot roast, that yeast is not always a predictable ingredient, and that ovens are not precision instruments and need to be watched closely. Like good musicians, good cooks realized that restricting one's repertoire has great advantages: It allows one to focus on the underlying technique instead of just a new set of notes.

So, my suggestion is to start with a shortlist of 25 recipes that you make most often, and stick with them for a bit. As you get better, slowly increase your range. You will soon learn what a biscuit, a roast chicken, or a chicken soup is really supposed to taste like. That is the first step in learning anything.

Rediscovering Chicken Salad

One summer day in the 1960s, I was haying with a Vermont farmer, when he said, "Let's take a walk." We stretched our legs and walked down the dirt road to a spring that flowed from a gravel bank. Having had nothing but second-rate tap water all my life, my first taste from this wild spring was a revelation, elevating this common drink to a higher plane. Chicken salad is much the same. For those of us used to the ubiquitous pureed scoopfuls offered at diners and ho-hum sandwich shops, the real thing is no less of a surprise, full of competing flavors, chunky textures, and lively bits of surprising ingredients. ▶◀

The first question, of course, was how to cook the chicken. You can boil it, poach it, or roast it. (Broiling makes for tough meat, and grilling is not always possible.) The boiled chicken was a bit too soft, although the flavor was good. Poached chicken (I used a flavored chicken stock for the poaching liquid) was good but is fussy — the heat level must be constantly adjusted, and, of course, one needs to prepare the liquid. Roasted chicken was the winner, because it had more real chicken flavor, the texture was good, and it is a relatively simple method. Roasting with both the skin and bones produces the most flavor and the moistest meat. I used my standard roasting method, which is 375 degrees for about an hour.

The next issue was the salad itself. Really large chunks of chicken make for a sloppy sandwich, so I settled on ½-inch dice. (Anything smaller feels like tuna salad.) For binder, I tried the usual suspects: mayonnaise, yogurt, sour cream, buttermilk, and cream cheese, both alone and in combination. I settled on mayonnaise. Two-thirds cup of chopped celery was great, as were chopped scallions. I tried capers, pickles, apples, cucumbers, and onion and had no luck, but I did find that halved seedless grapes worked well, adding a nice counterpoint of texture and flavor. Lemon juice perked up the flavor as did 1½ teaspoons Dijon mustard. For herbs, tarragon was the winner, and salt and pepper rounded out the flavors.

For a variation, I turned to a curried chicken salad; I tried a method listed in the new *Joy of Cooking*. The curry powder is cooked briefly in a skillet with a small amount of oil and then added to the mayonnaise. This greatly enhanced the flavor. I then added apple, raisins, and almonds. Be sure to use fresh, high-quality curry powder for the best flavor.

Chicken Salad with Tarragon and Grapes

MAKES ABOUT 5 CUPS, ENOUGH TO SERVE 4 TO 6

This is a snap to make — you can even purchase a roasted chicken at the market, if you like. I often roast 2 chickens at a time, serving 1 for dinner and using the other for chicken salad the next day. Although the quality of the chicken is not as good, you can also simmer a cut-up chicken in 2½ quarts water for 30 to 40 minutes, or until the meat is cooked. (You can add vegetables and herbs such as celery, parsley, and 1 or 2 carrots along with the chicken, if you like, but this is not necessary.) Use the liquid for homemade stock and the meat for this recipe.

1	whole high-quality chicken (about 3½ pounds), roasted (see recipe at right), cooled, skinned, boned, chilled, and chopped into ½-inch pieces (about 4 cups)
2	medium celery ribs, finely chopped (about ⅔ cup)
¼	cup finely sliced scallion
⅔	cup mayonnaise
1	tablespoon lemon juice
1½	teaspoons Dijon mustard
2	teaspoons finely chopped fresh tarragon
1	cup halved seedless grapes
1	teaspoon table salt
	Freshly ground black pepper

Mix all of the ingredients in a large bowl. Serve immediately or refrigerate overnight.

VARIATION

Curried Chicken Salad

Heat a small skillet over medium heat until hot. Add 1 tablespoon canola oil and 2 tablespoons fresh curry powder. Stir to form a paste, about 1 minute. The mixture will smoke a bit and become aromatic. Cool for 5 minutes and mix with the mayonnaise. Omit the celery, lemon juice, mustard, tarragon, and grapes from the recipe above. Add ⅔ cup chopped apple, ¼ cup golden raisins, and ¼ cup sliced almonds.

Easy Roast Chicken

Place a shallow roasting pan on the center oven rack and heat to 375 degrees. Remove the pan, add a V-rack, and place the chicken on its side on the rack. Roast the bird for 20 minutes. Turn the bird to the other side and roast for 20 minutes. Turn it breast-side up and roast for 20 minutes. When the thickest part of the thigh reaches 165 to 170 degrees measured on an instant-read thermometer, the chicken is done; the cooking time is about 1 hour total for a 3½-pound bird.

GIVE MEAT A REST

CUT RIGHT AWAY

If you cut into a steak as soon as it comes out
of the skillet or off the grill, the juices will flow out of
the meat and onto the cutting board.

CUT AFTER 10-MINUTE REST

If you wait 10 minutes and then cut into the steak,
the juices will have been redistributed
evenly throughout the meat and won't be lost.

Skillet Steak, the French Way

Most of us think of steaks and grilling as inseparable, yet a quick (10-minute) skillet steak is one of life's great pleasures, as it requires no preheated grill and can be done in the middle of a snowstorm. Cooking the steak itself is not too difficult, and an easy pan sauce transforms this dish from everyday steak to a Saturday night dinner, the perfect marriage of meat and sauce leading to a luxurious, extraordinary main course. ▶◀

First, the steak itself. Much testing has led me to select either rib-eye or boneless strip steaks, as these have the most flavor and are quite juicy. (Rib-eye steaks are also boneless; if they include the bone, they are called rib steaks.) One-inch-thick steaks are the most common supermarket size, and a heavy-duty preheated skillet is a must. The steak is seasoned liberally with salt and pepper, slapped into the hot greased pan, cooked for five minutes, turned, and then cooked another five minutes or so for a medium-rare steak. The meat is then removed from the pan, and the sauce is made.

A classic French pan sauce has four main ingredients: shallot or onion, wine or stock, herbs, and butter to finish. Of course, there are easier, more pedestrian approaches, such as a simple combination of Worcestershire sauce, water, and butter. But for a good rib eye and with only a few minutes of work, I wanted more complex flavors. I preferred shallot to onion for the improved flavor. After the shallot had been softened, I tried a variety of liquids. Chicken stock was wan and incapable of standing up to the beef, red wine was good but a bit lackluster in terms of taste, Marsala was too sweet, but sherry was just right. Next, I tried adding vinegar, but it was a poor match with the sherry, as were capers and green peppercorns. To add some bite to the sauce, I preferred a combination of Dijon mustard and lemon juice. For the herbs, I preferred thyme and parsley, although you can experiment with what's on hand. (Tarragon is one of my favorite herbs with steak.) To round out the sauce, I added some anchovy fillets at the beginning of cooking so that they would dissolve and add a subtle flavor. Although I am apt to poke fun at classic French cooking, mounting the sauce with butter is, in fact, a great idea and adds a bit of luxury and smoothness. Four tablespoons of cold butter are whisked into the sauce just before serving, 1 tablespoon at a time.

Steaks with Sherry-Shallot Pan Sauce

SERVES 2

This recipe serves 2, and both steaks can be prepared in the skillet at the same time. For 4 people, increase the pan size and increase the cooking time a bit (the meat will cook more slowly), but you can leave the ingredients for the sauce the same — there will be enough for all.

FOR THE STEAKS

2   rib-eye or boneless strip steaks, about 1 inch thick (8–10 ounces each)
    Salt and freshly ground black pepper
1   tablespoon vegetable oil

FOR THE SAUCE

1   tablespoon vegetable oil
1   large shallot, finely chopped (about ¼ cup)
1¼   cups dry sherry
4   anchovy fillets, coarsely chopped
1   teaspoon Dijon mustard
1   teaspoon finely chopped fresh thyme
1   tablespoon lemon juice
1   tablespoon finely chopped fresh flat-leaf parsley
4   tablespoons cold unsalted butter, cut into tablespoon-size pieces
    Salt and freshly ground black pepper

1. For the steaks: Season the steaks liberally with salt and pepper. Set a large heavy-duty skillet over high heat. When hot, add the oil, swirl to coat the bottom of the pan, and then add the steaks and stand back — they will splatter. Cook for 5 minutes and turn. Cook on the second side for 4 minutes for rare, 5 minutes for medium rare, and 6 minutes for medium. (Start checking at 4 minutes; the steaks will continue to cook as they rest.) Remove the steaks from the skillet and keep warm on a plate in a low oven or tented with foil.

2. For the sauce: Pour off any fat from the skillet and lower the heat to medium-high. Add the oil and then the shallot. Cook for 1 to 2 minutes or until the shallot has softened but not browned. Add the sherry and anchovies. With a wooden spoon or heatproof spatula, scrape the browned bits from the bottom of the pan. Boil until the sherry is reduced by about half and syrupy, about 5 minutes. Add the mustard and thyme and cook for an additional 2 minutes. Off heat, add the lemon juice and parsley and whisk in the cold butter 1 tablespoon at a time. Season to taste with salt and pepper and serve over the steaks at once.

Quick and Easy Steak au Poivre

The basis of this dish is simple enough: a pan-seared steak impregnated with peppercorns and finished in a brandy-cream sauce. It's the prince and pauper of French cooking. At its best, it marries the rough-and-tumble taste of steak and pepper with a creamy, four-star pan sauce. Yet, poorly executed, steak au poivre has a pale crust, an insipid sauce, and so many peppercorns that one is forced to wash it down with tumblers of high-octane wine. ▶◀

The first step is choosing a steak. Steak au poivre is typically made with strip steak, but I also tried rib eye, shell steak, and sirloin tip, the latter two in hopes of keeping down the price. (I didn't try tenderloin, as it has less flavor and is wildly expensive.) The shell steak was dry and tough, the sirloin tip was juicy but tough, and the rib eye was the winner—more flavorful and slightly juicier than the strip. However, it ain't cheap, running $6.99 to $10.99 per pound. The steaks are best when cut to a 1-inch thickness. This allows for a well-browned crust without an overcooked interior. (Thinner steaks quickly dry out.)

The problem with the pepper is that, when pressed into the steak, it provides a barrier between meat and pan, thus preventing browning and the development of a nice fond, those browned bits that are used to make a rich sauce. After much testing, I decided to simply add the peppercorns to the sauce instead, a method that worked just fine. The heat of the pan was also an issue. When I tried high heat, the fond became too dark and bitter by the time the steak was cooked; medium-high heat, therefore, worked best. I also found it necessary to weigh down the steak to produce the best crust. A second skillet placed on top of the steak worked fine.

The sauce is usually made from shallots, brandy, cream, stock, butter, and lemon juice or vinegar. In my case, I was adding the pepper directly to the sauce, and I preferred black to green peppercorns and liked them crushed instead of whole or ground. I found stock to be unnecessary, as it watered down the sauce, requiring extra time to reduce it back to the proper thickness. Without the stock, the sauce cooked very quickly, and the tastes were fresher. One-third cup brandy or cognac and ⅔ cup heavy cream were just right. Cognac is a bit sweeter than brandy, but the choice is yours. I dumped the butter as being superfluous.

The shallots didn't add much, given the horsepower of the peppercorns, and the lemon juice/vinegar was unnecessary, because the sauce now cooked so quickly that it was bright and lively on its own. As for technique, I simply dumped all of the sauce ingredients into the pan at the same time and scraped the bottom of the pan to dissolve the fond. In just two minutes, the sauce was done. Now this simple sauce was made with only three ingredients, and I liked it better than more complex and more traditional recipes.

Four-Ingredient Steak au Poivre

SERVES 4

Place the peppercorns in a heavy-duty zipper-lock bag and whack them with either a rolling pin, a heavy saucepan, or a flat meat pounder. Note that the cooking times are approximate. Everything depends on the thickness of the steaks, the type of skillet, and the horsepower of your stovetop.

4	rib-eye or boneless strip steaks, about 1 inch thick (8–10 ounces each)
	Salt and freshly ground black pepper
⅓	cup brandy or cognac
⅔	cup heavy cream
1	tablespoon black peppercorns, crushed

1. Heat a 12-inch heavy-duty skillet over medium heat for 4 minutes. Season the steaks liberally with salt and pepper. Place the steaks in the hot skillet, adjust the heat to medium-high, and place another skillet directly on top of them. Cook the steaks without moving them for 6 minutes or until well browned. Flip the steaks and press on them again with the extra skillet. Cook them for about 4 minutes longer for rare, 5 minutes for medium-rare, and 6 minutes for medium. (Time will depend on the thickness of the steaks. Check them for doneness after 3 minutes.) Transfer the steaks to a large plate and tent loosely with foil.

2. Add the brandy, heavy cream, and peppercorns to the skillet. Bring to a boil, scraping the bottom of the pan with a wooden spoon or spatula to loosen the browned bits. Simmer until thick enough to heavily coat the back of a metal spoon, about 2 minutes. Adjust seasonings with salt if necessary.

3. Place the steaks on individual dinner plates. Spoon the sauce over the steaks and serve immediately.

Tender, Succulent Short Ribs

Short ribs are rarely made at home because they are unfamiliar to most cooks, they are fatty, and they take time to cook. However, most of the cooking time is unattended, the fat can easily be removed from the sauce, and the resulting fork-tender meat is so richly flavored that it far outshines a beef stew or a roast. ▶◀

The basic method is straightforward. The ribs are browned, usually on top of the stove but sometimes in the oven. Then, the meat is removed along with excess rendered fat, vegetables and aromatics such as garlic are sautéed, the meat is added back with liquid (such as stock or wine), the pot is covered, and the meat is cooked for two to three hours at a relatively low oven temperature. The long, slow cooking melts the collagen (connective tissue) in the meat until it is fork-tender and succulent. Bad short ribs, however, are fatty and tough, and the accompanying sauce is thin and acidic.

To solve the problem of short ribs, I started with the meat itself. I wanted to serve six to eight people, so about six pounds of ribs was about right. It is important to use ribs that are at least 1½ inches thick; the thicker, meatier ribs are more tender and flavorful. The length of the ribs varies from 3 to 7 inches, but I found that 4 to 5 inches makes for the best presentation and portion control. This is a fatty cut of meat, so purchase the leanest-looking ribs you can find and make sure that they are trimmed of excess fat. The ribs need to be seasoned and browned in a couple of batches over high heat in a large, heavy-duty skillet. (I found that I needed only 1 tablespoon vegetable oil, as the ribs provide plenty of their own fat.) It is important to brown the ribs on all sides to render as much fat as possible.

In terms of vegetables, my favorite accompaniments are onions, carrots, shallots, and garlic. I used two chopped medium onions, two chopped medium carrots, six chopped medium shallots, and one medium garlic head, cloves separated and crushed. This combination lends lots of flavor — earthy and sweet. I found that I didn't want the vegetables to brown, just to soften, for best results. This dish is a bit dull without a healthy dose of parsley, thyme, and rosemary. Using 10 sprigs of parsley, eight of thyme, and one of rosemary provided the flavor I was looking for. I also preferred the dish with a couple of bay leaves thrown into the pot.

As for the sauce, I immediately thought of chicken broth, as canned beef broth is inedible. As for the wine, a common additional ingredient, I preferred Pinot Noir,

How to Make Tough Meat Tender

I can neither count nor remember the number of times I have braised, roasted, or stewed tough cuts of meat that turned out, well, tough. What do I mean by tough cuts? Well, any shank (the lower leg), chuck roast (from the forequarter of the animal), round roast (the area from the hip to the knee), oxtail, brisket, etc. After trying hundreds of "tough-cut" recipes, I realized that most of them involved braising.

According to Madeleine Kamman in *The Making of a Cook* (Macmillan, 1971), the term comes from *braise*, which means "smoldering coals" in French. Meat was placed in a tightly covered pot called a *braisière*, which was placed on a bed of embers, and then additional coals were placed on the lid, which was slightly concave. This method was developed centuries ago in Europe, before stoves had been invented. Braising, therefore, was simply a method of roasting meats over a coal fire.

Since that time, braising has come to mean cooking foods either on top of or in an oven in a covered pot (think Dutch oven here) with a small amount of liquid. This liquid, which was most often chicken stock, wine, or water, was imbued with all sorts of magical properties by a variety of cooking experts. The steam from this liquid was supposed to penetrate the muscle fibers, somehow making them more tender. Well, it turns out that there is no magic involved. It is simply a matter of conductivity and temperature.

Water is a better conductor than air. That's why a swimmer will die of hypothermia a lot faster in 35-degree water than will a stark-naked man on the beach in the same temperature. Simply put, water and steam can get the inner temperature of a piece of meat up over 200 degrees a lot easier than air can. To test this proposition, we did a three-way test in the *Cook's Illustrated* test kitchen.

We took a 3-pound chuck roast and roasted it, braised it, and boiled it. The roasted piece was a disaster — it never reached an internal temperature higher than 180 degrees in a 250-degree oven. Both the braised and boiled roasts were excellent, because the interior sections had reached temperatures in excess of 200 degrees and stayed there awhile. Why is this temperature important? The collagen (those waxy rivulets you see in a tough pot roast) need to get up over 200 degrees to melt. That's all you need to know. Tough meat has to be cooked long enough to break down the collagen. This is best done at lower temperatures so that the outer layer of meat does not dry out. It just can't be done without some liquid to transfer enough heat to the roast.

A word of consolation to the braising bunch: Braising does provide one obvious advantage over boiling. It allows one to produce a sauce along with the roast, because the smaller amount of liquid has more concentrated flavors than the gallon or so of water used for boiling. So braising is a good idea for a tough cut; there just isn't anything magical about it. (If you find yourself serving tough meat, what did you do wrong? You were impatient. Just put the bloody thing back on the stove and cook until it is fork-tender!)

Burgundy, or Cabernet Sauvignon. (The dish has a slightly different taste depending on which wine you choose, but all were good.) A recipe for Beef Burgundy printed in *Cook's Illustrated* suggested reserving ½ cup of the wine for the final stages of the dish. This worked well, giving the sauce a fresher, more lively taste. A half cup of port also married nicely to the beef and was added at the onset of braising. The sauce must be thickened; there are three common methods: using a roux (butter and flour) before deglazing, using kneaded butter after the braising process, and sautéing flour into the vegetables before deglazing. I found that sautéing a few tablespoons of flour into the vegetables was the best method. The sauce thickens to a velvety consistency, provided you use the correct amount of flour: 3 tablespoons.

Cooking temperature is key in braising, oven heat usually being low for best results. At 375 degrees, for example, the meat turned out a bit stringy, and the liquid actually reached a vigorous boil. It turned out that 300 degrees was optimal — the meat was silky and tender, yet the cooking time was not extended to three or four hours as would be the case with a lower oven.

Finally, the sauce contains a lot of fat. If it is not removed, the liquid will be virtually inedible. The easiest method is to chill the sauce overnight. The fat will rise to the surface and solidify, and it can then be removed in seconds. If you do not make this dish the day before, simply pour off the liquid, let it sit for a half hour, and then spoon off the fat that rises to the surface.

Minor adjustments to the recipe included a small amount of tomato paste for color and flavor plus chopped fresh parsley; a side of garlic mashed potatoes or sautéed root vegetables makes a nice accompaniment.

Best Braised Short Ribs

SERVES 6 TO 8

Yes, this is not a quick dinner, but it can be made a day ahead of time, which is perfect for entertaining. During chilling, the fat will rise to the top of the sauce and solidify, making it very easy to remove. If you use canned chicken broth, choose a low-sodium brand. Serve with mashed potatoes or the root vegetable stir-fry on page 45.

1 tablespoon vegetable oil or olive oil

6 pounds bone-in beef short ribs, at least 1½ inches thick and 4–5 inches in length preferred
Salt and freshly ground black pepper

2 medium onions, cut into ½-inch dice

2 medium carrots, cut into ½-inch dice

6 shallots, quartered

1 medium garlic head, cloves separated and smashed with skin remaining

3 tablespoons flour

4	cups dry, full-bodied red wine such as Pinot Noir, Cabernet Sauvignon, or Burgundy
½	cup ruby port
3½	cups chicken stock
10	sprigs fresh flat-leaf parsley
8	sprigs fresh thyme
1	sprig fresh rosemary
2	bay leaves
1	tablespoon tomato paste
¼	cup chopped fresh flat-leaf parsley for garnish, optional

1. Heat the oil in a large heavy-duty skillet over medium-high heat. Adjust an oven rack to the center position and heat the oven to 300 degrees. Liberally season the short ribs with salt and pepper. When the oil just starts to smoke, brown half of the meat until deeply colored on all sides, using tongs to lean the ribs against each other for balance. Transfer the ribs to a Dutch oven. Repeat the process with the second half of the meat.

2. Pour off all but 2 tablespoons of the fat from the skillet and lower the heat to medium. Add the onions, carrots, and shallots. Sauté until soft and the onions and shallots become translucent, 6 to 7 minutes. Add the garlic and cook an additional minute. Stir in the flour until well combined, about 1 minute more. Add 3½ cups of the wine to the pan and bring to a simmer, scraping up any browned bits remaining at the bottom of the pan.

3. Add the contents of the skillet to the Dutch oven, along with the port, chicken stock, parsley, thyme, rosemary, bay leaves, and tomato paste. Set the Dutch oven over medium-high heat and bring to a boil. Cover and set the pot in the oven. Cook until the meat is fork-tender, 2½ to 3 hours.

4. Remove the Dutch oven from the oven. Using tongs, transfer the ribs to a large plate, removing excess vegetables and herbs that may cling to the meat. Discard any loose bones that may have fallen away from the meat. Strain the braising liquid through a large sieve into a bowl, pressing out the liquid from the solids. Cover the ribs and liquid separately with plastic wrap and refrigerate overnight. (If serving the ribs the same day, place the liquid in a glass bowl or large measuring cup and spoon off excess fat. It is best to let the liquid rest for at least 30 minutes to allow most of the fat to rise to the surface.)

5. Spoon off and discard the solidified fat from the braising liquid. Add the liquid to the clean Dutch oven and bring to a boil over medium-high heat. Briskly simmer until the sauce is reduced to the consistency of heavy cream, 5 to 10 minutes. Add the remaining ½ cup wine and the reserved ribs to the pot. Reduce the heat to medium-low, cover, and cook until the meat is heated through, about 10 minutes. Serve immediately, with or without chopped fresh parsley.

Four-Star Boiled Dinner

Boiled (the meat and vegetables are actually simmered) dinner sounds like something you would eat as a last resort, when all you have in the house are a tough piece of meat and some old vegetables. The French don't see it that way; they often make "pot au feu," and it isn't viewed as a second-class dish. The notion is simple: Take tough cuts of beef (some recipes also include chicken, sausage, etc.) and vegetables and simmer them in water. This produces a first-class broth (which the French serve as a first course) plus tender meat and flavorful veggies. The problem with this recipe is choosing the right meat and vegetables and coordinating the cooking times. ▶◀

Let's start with the key cooking principle: Simmering meat in water is a terrific way to cook tough cuts. In a test at *Cook's Illustrated*, we found that roasting never gets tough meat hot enough to become fork-tender (air is a lousy heat conductor) and that simmering inexpensive cuts is just as good as braising (cooking in a covered dish with a small amount of liquid). There is a simple bit of physics at work here. Tough cuts of beef must reach and maintain an internal temperature of more than 200 degrees in order for the collagen to break down, which results in fork-tender meat. So simmering in lots of water can be a very good thing indeed.

Okay, now for the cuts of beef. I tested chuck roasts, short ribs, beef shank, veal shank, oxtail, pork ribs, ham hock, lamb shank, chicken, and sausage. I learned that a combination of chuck roast (it slices nicely as well) with short ribs or beef or veal shanks (they add a lot of flavor) was just right. I also discovered that 3 quarts water was the best quantity. (Too much water produces a weak broth.) Simmering the meat the day before, chilling the broth, and then removing the solid fat that rose to the surface was the easiest method of defatting the liquid, a crucial step.

As for the vegetables and herbs I wanted to flavor the broth (these vegetables would be discarded), I settled on two medium-to-large onions, one leek, two carrots, one large ripe tomato, three medium garlic cloves, six whole cloves, 10 sprigs parsley, four sprigs thyme, and two bay leaves. I also added 1 teaspoon each of salt and peppercorns. The dish may need more salt at the finish, but you must be careful not to add too much salt early on, because the broth intensifies as it cooks.

As for the vegetables for serving, I found that cooking them separately in the defatted broth was best, as the meat didn't get in the way. Of the vegetables tested, the losers were leeks, sun-dried tomatoes, and artichokes. I liked potatoes, carrots, turnips, peas, pearl onions (frozen are fine), green beans, asparagus, fennel, parsnip, and rutabaga. They each have their proper cooking times, so I divided them into three categories: 20 minutes, 10 minutes, and five minutes. You can use any combination you like.

To finish the dish, I tried a variety of sauces, including horseradish cream, gremolata, ginger-garlic, and a simple Salsa Verde. The latter was the winner and appears on page 169. (It is, however, optional.)

French-Style Boiled Dinner with Salsa Verde

SERVES 8 TO 10

This is a good recipe for company, as most of the work can be done the day before. It also provides both meat and vegetables — all you need are bread and wine. Don't depend on the cooking time for the meat; keep cooking it until it is really fork-tender.

FOR THE MEAT AND THE BROTH

4 pounds chuck roast
4 pounds beef short ribs, beef shank, or veal shank, or any combination
2 medium or large onions, peeled and quartered through the core
1 leek, trimmed and cut into large pieces
2 medium or large carrots, cut into large chunks
1 large ripe tomato, quartered
3 garlic cloves, smashed
6 whole cloves
10 sprigs fresh flat-leaf parsley

4 sprigs fresh thyme
2 bay leaves
1 teaspoon table salt
1 teaspoon peppercorns

TO FINISH THE DISH

7–8 pounds prepared vegetables of your choice (see page 167)
1 cup Salsa Verde (page 169), optional

1. For the meat and the broth: Place all of the ingredients plus 3 quarts water into a large Dutch oven or soup pot. Bring to a boil. Reduce the heat to maintain a gentle simmer and cook, covered, for 2 to 3 hours or until the meat is fork-tender. Cool to room temperature and refrigerate overnight.

2. Remove the solid layer of fat that has formed over the broth. Reheat until warm over low heat. Strain the broth into a large saucepan. Separate the meat from the vegetables and discard the vegetables. Place the meat back into the Dutch oven and ladle about 2 cups broth over the meat. Continue to cook over low heat until hot.

3. To finish the dish: Bring the remaining broth to a boil. Taste for seasoning, adding additional salt if necessary. Add vegetables from the 20-minute category, and, once the broth comes back to a boil, cook for 10 minutes. Add vegetables from the 10-minute category and cook for 5 minutes once the broth has returned to a boil. Add vegetables from the 5-minute category and boil for 5 minutes. Place the meat on a large cutting board. Cut the chuck into thick slices on the bias. Serve the meat, vegetables, and broth in large bowls with Salsa Verde, if desired.

HOW TO PREPARE AND COOK THE VEGETABLES

20-Minute Cooking Time

CARROTS: Peeled, halved crosswise, thin end halved lengthwise, thick end quartered lengthwise
FENNEL: Tops cut off, bulb quartered through the core
RED POTATOES (SMALL): Washed and left whole
RUTABAGAS: Peeled and cut into 1-inch chunks
TURNIPS (MEDIUM): Peeled and quartered

10-Minute Cooking Time

PARSNIPS: Peeled, halved, thick end quartered lengthwise

5-Minute Cooking Time

ASPARAGUS: Thick ends snapped off
GREEN BEANS: Trimmed
PEARL ONIONS: Frozen
PEAS: Fresh or frozen

Investigating Salsa Verde

Salsa verde, or "green sauce," is simple enough. It's usually made with parsley, capers, vinegar, anchovies, garlic, and olive oil. The problem with this recipe is achieving the proper marriage of flavors. Having tried a half dozen recipes from Marcella Hazan, Patricia Wells, Penelope Casas, and others, I found that salsa verde can be a rough customer indeed, reeking of garlic and anchovies with a strong sour undertone to boot. My goal was to find the perfect marriage of flavors, toning down the brutish high notes while delivering a good jolt of flavor. ▶◀

I started with the ingredients above and then tried a series of additions. I liked capers — they added a nice briny undercurrent — but mustard, a common ingredient in many salsa verde recipes, was often overpowering if used in large quantities. Onions, fish stock, and white wine did nothing for the flavor. And a thickened sauce, using flour as a thickener, was also a dud; it lacked the bright flavors and fresh taste of a good green sauce.

The recipe I liked the best was from Biba Caggiano's *Trattoria Cooking*. First, I reduced the garlic to one medium clove, as I felt that the sauce had too much bite. For the same reason, I reduced the number of anchovy fillets from four to two. The fishy taste was gone, and what remained was a pleasant hint of anchovy. The best part of this recipe was the use of good-quality bread, which bound the ingredients together and also made the mixture less harsh. I found that ¾ cup of firm or day-old bakery- or European-style white bread to be best. I removed the crust and cut it into cubes for best results. To soften it, an important step, I simply added the bread, oil, and vinegar to the food processor bowl and let the bread sit in the liquid for a couple of minutes before adding the balance of the ingredients and blending.

Next I played around with lemon juice and vinegar. I preferred red wine vinegar or white balsamic vinegar to either lemon juice (too sweet) or white wine vinegar (too harsh). I tried substituting cornichons for capers but found that the flavor was too sour. I also needed to add salt, about ⅛ teaspoon, and a few grinds of fresh pepper.

The Best Salsa Verde

MAKES ABOUT 1 CUP, ENOUGH TO
ACCOMPANY 6 TO 8 SERVINGS OF BEEF,
CHICKEN, OR FISH

*I guess that one could argue about what
constitutes the "best" green sauce, but I am
happy to put this one into the competition.
It has a richer, less acidic texture and flavor
than many recipes I have tried.*

- ½ cup best-quality olive oil
- 2 tablespoons red wine vinegar or
  white balsamic vinegar
- ¾ cup day-old or firm bakery-style
  white bread, crusts removed and
  broken into 1-inch pieces
- 2 tablespoons capers, drained well
- 1 medium garlic clove, coarsely chopped
- 2 cups coarsely chopped loosely
  packed fresh flat-leaf parsley
- 2 anchovy fillets, coarsely chopped
- 1 teaspoon Dijon mustard
- ⅛ teaspoon table salt
  Freshly ground black pepper

Add the oil and vinegar to the bowl of
a food processor. Place the bread in the
bowl, letting it sit for 5 minutes in the
puddles of oil and vinegar and not on top
of the blade. Add the remaining ingredients and process for about 40 seconds or
until the mixture is finely chopped and
homogenous, stopping to scrape the sides
of the bowl if necessary. Serve immediately or refrigerate for up to 2 days.

Veal Shanks Rediscovered

I know the statistics. Whereas Americans consume more than 60 pounds of beef per capita per year, we eat less than 2 pounds per year of veal. Perhaps that is because veal and rabbit have that same baby thing going — we don't like to eat cartoon characters, and although baby vegetables are okay, we turn our back on calves. It is, no doubt, a reasonable moral position, but, speaking as someone who raises his own beef and pork, I am not sure that heaven makes moral distinctions between killing and eating animals that are 2 years old versus 2 months. Oh, and rabbit is about the most delicious meat there is — I even shoot my own. So if you haven't thrown this book down in disgust, let's talk about the best way to cook veal shanks, one of the world's most succulent and satisfying foods. 🎀

The shank is the lower foreleg of the animal and is my favorite cut, as it is incredibly tender when properly cooked. (Osso buco is made from this cut.) But over the years, I have had mixed results cooking shanks. Some were perfectly tender after two hours; other shanks were still tough after three hours of cooking time. I wanted to discover a foolproof method for determining just when they were done as well as home in on the best oven temperature.

I have found that long, slow cooking is the best method for most cuts of meat, the exceptions being lamb and very expensive cuts such as tenderloin. I have tried a variety of temperatures with shanks and found that a low 250 degrees is ideal. Low temperatures allow the meat to cook evenly without overcooking the outer layers before the middle of the meat is properly cooked. The big problem, however, was how to determine exactly when the shanks were done.

It turns out that an old-fashioned pot roast held a valuable clue. When meat's internal temperature reaches a bit over 100 degrees, the meat starts to lose moisture. The fibers twist like a bath towel, exuding juices. That's why rare or medium-rare meat is usually juicier than medium or well-done meat. However, when meat starts to reach temperatures in excess of 160 degrees, the collagen, those tough jelly-like ripples in the meat, start to melt, softening the meat and making it more tender. What I didn't know is that the meat must reach a whopping 200 to 210 degrees for this process to be fully realized. Meat cooked to, say, 180 degrees, will still be tough and dry. That's why many of the shanks I had cooked were still tough; I just hadn't cooked them long enough. The best way to measure the internal temperature, by the way, is to use an instant-read thermometer.

I also noted that both the pan and the shank itself might dramatically change the cooking time. A cast-iron Dutch oven, for example, will cook much faster than stainless steel. Large pieces of shank cook slower than smaller, thinner slices. As a result, the recipe below simply states two to four hours of cooking. (This dish can be held and then reheated.) Let the thermometer or your fork be the guide. Continue cooking until the shanks are fully "pot-roasted" and meltingly tender. By the way, this dish is a model for hundreds of similar recipes. You can use lamb shanks or beef short ribs instead. You can change the herbs or the seasonings to make endless variations.

Veal Shanks with Olives, Anchovies, and Sage

SERVES 4

Be sure to cook the shanks long enough — the meat should be falling off the bone, and the internal temperature should reach at least 200 degrees. This dish can be made earlier in the day and then reheated on top of the stove over low heat (about 15 minutes). If you refrigerate this dish before reheating, any fat will solidify and come to the surface, where it is easy to remove. I like to serve this dish with Seven-Minute Polenta (see page 114).

4   small to medium veal shanks,
    2-inch-thick center-cut pieces
    (2½–3 pounds total)
    Salt and freshly ground black pepper

2   tablespoons unsalted butter
2   tablespoons olive oil
¼   cup flour
1   medium onion, chopped
6   anchovy fillets, chopped
1   garlic head, cut in half and excess
    paper removed
½   cup dry white wine
1   cup chicken stock
1   cup canned diced tomatoes, drained
1   cup pitted and chopped Kalamata
    olives
2   tablespoons minced fresh sage

1. Adjust an oven rack to the center position and heat the oven to 250 degrees. Tie a string around the circumference of each shank (or have the butcher do it for you). Season shanks with salt and pepper. **2.** Heat the butter and olive oil in a

12-inch-wide Dutch oven or sauté pan with a lid over medium-high heat. When the butter-oil mixture is very hot but not smoking, lightly flour the seasoned shanks and then add them to the pot. Sauté for 4 minutes per side, shaking the pan occasionally to stop the shanks from sticking. The shanks should be golden brown on each side. Remove the shanks from the pot and reserve on a plate. Add the onion and anchovies to the pot, stir, and cook for 2 minutes. Add the garlic, wine, chicken stock, tomatoes, and ¾ cup of the olives along with the veal shanks and bring the mixture to a boil. Cover and place in the oven.

3. Cook for 2 to 4 hours or until the meat falls off the bone and is very tender. Remove the garlic head and squeeze out the contents, adding the cooked garlic back to the liquid. (Cooking time will depend on the size of the shanks, your oven, and your pot. You can make the recipe to this point, refrigerate, and reheat later for serving.)

4. Place the pot on the stove and bring the liquid to a simmer. Add the sage and the remaining ¼ cup olives. Cook, uncovered, for 4 minutes. Adjust the seasonings, adding salt and pepper to taste. Transfer one shank to each plate and spoon the sauce over the shanks.

Searing Meat to Seal in the Juices

Forget it. Searing does nothing more than add flavor—it doesn't seal in anything. Meat dries out because it starts to lose liquid at temperatures above 110 degrees. The meat fibers twist (like wringing a wet towel), and juices are lost. The higher the internal temperature, the drier the meat, and searing isn't going to slow down this process. Beef cooked to 160 degrees will be dry no matter how much searing you do.

How to Roast Pork Tenderloin

Pork tenderloin is a relatively small, tapered cut of meat, often weighing just 1 pound. Since it is both small and a premium cut, it lends itself to high-heat cooking and is ideal for a quick supper. The question was how to roast the tenderloin so that the exterior browns nicely while the inside remains juicy and tender. ▶◀

I began my testing by rubbing pork tenderloins with olive oil, sprinkling them with salt and pepper, and roasting them in a hot oven. At 450 degrees, the tenderloin cooked to an internal temperature of 145 degrees in 38 minutes. The top of the roast was visually unappealing, although the meat was tender and juicy. At 475 degrees, the tenderloin cooked in just about 30 minutes, and the exterior was a bit more browned. At 500 degrees, the tenderloin cooked in only 20 minutes (at this temperature, the roast was easy to overcook), but the pan drippings burned and the roast, once again, was still not properly browned. A lower temperature, 350 degrees, was also unproductive.

Putting aside the oven for a moment, I decided to try sautéing the tenderloin in a skillet before roasting. The bad news was that the meat shrank too much and was not tender. I decided to return to the 475-degree oven, the highest temperature I could use without burning the drippings. I noted that the bottom of the roast browned nicely, so I decided to turn the roast in the pan after 15 minutes. Voilà! Now the exterior was deeply caramelized, the roast had lots of flavor, and the meat was tender and juicy.

Since I often brine pork, I tested this method here as well, submersing the tenderloin in a solution of ½ cup kosher salt to 4 cups water. The brined roast was saltier tasting than the unbrined roast and had less pork flavor. Pork tenderloin is clearly too tender and delicate for brining. I also wondered if one pork tenderloin was enough for four people. In fact, I thought that a pound of meat was a bit skimpy, but because tenderloins are often sold two to a package, it was easy enough to roast two at once. I tried tying them together to create a uniform roast (tenderloins are tapered toward one end, so I tied them together head to toe), but this doubled the cooking time. The easiest solution was simply to roast two tenderloins together in the same pan.

Now I wanted to produce a quick pan sauce, so I deglazed the pan with ⅓ cup white wine; once it reduced, I added 1 cup chicken stock along with 1 teaspoon chopped thyme. Once that liquid was cooked down, I whisked in a tablespoon of butter and was done. You can also use a spice rub (instead of the sauce); I have included a recipe.

Charlotte's Web

Millions of tiny tears have been shed for this fictional pig, and rightly so. It was a great story. But the result is that every time I mention that our family raises two pigs each year, I am immediately categorized as some sort of barbarian, the type who murders with premeditation. Then I mention that I help shoot, bleed, skin, and clean the pigs, and all forms of polite conversation come to a sputtering halt. "How could you?" "Couldn't you keep them as pets?" "Your kids don't watch, do they?" (Yes, in fact, our kids do watch and find the process both sobering and fascinating, even my 4-year-old. My 7-year-old even mutters "bacon" under his breath every time he walks by the pigs' yard, which I inform him is in very bad taste.)

Of course, the affronted individual is perfectly happy to go to the supermarket and purchase meat that is nicely packaged, having already slipped off its mortal coil behind closed doors at the slaughterhouse, a place that Dante or Bosch would have understood completely as being representative of hell on earth. In fact, I raise almost all of my own meat (I even shoot rabbits), because the notion of inflicting pain, torture, fear, and suffering on a poor animal during its life (beyond those last fatal moments) is beyond me. There is a movement afoot (started by Peter Singer, an Australian philosopher, who wrote a book in 1975 entitled *Animal Liberation*) that has a simple premise: If we feel that we are morally superior to animals because of our superior intelligence, then why do we treat human beings with virtually no brain function (due to accidents or other causes) with dignity yet torture chimpanzees who exhibit many of the same abilities to think independently as we do, including fashioning tools and behaving in a manner consistent with the development of culture? Got me. And, if we are superior to animals because we have a soul, then let's be good shepherds of our flock and treat them well.

There are two ways to proceed here: One can become a vegetarian, which gives one, admittedly, the high moral ground. I have no quarrel with those who have the moral fiber to not eat meat or purchase leather products. Good for you. I tried that for two years but eventually became weak-kneed at the thought of a Sunday pot roast and a crisp rasher of bacon with my eggs. The other path is to accept the notion that some animals are raised for food, to treat them with respect while they are alive, and then to dispatch them with as much dignity and honor as we can muster as a civilization. Kosher food laws insist that animals be slaughtered one at a time by a rabbi with a knife (not a stun gun that delivers a metal slug to the back of the head). He also says a prayer, which seems the least one can do when taking a life.

Until then, I am going to have to endure the smirks and looks of horror from those of you who like your bacon but think that butchering pigs is barbaric. Our pigs have plenty

Roast Pork Tenderloin

SERVES 3

Tenderloins are usually sold 2 per package; 2 of them serve 6 adults. Do not cook the tenderloin to an internal temperature higher than 145 degrees. It will quickly dry out and become tough. (For safety, the internal temperature has to reach at least 140 degrees.)

FOR THE PORK

1 pork tenderloin (about 1 pound), rinsed and patted dry with paper towels
1 tablespoon olive oil
   Salt and freshly ground black pepper

FOR THE SAUCE

⅓ cup dry white wine
1 cup low-sodium chicken broth
1 teaspoon chopped fresh thyme
1 tablespoon butter

1. For the pork: Adjust an oven rack to the center position and heat the oven to 475 degrees. Tuck the thin end of the tenderloin under the larger part and secure with kitchen twine. Rub the meat with the oil and sprinkle with salt and pepper. Place the tenderloin in a small flameproof roasting pan and into the hot oven. Cook for 15 minutes. Turn the tenderloin using tongs or a meat fork and cook for an additional 15 minutes or until the internal temperature reaches 145 degrees measured on an instant-read thermometer. The time will vary slightly depending on the size of your tenderloin. Place the tenderloin on a warm plate, cover with aluminum foil, and let sit for 15 minutes before slicing.

2. For the sauce: Place the empty roasting pan over medium-high heat and add the wine. Scrape any browned bits from the bottom of the pan and let the wine reduce almost completely. Add the chicken broth and the thyme and bring to a boil. Cook until syrupy and reduced by two thirds, 5 to 6 minutes. Taste and adjust seasoning with salt and pepper if necessary. Off heat, stir in the butter. Serve over the carved roast.

of room to run, have shelter from the elements, eat table scraps as well as cornmeal, have plenty of fresh water, and seem to have a pretty good time rooting around their pen, squeezing into the water trough like hippos on a hot day, running in circles just for the fun of it, and generally being happy pigs. The day does come when they are turned into meat, but it is done as quickly and humanely as possible. If we are going to eat meat, let's be good caretakers of the animals and treat them with respect. No animal should suffer needlessly because, eventually, we are all going to come out on the short end of that stick.

Oh, and stop confusing children's books with reality. Death is sad, but there are worse things than death with dignity.

Two Pork Tenderloins

If you are feeding more than 3 people, you can easily roast a second tenderloin alongside the first. After turning the tenderloins in step 1, increase the cooking time to about 20 minutes or until they have reached an internal temperature of 145 degrees. (You will need a large flame-proof roasting pan.)

Pork Tenderloin with Spice Rub

Omit the olive oil, salt, and pepper in the recipe on page 175. Omit the sauce. Combine the spices below and liberally apply to the tenderloin before roasting. If using 2 tenderloins, double the amount of the spices.

1	teaspoon ground cumin
1½	teaspoons chili powder
¼	teaspoon ground allspice
⅛	teaspoon ground cinnamon
¾	teaspoon light brown sugar
1	teaspoon table salt
½	teaspoon freshly ground black pepper
	Pinch cayenne pepper

Pork Chili for Sissies

Chili has become the stuff of regional flag-waving. "Real" chili means one thing to Texans and something completely different to a denizen of Chicago. But most everyone agrees that chili should contain neither tomatoes nor beans. Having tried more than my share of these manly concoctions, I have to admit a retrograde weakness for chili recipes with both of these unfashionable ingredients. And, just to be even more persnickety, I prefer to use chili powder for most of my heat, as I prefer that my chili NOT bring tears to my eyes. ▶◀

So I started with a basic pork chili recipe and did a taste test of chili powders, including McCormick (in both plastic and glass bottles), Frontier, and Penzeys Medium (a mail-order chili powder). Penzeys was the clear winner, as it had a deep, authentic chile flavor. Frontier, which is usually found in natural food stores, took second place, and McCormick in the glass bottle wasn't half bad. (The stuff in the plastic bottle wasn't nearly as good.) I also discovered that pork can't handle the same amount of chili powder as beef, so I used only a bit more than 2 tablespoons for 2½ pounds of meat. I also decided to add ½ teaspoon each dried oregano and ground cumin as well as a couple of bay leaves.

Next, I moved on to the meat. I tested pork loin, boneless spareribs, and pork butt (this is cut from the shoulder of the pig) and found the pork butt to be the juiciest and most flavorful. Boneless spareribs were a close second, and the loin was the driest, stringiest, and least flavorful of the lot. I cut the pork into 1-inch pieces, seasoned them with salt and pepper, and browned them for the most flavorful results.

As for other ingredients, bacon was overwhelming in a pork chili, lime juice (a common ingredient in "authentic" chili recipes) was a nonstarter, 1 cup of canned crushed tomatoes was a winner, a modest half of a jalapeño added plenty of heat for this family dish (which I also wanted to be kid-friendly), and substituting chipotle for jalapeño added a hint of smoky heat without being an unwelcome guest.

I like my chili with beans, so 1 cup dried red kidney beans was a must. I also found that the starch in the beans helped to thicken the chili without having to add a thickening agent. The beans also cooked in the same amount of time as the meat, which worked out nicely. For liquid, water was just fine; chicken stock proved to be a waste of money, as I wanted the clean, bold flavors of the pork and chiles to shine through.

Pork Chili with Beans, Tomatoes, and Cumin

SERVES 6 TO 8

For those of you who prefer your pork in smaller pieces, simply take a potato masher to the pot after cooking, which will do the trick in seconds. If you like your chili hot, use up to 2 jalapeños or chipotles. Serve with white rice and garnish with any of the following: sour cream, shredded cheddar or Jack cheese, chopped cilantro, or chopped scallions.

3	tablespoons vegetable oil
2½	pounds pork butt or boneless spareribs, trimmed and cut into 1-inch cubes
	Salt and freshly ground black pepper
1	medium onion, cut into ½-inch pieces
3	medium garlic cloves, finely chopped or pressed
½	jalapeño chile, seeded and finely chopped, to taste, or like amount of chipotle for a smoky flavor
1	cup dried red kidney beans, rinsed and picked over
1	cup canned crushed tomatoes
2	tablespoons plus 1 teaspoon chili powder
½	teaspoon ground cumin
½	teaspoon dried oregano
2	bay leaves
2	teaspoons honey or more to taste

1. Heat 1 tablespoon of the oil in a large, heavy-duty Dutch oven over medium-high heat. Season the meat with salt and pepper and add a third of the chunks to the pot. Brown well on all sides, about 5 minutes. Set aside in a bowl. Repeat with the remaining oil and meat in two more batches. Reduce the heat to medium and add the onion. Cook, stirring frequently, until it is softened, about 5 minutes. Add the garlic and jalapeño and cook 1 minute. **2.** Add the browned meat, 4 cups water, 1 teaspoon salt, and all of the remaining ingredients except the honey to the pot and stir to combine. Bring to a boil and reduce the heat to maintain a very slow simmer. Cook for 2½ to 3 hours or until the meat and beans are very tender. Adjust the seasonings with salt and pepper. (If desired, use a potato masher to break apart the chunks of meat before serving.) Add the 2 teaspoons honey, taste, and add more if you like. Serve.

CHILI POWDER TASTE TEST

PENZEYS MEDIUM

With a deep, authentic flavor, this mail-order brand was the clear winner.

FRONTIER

This brand found in health food stores took second place.

MCCORMICK
(glass bottle)

Not half bad and far better than the lower-priced version sold in a plastic container.

MCCORMICK
(plastic bottle)

Bland and boring.
You get what you (don't) pay for.

Investigating Indian-Style Lamb Stew

American beef stew is satisfying, dependable, and, unfortunately, a bit dull. With just a few flavoring additions, the use of lamb instead of beef, and a couple of changes in cooking method, I set out to transform an American classic into something special. ▶◀

I started with a boned leg of lamb weighing in at 3¾ pounds. After trimming away the fat and silver skin, I was left with 3¼ pounds of lamb, which easily serves six. In order to reduce cooking time, I cut the lamb into 1-inch cubes, which allows it to cook to the point of being tender in just an hour. Although all stew recipes call for browning the meat, I knew that Indian curries do not include this step, because Indian cooks prefer a brighter flavor, one in which the taste of the spices shines through. I tested both methods, however, and preferred the stew with browned lamb. It had a deeper, darker flavor, and, in this particular recipe, this richer flavor married well with the spices.

Next, I investigated flavorings. I quickly eliminated cilantro and chiles, ingredients that are often found in restaurant versions of this dish. Sticking closer to an authentic Indian combination of spices, I settled on the foursome of cinnamon, cloves, cumin, and coriander married to garlic and ginger. (I found that the cumin and coriander are best purchased whole, not ground, for maximum flavor. They are then ground at home in a coffee grinder.) Over the years, I have discovered that the essence of Indian curries is the method by which the flavors of the spices are brought out. To release their full flavors, the spices need to be fried in oil for at least five minutes. This is where Americanized versions of Indian recipes often fall short — we sauté them briefly or simply add them to vast amounts of liquids. Neither method is effective at producing full flavors. After much testing, I finally settled on sautéing the onion, cinnamon, and cloves and then adding the remaining spices along with the ginger, garlic, and tomatoes. This mixture is then cooked for five to six minutes or until the oil starts to separate out and turn orange. (This separating of the oil is the key moment in preparing this dish; it ensures that the flavors of the spices have blossomed.)

Other ingredients included 2 cups chopped tomatoes (canned work fine here) as well as 2½ cups chicken stock (water tasted flat). A small food processor can be pressed into service for pureeing the garlic and ginger; just add one or two tablespoons of water. This will prevent the garlic from burning in the pan and also makes the pureeing process easier. You can also use a garlic press if you like.

Lamb Stew with Cinnamon, Cloves, Cumin, and Coriander

SERVES 6

This dish is great served over rice (preferably basmati) and accompanied with root vegetables, especially carrots and parsnips. (The root vegetable stir-fry on page 45 works well.) Use a small, clean coffee grinder to grind the whole spices. If using canned chicken broth, choose a low-sodium brand.

3	tablespoons vegetable oil
1	boneless leg of lamb (3½–4 pounds), trimmed of visible fat and silver skin and cut into 1-inch chunks
	Salt and freshly ground black pepper
1	(1½-inch) piece cinnamon stick
6	whole cloves
2	onions, cut into ½-inch dice
6	medium garlic cloves, pressed or pureed
1	(2-inch) piece ginger, peeled and grated or pureed
1	tablespoon coriander seeds, ground
1	tablespoon cumin seeds, ground
2	cups drained canned diced tomatoes
2½	cups chicken stock

1. Heat 2 tablespoons of the oil in a large heavy-duty Dutch oven, deep skillet, or sauté pan over medium-high heat. Liberally season the lamb cubes with salt and pepper. When the oil just starts to smoke, brown the lamb in batches. Set the browned meat aside.

2. Lower the heat to medium-low and add the remaining 1 tablespoon oil. Add the cinnamon stick, cloves, and onion and sauté for 5 to 6 minutes or until the onion is softened and just beginning to color. Add the garlic, ginger, coriander, cumin, and tomatoes and cook, stirring almost constantly, until the liquid evaporates, the tomatoes soften, the oil separates and turns orange, and the spices become very aromatic, 5 to 6 minutes.

3. Add the lamb and chicken stock to the pan and stir to combine with the other ingredients, scraping the browned bits from the bottom of the pan. Raise the heat to medium-high and bring the liquid to a boil. Lower the heat to maintain a gentle simmer and cook for about 1 hour (this time may vary) or until the lamb is very tender and the liquid has thickened. (If the lamb needs more than 1 hour to soften, you need to cover the pot to keep the sauce from reducing too much.) Adjust seasonings with salt and pepper. Serve immediately.

Quick sautés are the easiest way to get dinner on the table fast, and pan sauces are the best method for enhancing what might otherwise be lackluster meals. A good cook has an inventory of these simple recipes so that a steak, a pork chop, a chicken breast, or a piece of fish is easily transformed into a special dish. ▶◀

First, a few basics about sautéing: Use a large, heavy-duty skillet (for fish, nonstick is recommended). The pan must be thoroughly preheated over medium-high heat. In most cases, equal portions of olive oil and butter allow for the best color and flavor. Well-marbled cuts of beef such as sirloin strip or rib eye can and should be seared in a dry pan over high heat for superior color and crust. The pan should never be crowded, so if your pan is small or your crowd is large, cook the food in batches. An instant-read thermometer is the easiest way to determine the doneness of steak, pork, or chicken, while visual cues work well for fish. Piercing with the tip of a paring knife works well in all cases.

As for the sauce itself, the key is the fond—the caramelized bits of food found on the bottom of the pan after the beef, pork, or chicken has been removed. The pan is deglazed with liquid to release the fond, which adds flavor, color, and body to the sauce. (Because fish is preferably done in a nonstick pan, the fond is minimal.) After deglazing (the liquid lifts the caramelized bits from the pan surface and dissolves them), the liquid is cooked down until it intensifies in flavor and thickens. Additional ingredients add complexity, balance, and texture.

Caper, Olive, and Anchovy Sauce

MAKES ENOUGH SAUCE FOR
4 SERVINGS OF FISH

Use this sauce with fish. A high-quality extra-virgin olive oil is recommended.

- 2 medium anchovy fillets, finely chopped
- ⅔ cup dry white wine
- 1 tablespoon drained capers
- ¼ cup pitted and coarsely chopped black olives, oil-cured Italian or French or Kalamata preferred
- 1 tablespoon best-quality extra-virgin olive oil
- 1 tablespoon finely chopped fresh flat-leaf parsley
  Freshly ground black pepper

Once the fish fillets have been removed from the skillet, add the anchovies and cook, stirring constantly, until they have dissolved, about 1 minute. Add the wine, capers, and olives and cook over medium heat until the liquid has thickened slightly, about 2 minutes. Off heat, stir in the olive oil, parsley, and pepper to taste. Spoon over the fish and serve immediately.

Worcestershire Steak Sauce

MAKES ENOUGH SAUCE FOR
4 SERVINGS OF STEAK

The idea for this sauce was suggested by Jasper White, a well-known chef in Boston. Chicken broth gives the sauce a bit more body, but water is fine.

- ¾ cup water or low-sodium canned chicken broth
- 1 tablespoon Worcestershire sauce
- ¼ teaspoon lemon juice
- 1 tablespoon unsalted butter
  Salt and freshly ground black pepper

Once the steaks have been removed from the skillet, add ¾ cup water and the Worcestershire sauce. Using a wooden spoon or spatula, scrape any browned bits from the bottom of the pan. Cook over high heat until reduced and thickened slightly, about 3 minutes. Off heat, add the lemon juice and butter. Taste and adjust seasonings with salt and pepper if needed. Spoon over the steaks and serve immediately.

Apple Cider, Chives, and Cumin Sauce

MAKES ENOUGH SAUCE FOR
4 SERVINGS OF PORK OR CHICKEN

This recipe pairs nicely with pork or chicken.

- ¾ cup low-sodium canned chicken broth
- ¼ cup apple cider
- 1 teaspoon ground cumin
  Pinch cayenne pepper, optional
- 1 tablespoon chopped fresh chives or cilantro
  Salt and freshly ground black pepper

Once the pork or chicken has been removed from the pan, add the chicken broth. Using a wooden spoon or spatula, scrape up the browned bits from the bottom of the pan. Add the cider, cumin, and optional cayenne pepper. Cook over high heat until reduced and thickened slightly, about 3 minutes. Off heat, add the chives or cilantro. Taste for seasoning, adding salt and pepper if necessary. Spoon over the pork or chicken and serve immediately.

Maple Syrup, Vinegar, and Chicken Broth Sauce

MAKES ENOUGH SAUCE FOR
4 SERVINGS OF CHICKEN

I prefer to use white balsamic vinegar (my favorite vinegar for salad dressings as well), but any white wine vinegar will do. This recipe was inspired by Gray Kunz and his book, The Elements of Taste. *Serve this sauce with chicken.*

1 cup low-sodium canned chicken broth
2 tablespoons white balsamic vinegar or white wine vinegar
2 tablespoons maple syrup
Salt and freshly ground black pepper

Once the chicken breasts have been removed from the pan, pour off any remaining fat and add the chicken broth. Using a wooden spoon or spatula, scrape up the browned bits from the bottom of the pan. Add the vinegar and maple syrup and cook over high heat until glossy and thickened, about 3 minutes. Taste for seasoning, adding salt and pepper if necessary. Spoon over the chicken and serve immediately.

Lime, Fish Sauce, Honey, and Chile Sauce

MAKES ENOUGH SAUCE FOR
4 SERVINGS OF FISH

This sauce, which is best with fish, has a great combination of sweet, salt, sour, and heat. The chile should be added to taste, anywhere from ½ teaspoon to a couple of teaspoons, depending on the heat of the chile and your tolerance.

2 tablespoons rice vinegar
2 tablespoons fish sauce
1 tablespoon lime juice
1 tablespoon honey

½–2 teaspoons finely chopped fresh chile of your choice or ¼–½ teaspoon red pepper flakes or to taste
1 tablespoon chopped fresh cilantro

Once the fish is removed from the skillet, add the rice vinegar, fish sauce, lime juice, honey, and chile. Bring to a boil and cook for 1 minute. Off heat, stir in the cilantro. Spoon over fish fillets and serve immediately.

White Wine, Butter, and Thyme Sauce

MAKES ENOUGH SAUCE FOR
4 SERVINGS OF FISH

This classic combination is designed for fish. Chicken stock works well in place of fish stock or clam juice. (Frozen fish stock is sold in many upscale markets, and it works well here.)

6 tablespoons unsalted butter
¼ cup dry white wine
¼ cup fish stock, clam juice, or chicken stock
1 tablespoon lemon juice
1 teaspoon chopped fresh thyme or 1 tablespoon capers
Salt and freshly ground black pepper

Once the fish has been removed from the pan, add the butter, wine, fish stock, lemon juice, and thyme. Bring to a boil and cook until the sauce is reduced and slightly thickened. Taste for seasoning, adding salt and pepper if needed. Spoon over fish fillets and serve immediately.

Home of the Whopper

According to Greg Critser, author of *Fat Land* (Houghton Mifflin Company), Americans are the most overweight group on earth other than the inhabitants of a few South Seas islands. Today, 61 percent of us are technically "overweight," and more than 5 million Americans "now meet the definition of morbid obesity," which means that they qualify for radical surgery wherein the stomach is altered to stop it from digesting most foods. And this phenomenon is not restricted to adults. About one quarter of Americans under the age of 19 are considered obese, a figure that has doubled in the last 30 years.

So, am I to blame? I promote cooking, eating, and the liberal use of butter and salt. Should I be hauled up in front of a Senate committee and given the once-over? Well, actually, no. Home cooking is not the culprit. The food industry is.

Critser makes the case that the economics of food production is the enemy. When the United States produced huge surpluses of corn in the 1970s and sugar prices were high, the easy answer was high-fructose corn syrup (HFCS). This reduced the cost of any packaged food that required lots of sweetener. It turned out, however, that HFCS did some other things pretty well, too. It protected against freezer burn, it helped to promote fresh flavor for long-shelf-life products, and it made bakery products look more natural. In other words, it was a "super-food," because it was cheap and it helped sell product. As a testament to its success, in the 1980s Coke and Pepsi switched from a "50-50 blend of sugar and corn syrup to 100 percent high-fructose corn syrup."

At the same time, Earl Butz, the Secretary of Agriculture under Gerald Ford, cut a deal with Malaysia, opening the doors for large increases in the importation of palm oil. (In return, Malaysia would start importing products from the United States.) Palm oil was cheap and stable, thus increasing the shelf life of supermarket foods made with it. In essence, it was the fat equivalent of high-fructose corn syrup, and its popularity was based on economics and its ability to increase the shelf life of convenience foods.

Of course, one small problem was, for the most part, overlooked. Hog lard is 38 percent saturated fat; palm oil is 45 percent saturated fat! HFCS had a similar problem. Sucrose and dextrose go through "a complex breakdown process before arriving in the human liver." HFCS, however, does not. It arrives at the liver mostly intact, a distinction that turned out to be critical. The result? Consumption of HFCS rather than sucrose or dextrose results in more calories and thus more obesity.

Before we start picketing the various headquarters of the American food industry, keep in mind that both these events were tied to consumer demands. In the early 1970s, food prices had increased substantially, and reducing prices was a key political concern. So, we simply got what we asked for: cheap food. We also got long-shelf-life supermarket products that looked natural and tasted good. Who should we blame?

FINDING THE BEST COATING FOR FISH

FRESH BREAD CRUMBS

Although I usually like fresh crumbs, they overwhelmed
the delicate fish. The coating was too thick
and chewy (almost like stuffing), but it did look good.

DRIED BREAD CRUMBS

Dried crumbs made a thin, crisp coating that let the flavor
of the fish (not the breading) take center stage.

Better Fried Fish

Fried fish fillets run the gamut from pedestrian to horrible, the coating gummy and tasteless and the fish bland and overcooked. Yet this simple dish cooks in just minutes, takes little preparation, and, when made properly, produces juicy, tender fish encased in a crisp, flavorful coating. What's not to like? ▶◀

First, the fish. I tested a variety of fillets and found that only the thinnest will do for this recipe. (Thicker fillets such as cod turn out overcooked on the outside and undercooked on the inside.) The best choice turned out to be sole, with flounder a distant runner-up. Flounder fillets are a bit too small (about two ounces) for this recipe. Sole fillets run 4 to 6 ounces.

The coating consists of three parts: a liquid such as milk or egg, bread crumbs, and flavorings. I tested egg whites, whole egg, milk, and buttermilk. (The fillets are dipped into the liquid, coated with bread crumbs, and then pan-fried.) The egg-white version was crisp and clean, the milk was good but not quite as clean tasting, the whole egg was too rich, and the buttermilk added a tang that was unwelcome. I also determined that seasoning the fillets directly was preferable to letting the coating do all of the work.

For the bread crumbs, I tried a flour-cornmeal coating, fresh bread crumbs, and dried bread crumbs, all of which were fried in an olive oil–butter combination. The flour-cornmeal was gummy and the least flavorful, the fresh bread crumbs tasted like a bad church supper stuffing, and the dried bread crumbs were the crunchiest, adhered well, browned nicely, and contributed just the right amount of buttery bread-crumb flavor. Next, I tasted flavor additions to the bread crumbs: I liked the addition of chopped parsley and/or chives, because their flavor complements the breaded fillets. For 1½ cups bread crumbs (enough for eight fillets), I used ¼ cup chopped fresh herbs. I tried dried thyme, but it was overpowering, so I stuck with fresh parsley or chives. Next, I experimented with Parmesan cheese, but it simply interfered with the flavor of the fish. Lemon zest was an interesting addition, but I quickly found that I needed a lot of zest to get any lemon flavor. When I added enough zest, it then turned bitter, so I simply squeezed fresh lemon juice over the fillets after cooking.

Finally, I wanted to confirm the cooking technique. A combination of butter and oil was my first choice, but I also tested peanut oil (too much flavor) and canola oil (flavorless and not crispy). Using the butter–olive oil combination and a 12-inch skillet, I found that eight fillets could be cooked in two batches, 60 to 90 seconds per side. I found that I needed to add 2 additional tablespoons of olive oil to cook the second batch. For best results, the heat should be medium-high. If the fish cooks at low heat, the fillets become oily and soggy. At high heat, the butter burns. These quick-fried fillets are great served with salad, bread, and a glass of wine.

Pan-Fried Fish Fillets

SERVES 4 TO 6

Note that you should use store-bought dried bread crumbs, not fresh bread crumbs. Also, be sure to purchase unflavored crumbs, because many brands also include herbs and seasonings.

1½	cups unseasoned store-bought bread crumbs
	Salt
½	teaspoon freshly ground black pepper, plus additional for seasoning the fish fillets
¼	cup finely chopped fresh flat-leaf parsley or chives or a combination
2	egg whites
8	very thin fish fillets such as sole, 4–6 ounces each
5	tablespoons olive oil
3	tablespoons unsalted butter
	Lemon wedges for serving

1. Place the bread crumbs, 1 teaspoon salt, pepper, and parsley in a shallow bowl or pie plate. Stir with a fork to combine well. Whisk the egg whites in another shallow bowl or pie plate until slightly foamy. Season the fish fillets lightly with salt and pepper. Line a baking sheet with waxed or parchment paper. Place a large platter in a low (200-degree) oven to preheat.

2. Heat a heavy-duty 12-inch skillet over medium-high heat. One at a time, dip the fish fillets first into the egg whites and then into the bread-crumb mixture. For best results, flip the fish a couple of times in the crumbs, pressing down to adhere the coating. Set the breaded fillets aside in a single layer on the baking sheet.

3. Place 3 tablespoons each of olive oil and butter in the hot skillet. Swirl to coat the bottom of the pan. The butter will melt and foam very quickly at this point. Once the butter has stopped foaming, place 4 fillets (or as many as you can fit in a single layer) in the skillet. Cook for 60 to 90 seconds or until dark golden brown. With a large spatula, turn the fillets and cook on the other side until dark golden brown. Remove and place on the warm platter. Repeat with the rest of the fillets, adding the remaining 2 tablespoons olive oil before cooking the second batch. Serve immediately with lemon wedges.

Secrets of Salmon Teriyaki

Salmon teriyaki is fish marinated, cooked, and then finished with a simple teriyaki-style sauce. (*Teri* means "shiny," and foods prepared in this manner have a shellacked appearance.) The problem is that no two cookbooks agree on ingredients or methods. Some marinades include apple juice and maple syrup, other more authentic versions use soy sauce and mirin, and some use only sake. The marinating times vary greatly, as do the finished dishes — some taste oversalted, while others have little flavor. ▶◀

To find the best method of making salmon teriyaki, I started with the salmon itself. I chose center-cut fillets over steaks; the latter do not cook evenly, plus they include skin and bones. (*Center-cut* means that it is cut from the center of the salmon fillet where the meat is of a relatively even thickness. I wanted fillets in the 6- to 8-ounce range with a thickness of 1 to 1¼ inches.) For the marinade, I tested a handful of recipes and found that sake by itself did not add much flavor, whereas a soy sauce–based marinade was best. I ended up with a combination of soy sauce, mirin (a sweet rice wine used for cooking), and sake. Then I set out to determine how to use it. The first question was whether the fillet should be skinned. The answer was yes, because it was easier for the marinade to be absorbed. Next I tried adding a bit of sugar to the marinade (½ teaspoon) and thought it balanced the flavor nicely. I wasn't happy about having to use mirin, although it is available in larger supermarkets, but rice vinegar was a poor substitute. The last issue was marinating times. I tested times from 15 minutes to three hours and found that anywhere from one to two hours was best, as quicker times did not add enough flavor and longer times compromised texture.

The next question was the sauce. Many recipes simply use the marinade and then reduce it through cooking, but I found that this produced a very salty, intense sauce that overpowered the salmon. The simple solution was to use a light soy sauce. Other ingredients such as garlic and ginger were unwelcome and unnecessary.

The salmon fillets are best grilled over medium-high heat; you should be able to hold your hand 5 inches above the grill for three to four seconds. The salmon can stick, so clean the hot grates using tongs holding paper towels soaked in a bit of vegetable oil. The fillets are just cooked through after three minutes on each side. Thicker fillets may take 30 seconds to one minute longer. You know they are done when they are firm but not hard when the sides are pinched. (The fillets do cook a bit more on the way to the table, so they are best pulled from the grill when the center is still translucent.) In a pinch, you can use the tip of a small, sharp knife to check for doneness.

If you want to cook this dish in a skillet, a heavy-duty 12-inch pan works best for four fillets; you can also use cast iron if it is well seasoned. One teaspoon of oil is necessary to prevent sticking, and peanut oil was the winner. The fillets should be placed in the pan without touching each other (or the evenness of cooking will be affected) and then sit undisturbed for four minutes; lower the heat to medium-high after one minute. The fillets are then flipped and cooked on the second side for another four minutes. Be sure to check the salmon for doneness after two minutes on the second side. After the fillets are removed from the skillet, add the sauce ingredients and reduce until thickened, about one minute. Spoon over the fillets and serve.

Grilled or Pan-Seared Salmon Teriyaki

SERVES 4

Be sure to purchase center-cut fillets that are 1 to 1¼ inches thick for best results.

FOR THE SALMON

- ¼ **cup soy sauce**
- 2 **tablespoons mirin**
- 2 **tablespoons sake**
- ½ **teaspoon sugar**
- 4 **center-cut salmon fillets (6–8 ounces each), skin removed**

FOR THE SAUCE

- ¼ **cup light soy sauce**
- 2 **tablespoons mirin**
- 2 **tablespoons sake**
- ¼ **teaspoon sugar**

Vegetable oil for grill grate

1. For the salmon: Combine the soy sauce, mirin, sake, and sugar in a medium baking dish (the salmon can sit in one layer) and stir to dissolve the sugar. Add the salmon and allow it to marinate in the refrigerator for 1 to 2 hours, turning the fillets occasionally.

2. For the sauce: Combine the ingredients in a small skillet or medium saucepan and allow to cook over medium heat until the mixture is reduced by half and the sauce is slightly thickened, 1 to 2 minutes. Set aside.

3. Ignite the grill. When the fire is medium-high (you can hold your hand 5 inches over the flame for 3 to 4 seconds), rub the cooking area with a vegetable oil–soaked paper towel wad using tongs. Place the fillets on the grill and allow to cook for 3 minutes. Turn the fillets and cook for an additional 3 minutes or until both sides have dark grill marks and the salmon feels firm but not

THE SECRET TO FISH

THAT DOESN'T STICK

A COSTLY MISTAKE

We've all grilled fish and had it stick to the grill.
That flavorful, crunchy crust just peels right off, and the
end result looks and tastes pretty bad.

PERFECT RESULTS

By rubbing the hot grill with vegetable oil–soaked
paper towels (hold them with tongs), you can be
guaranteed that fish won't stick.

hard when pinched on its sides. (You may peek with the tip of a small knife; the very center should remain translucent.) Remove the fillets from the grill onto a warm platter, spoon the sauce over each, and serve immediately.

Pan-Seared Salmon Teriyaki

Do not prepare the sauce ahead of time. Instead, heat a large skillet over high heat for 3 minutes. Add 1 teaspoon peanut oil and swirl to evenly coat. Arrange the salmon fillets in the skillet so they are not touching and cook for 4 minutes, reducing the heat to medium-high after 1 minute. Turn each fillet and cook for an additional 4 minutes or until firm but not hard when pinched and well browned on each side. (See the end of step 3, this page, for tips on doneness.) Remove the fillets to a warm platter and combine all the sauce ingredients in the skillet. Cook until the sauce thickens and is reduced to about 3 tablespoons, about 1 minute. Spoon the sauce over the fillets and serve immediately.

Restaurant-Style Tuna Steak

Tuna is the seafood equivalent of beef, as it is cut into thick, dark steaks and tastes rich rather than fishy. It poses two problems, however. It is pricey — more than $15 per pound — and, for the most part, it can use some dressing up without overpowering the flavor of the fish. So I set out to find a recipe that added a modest amount of complementary flavor while also making the fish special enough to serve in modest portions as an appetizer. ▶◀

The first question was the basic cooking method: I like simple, so a sauté seemed best. Since a 1-inch-thick steak is the most common size, I tested a variety of cooking times and found that three minutes per side was about right if cooked in a hot pan. This turns out a tuna steak that is the equivalent of medium-rare — nicely browned on the outside yet still red in the middle.

The most obvious method for adding flavor was to use ground spices for a simple crust. I began with a combination of cumin, fennel, white peppercorns, and coriander, but I had a hard time making this work, because the cumin was overpowering and the white peppercorns had an unpleasant flavor. After much testing, I finally settled on 1 tablespoon fennel seeds, 1 tablespoon coriander seeds, and ½ teaspoon black peppercorns; each ingredient maintained its character, as did the tuna steak. I found that either a spice grinder (a coffee grinder works well) or a simple mortar and pestle helped to grind the whole spices without turning them into a powder. (A rough texture improves the dish.) Some recipes suggest using egg whites to help bind the spices to the steak. I tested this and found them to be unnecessary. Other recipes suggest coating only one side of the fish with spices, but I preferred coating both sides.

Next, I considered adding a simple sauce that could be drizzled over the finished tuna that had been sliced and fanned on a plate. A colleague at Cook's Illustrated suggested a simple maple syrup–soy sauce combination that is simmered for a few minutes and then allowed to cool. After testing various proportions as well as the addition of rice vinegar, mirin, and sherry, I finally settled on ¼ cup maple syrup and ⅓ cup soy sauce. I combined the two ingredients in a 10-inch skillet over moderate heat. Once the sauce started to boil, I reduced it by half in just two to three minutes. At that point, it had thickened but was not quite syrupy. (It thickened further as it cooled.)

Finally, a few pointers. The time it takes to cook the tuna may vary a bit based on your pan and your stovetop. Some folks like their fish very rare; if that is your preference, two minutes per side is enough. I prefer three minutes on the first side and then two to three minutes on the other. Be prepared, however, to check the tuna at this point and continue the cooking process until it is done to your satisfaction. A single large steak works best in this recipe, because it makes for the nicest presentation — the slices are long and look pretty fanned out on the plate. I also found that the tuna was juicier and easier to slice if the cooked steak sat for three or four minutes before slicing. The tuna and sauce can be served alone, but it can easily be stretched to serve six people if you accompany it with a bed of greens or a salad.

Six-Minute Tuna Steak with Spice Crust

SERVES 4 TO 6 AS AN APPETIZER

This recipe is equally good served alone, over a bed of greens, or alongside a simple salad.

FOR THE SAUCE
⅓ cup soy sauce
¼ cup maple syrup, darker syrup preferred

FOR THE TUNA
1 tablespoon fennel seeds
1 tablespoon coriander seeds
½ teaspoon black peppercorns
   Salt
1 tuna steak, 1 inch thick (about 1 pound)
1 tablespoon vegetable oil

1. For the sauce: Place the soy sauce and maple syrup in a heavy-duty 10-inch non-stick skillet over medium-high heat. Once boiling, cook until the mixture is reduced by about half and thickened, 2 to 3 minutes. Remove the sauce to a small bowl and set aside. The mixture will continue to thicken and become syrupy as it cools. Wash and dry the skillet in preparation for the tuna.

2. For the tuna: Using a spice grinder or coffee mill, grind the fennel, coriander, and peppercorns until well broken down but not powdery. Transfer the mixture to a plate large enough to accommodate the tuna. Lightly salt the tuna and dip each side into the spice mixture, pressing lightly on the steak to help the spices adhere. Place the clean skillet over medium-high heat until hot, about 4 minutes. Add the oil and swirl to coat the bottom of the pan. Place the tuna steak in the pan and cook, without moving, for 3 minutes. Turn the steak and cook for an additional 2 minutes for rare or 3 minutes for medium-rare. (The time may vary; check the steak at this point and continue cooking if necessary.) Transfer the fish to a cutting board and allow it to sit for 3 to 4 minutes. Cut the tuna into ¼-inch slices and divide evenly among the plates. Drizzle with the sauce and serve immediately.

Discovering Shrimp Curry

Curry is often thought of as a time-consuming ethnic specialty, something one might make once per year for a dinner party. Instead, think of curry as a means of infusing almost any dish with the fully blossomed fragrance of rich spices married to a subtle foundation of onions, ginger, and garlic, and you are coming closer to the truth. Best of all, if one opts for shrimp, this dish can be prepared in less than 45 minutes. ▶◀

Curry is nothing more than a stovetop stew. Most recipes begin by cooking onions; after testing, I preferred sliced to chopped. I also tried heavily browning the onions, but this flavor was more appropriate for a darker curry such as lamb. Here, I wanted a soft, sweet flavor to complement the shrimp. The next ingredients are garlic and ginger. Much testing has been done in our kitchens at *Cook's Illustrated* on this topic, and we have found that pureeing the garlic and ginger produces a smoother, more integrated flavor than if these ingredients are just chopped. A simple rasp-style grater works well, or one can opt for a small food processor.

The essence of curry is the spices and how one releases their flavor. A bad curry is either weakly flavored — the spices are wan and undercooked — or acrid — the spices have been burned. The usual suspects include coriander, cumin, and turmeric. Other curries also call for whole spices such as cinnamon, cloves, cardamom pods, peppercorns, etc. In my testing, I found that the whole spices were overpowering with shrimp, so I stuck to the basics with the addition of a bay leaf. The critical process in any curry is the cooking of the spices, which serves to release and develop flavor. To test this theory, I made a curry in which I simply simmered the spices along with the other ingredients. I found it to be raw tasting, watery, and flat. When the spices were added to hot oil, however, the flavor was greatly enhanced. To determine when the spices are properly cooked, simply look for the point at which the bright-orange oil starts to separate from the other ingredients. At this point, the mixture only needs to cook another half minute with constant stirring before adding water. (A nonstick pan is particularly helpful, as the oil-spice mixture has a tendency to stick.)

Some curry recipes have tomato, some have yogurt, some have both, and most have water. I found the combination of yogurt and tomato to be ideal with shrimp and decided to use two chopped plum tomatoes and ½ cup plain yogurt. Once this mixture has cooked for about 20 minutes along with the onion-spice mixture and 1 cup water (I also tested stock instead of water, which gave no additional flavor), the shrimp are added for a five-minute simmer to complete the dish.

Other ingredients that complemented this dish included a last-minute dash of freshly chopped cilantro and frozen peas (added straight from the freezer), which only need five minutes of cooking. For the shrimp, I use 1½ pounds large (31–40) shrimp. Smaller sizes are too hard to clean and add little texture; larger sizes are too expensive. An added benefit is that most freezer sections offer 1½-pound bags of frozen shrimp and, as most shrimp are previously frozen anyway, this is a quick and easy solution.

Shrimp Curry with Peas and Cilantro

SERVES 4 TO 6

A garlic press and a rasp grater are 2 valuable kitchen tools that will dramatically improve the flavor of this dish. Diced garlic and ginger add less flavor to a curry than the grated or pureed varieties. Vary the amount of cayenne to adjust the heat level in this dish. Serve with basmati rice.

- 3 tablespoons vegetable or canola oil
- 1 medium onion, thinly sliced
- 1 bay leaf
- 6 medium garlic cloves, pureed or pressed
- 1 (2-inch) piece ginger, pureed or grated
- 2 teaspoons ground cumin
- 2 teaspoons ground coriander
- 1 teaspoon ground turmeric
  Pinch–½ teaspoon cayenne pepper
  Salt
- 2 plum tomatoes, chopped (about ¾ cup) or ½ cup crushed canned tomatoes
- ½ cup plain yogurt (whole milk or low fat)
- 1½ pounds large (31–40 per pound) shrimp, peeled and deveined
- 1 cup frozen green peas
- 2 tablespoons chopped fresh cilantro

1. Heat the oil in a large skillet, preferably nonstick, over medium-high heat. Add the onion and bay leaf and cook about 5 minutes or until the onion is softened and translucent. Stir in the garlic, ginger, ground spices, cayenne, ½ teaspoon salt, the tomato, and yogurt. Cook, stirring constantly, until the liquid evaporates and the oil separates and turns orange, 5 to 7 minutes. Continue frying for an additional 30 seconds, stirring and scraping the bottom of the pan constantly.

2. Add 1 cup water and stir to combine. Reduce the heat to maintain a simmer, cover, and cook for 20 minutes or until the mixture is slightly thickened. Add the shrimp, peas, and cilantro and cook, uncovered, for 5 minutes longer, stirring occasionally, to evenly cook the shrimp. Discard the bay leaf, season to taste with salt, and serve immediately.

Why would anyone need a recipe for scrambled eggs? Simply put, most folks make dry, overcooked eggs that are tough and tasteless. When made properly, however, scrambled eggs are light and luscious and can also pull extra duty as the centerpiece of a light supper or lunch. ▶◀

Most cooks, especially the French, tell you to cook scrambled eggs over low heat. This can take 10 or 15 minutes for larger batches, requires constant stirring, and results in eggs that are good but on the mushy side. I wanted a lightning-fast recipe that produced big fluffy curds, so I turned to a recipe published in *Cook's Illustrated* by Elaine Corn. She suggests using high, not low, heat, and when I tested her approach, it worked well. The eggs are pushed back and forth in a nonstick skillet, which rolls up the eggs into large curds, and, best of all, the eggs are done in less than two minutes.

So, my starting recipe was 2 tablespoons butter, six eggs, 6 tablespoons milk, and salt and pepper to taste. After a few tests, I settled on 1½ tablespoons butter, as long as one is using a heavy nonstick skillet. (This recipe shouldn't be made in a conventional skillet, because the eggs will stick.) As for the milk, I tested milk, half-and-half, light cream, heavy cream, and water. The winners were half-and-half and light cream, although milk will do in a pinch. I tested adding salt to the eggs before cooking versus after (one cookbook suggested that adding salt to the uncooked eggs makes them tough) and found that ⅜ teaspoon salt was necessary at the outset; it did not toughen them and was crucial to boosting flavor.

The eggs need to be lightly beaten with the salt and half-and-half. Overbeaten eggs turned out tough, so beat lightly until they are almost homogenous, showing no streaks of white or yolk. I was keen to avoid any sort of browning, so I added the butter to a cold pan and then put the skillet over high heat. (This method avoids the problem of butter browning in a hot pan.) When the foam subsided, I added the eggs and immediately started pushing them around the pan with a heatproof rubber spatula. (A flat-edged wooden spatula also works well. I also tested medium heat but found the eggs to be disappointing, as they turned out dull, tough, and dry.) I did find that the action of pushing and folding must be constant. The eggs have to be removed from the heat when they are moist but not runny to prevent them from drying out and overcooking. It is true what many recipes say: The eggs finish cooking on the way to the table, so they do have to be removed just before you think they are done.

High-Heat Scrambled Eggs

SERVES 4 TO 6

Be sure to use the correct skillet size for this recipe and make sure that it is nonstick. A conventional pan requires double the amount of butter. Two eggs can be made in an 8-inch pan; 4 eggs work well in a 9- or 10-inch pan. When making smaller or larger amounts, use 1 tablespoon half-and-half per egg and adjust the salt accordingly. If you do not have half-and-half or cream, use milk. Smaller recipes cook more quickly — 2 eggs are done in 30 seconds or less.

- 6 large eggs
- 6 tablespoons half-and-half or light cream
- 3/8 teaspoon table salt
  Freshly ground black pepper
- 1½ tablespoons unsalted butter

Crack the eggs into a medium bowl. Add the half-and-half, salt, and pepper to taste and mix with a fork until no longer streaky. Do not overbeat. Put the butter in a heavy-duty nonstick 10-inch skillet and place over high heat. Once the butter has melted and the foaming has started to subside, add the egg mixture. Immediately begin pushing and folding the eggs, starting at the outside edges of the pan and working toward the center. This is best done with a heatproof or wooden spatula. Continue with this motion until the eggs are a tidy mound of large curds that appear wet but not runny, 1½ to 2 minutes. Remove the eggs from the heat. The residual heat will finish cooking the eggs on the way to the table.

VARIATIONS

Scrambled Eggs with Cheese
Add ½ cup grated cheddar, Swiss, or Gruyère cheese to the beaten egg mixture.

Scrambled Eggs with Ham
Add ½ cup finely diced ham to the beaten egg mixture.

Scrambled Eggs with Smoked Salmon
Add ½ cup finely diced smoked salmon to the beaten egg mixture and top the finished eggs with a bit of chopped chives.

The Wrong Egg

The first thing you should know about eggs is that egg cartons are dated. They use the Julian calendar (001 is January 1, and 365 is December 31); the date is stamped on the carton when the eggs are put into the carton. Unfortunately, some rumors suggest that if eggs don't sell, they are sometimes put into a new carton with a more recent date.

The problem with old eggs is that they lose moisture, and the contents start to shrink. Eggshells contain about 15,000 tiny holes, so the eggs do breathe (and also dehydrate). As a general rule, try to use eggs within three weeks of the date on the carton.

As for quality, the color of the shell does not matter at all. (This is simply a function of the breed of bird.) However, there is a big difference in the quality of eggs, depending on where you buy them. You want a white and yolk that stand up nicely when fried rather than running all over the pan. A recent taste test at *Cook's Illustrated* indicated that tasters did prefer farm-fresh eggs to supermarket eggs, though some of them were not used to the rich flavor of a real egg. As with beef or turkey, Americans are used to more subtle, delicate flavors, and when confronted with the real thing (grass-fed beef, free-range turkey, or small-scale, farm-fresh eggs), they find it overwhelming.

Now, what do you do when you want to make a recipe that calls for large eggs (as almost all do) and you have extra-large or medium on hand? This is a real problem when baking, as more or less egg often matters a lot. Well, here is a simple conversion table to make life easier.

LARGE EGG CONVERSION CHART

When a recipe calls for the number of large eggs indicated in the left column of the chart, use the equivalent number of extra-large or medium eggs listed in the other two columns. For a half egg, lightly whisk the yolk and white together and use only half of the liquid.

Large Eggs in Recipe	Extra-Large Eggs	Medium Eggs
1	1	1
2	2	2
3	2½	3½
4	3½	4½
5	4½	6
6	5	7
7	6	8
8	7	9

The Magical Souffléed Omelet

The concept is simple: Take three or four eggs, separate them, whisk the yolks together with seasonings, whisk the whites into peaks and fold them into the yolks, place the mixture in a skillet, and finish cooking in the oven. The result is a quick and easy breakfast pan soufflé for two. The problem with many of these recipes is that the mixture is too light in both texture and taste. I wanted more substance, more flavor, and a few variations on this simple theme. ▶◀

I started with three eggs, an amount I considered just right for an 8-inch skillet and two servings. I tried separating all three eggs, but the resulting omelet was too airy; leaving one egg whole was a better approach. It is important not to whip the whites until they are stiff; you want soft, 2-inch peaks so that they fold easily into the yolk mixture. Some recipes suggest beating the yolks until they are very light, but this method reduces their character; the recipe starts to taste more like a soufflé than an omelet. Simply whisk them until blended.

As far as the butter goes, a mere 2 teaspoons in a nonstick skillet was fine. Any more and the omelet became greasy and the bottom browned a bit too much, making it tough. Some recipes suggest adding water to the eggs, but I preferred a tablespoon of heavy cream (I also tested light cream and half-and-half), which provided a bit of richness and moisture. As for scrambled eggs, a nonstick skillet is essential; a nonstick surface is perfect for eggs, because it releases easily and therefore requires less oil or butter. Some recipes suggest cooking the omelet for two to three minutes on the stovetop and then transferring it to an oven. My tests indicated that just one minute on the stovetop followed by five minutes in a 400-degree oven eliminated the tough bottom crust that was often a problem.

My last thought was to develop variations. Since this is a relatively light dish, substantial additions such as ham or bacon seemed out of place. Cheese, however, is a natural, and I came up with two recipes: one with grated Gruyère or Swiss and the other using a combination of Parmesan and goat cheese. Finely chopped herbs are a classic (best for lunch or supper perhaps), and, finally, I liked a tablespoon of maple syrup added to the yolk mixture as a variation unto itself.

Souffléed Omelet

SERVES 2

If you want to serve 4 instead of 2, double the recipe and use a 10- or 12-inch skillet.

3	large eggs
1	tablespoon heavy cream
¼	teaspoon table salt
	Freshly ground black pepper
2	teaspoons unsalted butter

1. Adjust an oven rack to the center position and heat the oven to 400 degrees. Separate 2 of the eggs. Place 1 whole egg and 2 egg yolks in a medium bowl. Add the cream, salt, and pepper to taste and whisk to combine. Place the remaining 2 egg whites in a medium bowl and beat into soft peaks. (Do not overbeat, as this will make the whites difficult to incorporate into the yolk mixture.) Fold the whites into the yolk mixture.

2. Heat an 8- or 9-inch heavy-duty nonstick ovenproof skillet over medium heat. When hot, add the butter. Once the butter has stopped foaming, swirl to evenly coat the bottom of the pan. Add the egg mixture, spreading it evenly in the pan. Cook for 1 minute.

3. Place the pan in the hot oven and cook until the omelet is puffy and just set and may have started to brown ever so slightly on the top, 4 to 5 minutes. Slide the omelet onto a warm plate and serve immediately.

VARIATIONS

Maple Syrup Souffléed Omelet

Add 1 tablespoon maple syrup to the yolk mixture along with the cream. The more flavorful lower-grade dark-amber syrup is preferred.

Cheese Souffléed Omelet

Add ½ cup grated Gruyère, Swiss, cheddar, or Jack cheese to the yolk mixture along with the whites.

Goat Cheese Souffléed Omelet

Add 1 tablespoon grated Parmesan cheese and 2 ounces softened goat cheese to the yolk mixture along with the heavy cream, and whisk until the goat cheese is well incorporated.

Herb Souffléed Omelet

Add 2 teaspoons finely chopped fresh chives, flat-leaf parsley, tarragon, or thyme along with the whites. The herbs may be added along with the cheese or by themselves to suit your taste. The thyme is particularly good with the goat cheese variation.

Potato Frittata Simplified

A frittata is nothing more than a big, filled omelet. The omelet is not folded; it is cooked flat, the eggs and ingredients melded together, and then it is usually served in wedges. So what's the problem? Well, the eggs are usually tough and dry, the potatoes are soggy and take a long time to cook, and many recipes suggest slipping the frittata out of the pan, flipping it, and then slipping it back into the pan, a process that is prone to disaster. I wanted a quick potato frittata with crisp potatoes, just-cooked eggs, and plenty of flavor. ▶◀

I started testing with five different recipes from the likes of Carol Field, Penelope Casas, and Marcella Hazan and decided that the cooking method for the potatoes was key. Instead of using slices, I started with 1½ cups small diced potatoes and then fried them in a 10-inch nonstick skillet. This took just 10 minutes and only 1 cup of peanut oil. (Other oils either added no flavor or produced less-than-crispy potatoes.) I preferred Yukon Gold or russet potatoes, both of which have good flavor and a nice light texture.

For the eggs, six was the right amount, but I did not like the addition of milk or cream. Once the potatoes were cooked and removed from the pan along with the oil, I found that a tablespoon of butter to cook the eggs added flavor and also tenderness. The lightly whisked eggs were combined with the cooked potatoes and returned to the pan. Now the question was, what was the best method for cooking the eggs?

The problem with a frittata is that the bottom cooks before the top is ready, leading to overcooked eggs. Part of the solution is to pull in the edges of the frittata, tilting the pan so some of the uncooked egg on top runs down onto the hot pan. However, this still leaves one with eggs that are undercooked on the top. There are three ways to handle this issue: Use a broiler to finish the dish (a good solution if you have a good broiler), flip the dish onto a dinner plate and then slide it back into the pan (tricky, at best), or simply place the skillet in a hot oven to finish. This last method is least prone to error.

Other additions include chopped chives or parsley, sautéed onion, and roasted asparagus. One can also add grated Parmesan cheese, a great addition with the asparagus frittata. Note that salt and pepper are key ingredients and ought not to be reduced.

Quick and Crispy Potato Frittata

SERVES 4

It's important to use an even dice of potatoes for even cooking.

- 1 cup peanut oil
- 2 medium Yukon Gold or russet potatoes, washed and cut into ¼-inch dice (about 1½ cups)
- ¾ teaspoon table salt
- 6 large eggs
  Freshly ground black pepper
- 2 tablespoons finely chopped fresh chives or flat-leaf parsley
- 1 tablespoon unsalted butter

1. Adjust an oven rack to the center position and heat the oven to 450 degrees. Heat the oil in a heavy-duty 10-inch nonstick ovenproof skillet over medium-high heat. When the oil reaches 375 degrees (check with an instant-read thermometer), add the potatoes and cook, stirring occasionally, until they are dark golden brown, 5 to 8 minutes. Drain the potatoes in a mesh colander and then dump onto paper towels. Sprinkle with ¼ teaspoon of the salt. Wipe out the skillet. Lower the heat to medium.

2. Meanwhile, whisk the eggs in a medium bowl until foamy, about 2 minutes. Add the remaining ½ teaspoon salt, pepper to taste, and chives and stir to combine. Place the butter in the skillet. Once it has stopped foaming, add the potatoes and then the egg mixture. Stir

gently. As the eggs begin to set, push and lift the edges of the frittata to allow the loose egg to run underneath, tilting the skillet if necessary. Continue until the frittata is no longer runny but the surface is still wet, about 1 minute.

3. Place the skillet in the hot oven and cook until the surface is just barely set but still slightly wet, 2 to 3 minutes. Slide the frittata onto a plate and serve.

VARIATIONS

Potato-Onion Frittata

Before browning the potatoes, sauté 1 cup diced onion in 1 tablespoon peanut oil for 3 to 4 minutes over medium heat until soft and just starting to brown. Remove the onion from the skillet, set aside, and add the onion to the egg mixture when adding the chives.

Asparagus Frittata

Preheat the oven to 500 degrees. Omit the peanut oil, potatoes, and chives in the recipe at left. Snap the tough ends from 1 pound asparagus. Place the asparagus on a baking sheet and coat very lightly with olive oil. Place in the oven and roast until bright green and barely limp, 5 to 8 minutes depending on the thickness of the asparagus. Remove from the oven and lower the temperature to 450 degrees. Proceed with the recipe at step 2. Reduce the amount of salt to ½ teaspoon and add ¼ cup freshly grated Parmesan cheese to the egg mixture. Add the asparagus to the skillet in place of the potatoes in step 2.

HOW TO GET A PERFECTLY DICED POTATO

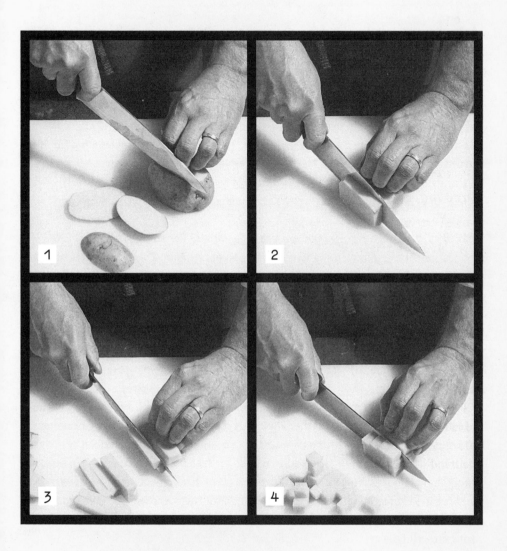

1 Using the claw grip, with your fingertips folded inward toward your palm to hold the potato in place, cut thin slices from all sides of the potato to make them flat. When you're done, the potato will look like a rectangular box. 2 Cut the potato into rectangular slabs. 3 Stack the slabs and cut them lengthwise into strips. 4 Cut the strips crosswise to make perfect dice.

On Whipping and Beating Egg Whites

When I started taking formal cooking lessons in the 1970s, most of the classes were devoted to French cuisine. That meant a lot of really silly recipes such as a coulibiac of salmon (salmon baked in brioche dough), beef birds, carved mushrooms, and all sorts of heavy, relatively indigestible sauces. In that context, the soufflé reigned supreme as being relatively practical, somewhat mysterious in its mechanics, and also temperamental — and therefore a great test of one's cooking skills. Somehow, beating egg whites to just the correct texture was the holy grail of French cookery, and folding in other ingredients was akin to a final exam. The perfect soufflé was part alchemy and part artistry. This, of course, led to thinking useless thoughts such as, "Are copper bowls really better for beating egg whites?" Who cares? When was the last time you saw a home cook with a copper mixing bowl?

So what is really going on when you beat egg whites? For starters, egg whites are about 90 percent liquid (water) and about 10 percent protein. This means that egg white foams are gas bubbles separated from each other by very thin liquid-protein films. When you agitate or beat egg whites, the tightly wound protein molecules relax and begin to unfold and stretch. With continued beating, the stretched proteins begin to overlap, creating a long, elastic surface. This is known as the "soft-peak" phase — the air bubbles are relatively large and the foam unstable, because the proteins have not sufficiently unwound and bonded to create a rigid enough structure for holding the air pockets. If one continues beating, then the proteins further bond and envelop the air bubbles, trapping and separating them. (Think of a sponge.) Consequently, you get smaller air bubbles but an increased quantity of them held in a three-dimensional network of united protein molecules. The key is to establish a fine, even foam that is still moist and elastic enough not to break. Without the addition of sugar (see page 208), the margin between beating to maximum volume and overbeating is slim. If you overbeat or heat foams too quickly or too slowly, the proteins will overcoagulate. They become too rigid and rupture, squeezing out the liquid held within their mesh. Technically called *syneresis*, this process is what home cooks recognize as weeping or curdling.

So, simply put, beating egg whites on their own is tricky business, the same message I received from my haughty French cooking instructor back in the 1970s. Yet, what I wasn't told was that there are two ingredients that pretty much solve this problem and make beating egg whites child's play. The first is sugar, which delays foam formation. It separates protein molecules, slowing the bonding process, thus it helps to prevent overbeating. It also stabilizes the foam, particularly in the oven, because it attracts water and thus delays water evaporation, giving protein structure time to set up. So, whether you are using a sugar syrup or plain granulated sugar, the risk of overbeating decreases as the amount of sugar increases, because it impedes the bonding of proteins. On the flip side, proteins also help to keep sugar crystals apart, which prevents a coarse-textured foam.

The second and less common ingredient is cream of tartar, an acid. But first, a word about what happens to a soufflé in the oven: Although rarely discussed in cookbooks, egg whites contain a variety of proteins that coagulate, or set, at different temperatures. Think of this as a house. Some of the proteins set early, forming the foundation, while others set later, forming the superstructure. For a successful soufflé, it is important to keep these latter proteins elastic (the cream of tartar does this) so that they set slowly, giving the trapped air bubbles time to expand and provide lift. (The air cells will come up against less resistance when they expand under heat.) The other benefit of cream of tartar is that acids enhance the whiteness of a foam, which is why cream of tartar is often used in angel food cake recipes.

The answer? Add cream of tartar and sugar (sugar is not usually added to savory recipes, however) to egg whites when you beat them. They will be more stable and harder to overbeat, and they will expand better in the oven. (I mix together ¼ teaspoon cream of tartar and 2 tablespoons sugar and add it to the whites about 20 seconds after I started beating them. This works well for four to six whites.)

If you are interested, I also tested the notion that egg whites are best whipped at room temperature. Actually, cold whites will produce 50 percent more foam than warm ones. However, this difference tends to even out in the oven; the final soufflé made with cold whites will be only slightly higher.

I also wondered if it matters if you slightly over- or underbeat the whites in terms of the final product. The answer is no. Slightly underbeaten whites will produce less foam but will make up for it in the oven by rising more. Slightly overbeaten whites will rise less but produce more foam to start with.

THE SECRET TO FLUFFY,

STABLE EGG WHITES

JUST EGG WHITES

Egg whites beaten without sugar or cream of tartar yield a relatively unstable foam, which is less dense, harder to fold into other ingredients, and likely to break relatively quickly.

EGG WHITES WITH CREAM OF TARTAR

Cream of tartar helps create a stable, glossy foam.
Adding a little sugar (when using the egg
whites in a dessert recipe) also improves their
stability and volume.

A Goat Cheese Soufflé?

For many home cooks, this recipe has two strikes against it: It uses goat cheese and it is a soufflé. Give me just a moment to sell you on this concept. It is simple to put together, cooks in just 23 minutes, and is an easy way to bring the elegance of restaurant dining home. ▶◀

The idea for this recipe came from the London chef Sally Clarke who, in turn, was inspired by Alice Waters. Although I loved Ms. Clarke's recipe, it was too rich for my taste, using a superabundance of cheese and cream. A few bites were enough to send one running for a health club. The soufflés were also supposed to be baked in shallow soup plates, a notion that is best suited for a restaurant, not a home, setting.

The first step was to lighten the load by severely reducing the quantities of cheese. The Parmesan went from a whopping 2¼ cups to 1½ cups, and the goat cheese was reduced slightly from 14 ounces to 12. I was not in Weight Watchers territory, but things were moving in the right direction. Light cream did not work as well as the heavy cream called for by Ms. Clarke. I took the eggs down a notch to five from six. Other ingredients included salt, pepper, and chopped fresh thyme. Now I had a very good soufflé, but I wanted to make the recipe as friendly as possible for the home cook.

The real breakthrough occurred when I added a bit of cream of tartar to the egg whites before beating them. Cream of tartar made the whites more elastic, easier to fold, and also higher rising. The cream of tartar stabilizes the whites so that they can be held a few minutes and I could use the same beaters for the yolks. (If the whites are beaten last, the beaters must be cleaned first to remove any traces of yolk.) I found that instead of simply beating the yolks until smooth, if I beat them for a couple of minutes, it further lightened the final texture of the soufflé. It also made the folding of the egg white and yolk mixtures that much easier.

The original recipe called for using soup plates as baking dishes. I have done this at home, but most folks don't have the right type of plate (they have to be shallow) nor the oven space to bake six or eight plates at one time. I tried a soufflé dish, but I preferred an oval casserole dish (1½ quarts or about 10 by 7 inches), which worked nicely when the soufflé was baked at 400 degrees for about 23 minutes. (Other oven temperatures were less successful.) I prepped the baking dish with butter and Parmesan per the original recipe, which made the soufflé release nicely and taste great. This recipe also works well in custard cups or ramekins.

Goat Cheese Soufflé with Thyme and Parmesan

SERVES 6 TO 8 AS A FIRST COURSE (IT IS VERY RICH)

Be sure that your oven is calibrated properly for this recipe; many ovens are off by 50 degrees or more. Do not use aged goat cheese. Instead, use the logs of fresh goat cheese that have a relatively light texture.

1	teaspoon unsalted butter for buttering casserole dish
1½	cups freshly grated Parmesan cheese
5	large eggs, separated
½	teaspoon cream of tartar
12	ounces fresh goat cheese, at room temperature
½	cup heavy cream
¾	teaspoon finely chopped fresh thyme leaves
½	teaspoon table salt
	Freshly ground black pepper

1. Adjust an oven rack to the center position and heat the oven to 400 degrees. Butter the inside of an oval casserole dish (10 by 7 inches works best) or a 1½-quart soufflé dish and dust with 2 tablespoons of the Parmesan cheese.
2. Add the egg whites and cream of tartar to a large mixing bowl. Using an electric mixer, beat on medium-low speed until combined. Increase speed to medium-high and beat until the whites form soft billowy peaks, about 2 minutes; be careful not to overbeat, in which case they will look dry and lumpy. Transfer the whites to a large bowl. Place the yolks in the mixing bowl and beat on medium-high until they are thickened and lemon colored, about 2 minutes. Add the goat cheese and beat on low to incorporate. Increase the speed to medium and continue beating until the mixture is smooth, about 1 minute. Add the cream, 1¼ cups Parmesan, thyme, salt, and pepper to taste and mix on medium until well combined, about 30 seconds longer.
3. Add the yolk mixture to the whites and fold together using a rubber spatula until homogenous. (You may find it easier to stir ¼ of the whites into the yolk mixture first.) Pour into the prepared baking dish and sprinkle with the remaining 2 tablespoons Parmesan. Bake until the soufflé is dark golden brown, is puffed, and barely jiggles in the center when shaken, 20 to 25 minutes. Serve immediately.

Individual Goat Cheese Soufflés

SERVES 8

Increase the butter to 2 teaspoons and the grated Parmesan to 1½ cups plus 2 tablespoons. Prepare eight ¾-cup ramekins or custard cups in place of the baking dish, using ¼ cup of the Parmesan for dusting. Place them on a baking sheet large enough to hold them without touching. Evenly distribute the soufflé batter among the cups, sprinkle with the remaining 2 tablespoons Parmesan, and bake until dark golden brown and very puffy, about 15 minutes. Serve immediately.

Perfect Pancakes

Second-rate pancakes are as common as the oversized, tasteless muffins one buys at diners and overrated coffee shops. I wanted my pancakes to be light, easy to make, and also adaptable to fruit variations such as blueberries. ▶◀

The first problem with most pancake recipes is that they use milk instead of buttermilk, and the pancakes turn out very thin. Buttermilk is a wonderful thickener; the huge amount of lactic acid in buttermilk reacts with baking soda to provide a lot of lift and fluff. With that basic ingredient out of the way, I then noticed that most pancake recipes use too much leavener — up to a tablespoon of baking powder and/or soda — and this produces a soapy flavor and also results in thinner pancakes, because they collapse on themselves toward the end of cooking due to an excess amount of lift. I finally decided to use ¼ teaspoon baking soda and ½ teaspoon baking powder. I found that a combination of soda and powder was best, because batter made with just soda tended to fizzle out by the time the last pancake was made; double-acting baking powder reserves some of its leavening activity until it comes in contact with heat, unlike baking soda, which reacts immediately with acid.

Now I had a basic recipe using 2 cups flour, baking powder and soda, 2 cups buttermilk, salt, eggs, and possibly sugar and melted butter. I found that mixing buttermilk and a small amount of milk was best; this produced a batter that was pourable yet thick enough to produce a fluffy cake. I finally settled on 1⅔ cups buttermilk to ⅓ cup milk. Two eggs are standard in pancake recipes; I tested one and three eggs with disappointing results. (If one separates the eggs and beats the whites, one produces an extremely light pancake. See the variation on page 212.) Melted butter does add some flavor, but it produces an unevenly browned pancake, and it is an extra step. (I smear my pancakes with butter anyway, so it seems a bit redundant.) For those reasons, I left it out. Two teaspoons sugar perked up the flavor, as did ½ teaspoon table salt.

Most folks go off the rails when they mix pancakes. The simple rule is to use a light hand and undermix instead of overmix. This is not a cake batter. Simply pour the wet ingredients into the dry and gently fold the batter for just a few seconds until the batter is thick and relatively lump free. (A few small lumps are okay — the batter should not be totally smooth.) The other issue is the griddle or skillet. Every griddle is different, so settings are irrelevant. You want a medium-high heat so that the exterior of the pancake does not overcook by the time the interior is cooked through. I use ⅓ cup of batter for each pancake and leave plenty of room between them. This recipe can be doubled for larger crowds.

Perfect Pancakes

SERVES 4

Remember to use a very light hand when mixing—a few lumps in the batter are just fine. If you have problems with the pancakes sticking to the griddle, use paper towels to coat it with a thin layer of vegetable oil (do not use corn oil, which is sticky) before cooking the pancakes. The separated-egg version that follows is more work but produces a much higher, fluffier pancake.

2	cups all-purpose flour
½	teaspoon table salt
2	teaspoons sugar
¼	teaspoon baking soda
½	teaspoon baking powder
1⅔	cups buttermilk
⅓	cup whole milk
2	large eggs

1. Heat a seasoned griddle or skillet. Whisk the dry ingredients in a medium bowl. Whisk the buttermilk, milk, and eggs together in a small bowl or large measuring cup. Pour the buttermilk mixture into the dry ingredients and gently fold until roughly combined; there should still be a few small streaks of flour. Small lumps in the batter are okay—do NOT overmix!

2. Pour ⅓ cup of the batter onto the heated griddle for each pancake, spacing them well apart. Cook until several large bubbles appear on the batter surface. Turn and cook until the underside is medium brown. Repeat with the remaining batter. It is best to serve pancakes as soon as they are cooked.

VARIATIONS

Blueberry Pancakes

Pick over, rinse, and dry 1 cup blueberries. Scatter a small handful over each pancake when they are first poured onto the skillet.

Extra-Fluffy Pancakes

Separate the eggs. Whisk the yolks with the buttermilk and milk. In a separate bowl, beat the whites to 2-inch peaks; they should still be very soft and moist. Add the liquid ingredients to the dry ingredients as directed and stir gently for 5 seconds. Now add the whites and gently fold them in. Do NOT overmix.

PANCAKE BATTER: EASY DOES IT

1 Whisk the dry ingredients together in a bowl, whisk the liquid ingredients together in a measuring cup, and then pour the liquid ingredients into the bowl. 2 With a rubber spatula, begin to fold the wet and dry ingredients together. 3 Once the large streaks of flour disappear, stop mixing. Note that the batter will still have some lumps. 4 If you continue to stir, the batter will become smooth. However, at this point you've overmixed the batter, and the pancakes will be tough.

The Best Bran Muffin

The typical coffee shop bran muffin is a huge, sticky beast of a confection, heavy and sweet enough to place it far outside the category of a health food. When it's attempted at home, one is immediately put off by the two-page ingredient list and the need to let the batter sit overnight as the bran absorbs liquid and swells. One quickly concludes that bran muffins are an unholy marriage of bad taste and inconvenience. ▶◀

My first task was to eliminate the overnight rest in the refrigerator. (This category of bran muffin uses a bran cereal that requires a long rest to absorb liquids; a second category uses wheat or oat bran, and the batter can be used right away.) I baked up samples from both methods and found that the refrigerator muffins tasted muddy; the simpler bran recipes had a lighter texture and an earthier flavor. So, bran was in; bran cereal was out.

Next, I tested a variety of recipes from *Baking with Jim Dodge, The New Basics,* and *The Fannie Farmer Cookbook.* None of them were what I was after, although Jim Dodge's recipe was the best of the lot. The most obvious problem was the use of cinnamon, allspice, nutmeg, and vanilla — it read more like a pumpkin pie recipe than a muffin. I tested reducing the quantities but finally ended up eliminating all four ingredients altogether. The recipe used 1¼ cups all-purpose flour combined with ¼ cup whole-wheat flour. This was indeed just the right proportion; more wheat flour made the muffins heavy, less made them flat-tasting. I tested rye flour, which I found to be superb, but whole-wheat or rye will do just fine.

The key ingredient is wheat bran, which is usually sold in flake form and looks nothing like a pebbly bran cereal; it is light in both texture and color. You can purchase either wheat or oat bran, but testing proved that wheat bran was best for this application, because the latter produced a heavier muffin.

I also wanted to streamline the recipe by melting the butter instead of creaming it. To my surprise, a blind taste test between these two methods proved that melted-butter muffins (by far the easiest method) were moister and also more flavorful. It is best to start the recipe by mixing the melted butter with brown sugar rather than adding the butter at the end. This makes it easier to whisk out any lumps in the sugar, and the butter has a chance to cool so that it does not jump-start the baking soda, making the batter swell too quickly before it is scooped into the muffin tin.

Molasses was a key ingredient for its rich flavor, but it had to be combined with dark brown sugar rather than white or light brown, the latter choices having too little flavor. Some recipes call for both buttermilk and sour cream. I found the latter to be unnecessary and dropped it, slightly increasing the amount of both butter and buttermilk. I adjusted the baking soda, increasing it to a full teaspoon, and found that adding the wheat bran at the end of the mixing process reduces the amount of mixing. Because the batter is heavy, an ice cream scoop is recommended for filling the tin. Paper liners are suggested for this recipe for easy cleanup but are not essential.

Best Bran Muffins

MAKES 12 MUFFINS

Be sure to use wheat bran, a light, flaked product that is nothing like the hard, pebbly cereal. You can use ½ cup oat bran with 1 cup wheat bran, which makes for a slightly heartier muffin.

1¼	cups all-purpose flour
¼	cup whole-wheat or rye flour
1¼	teaspoons baking powder
1	teaspoon baking soda
¾	teaspoon table salt
8	tablespoons (1 stick) unsalted butter, melted and cooled slightly
⅔	cup packed dark brown sugar
2	large eggs
3	tablespoons molasses
1¼	cups buttermilk
1½	cups wheat bran or 1 cup wheat bran and ½ cup oat bran
1	cup raisins

1. Adjust an oven rack to the center position and heat the oven to 375 degrees. Place paper liners in a 12-cup standard-size (½ cup) muffin tin or butter each cup. Whisk the flours, baking powder, baking soda, and salt together in a medium bowl. Add the melted butter and sugar to the bowl of an electric mixer and beat on medium speed until well combined, about 1 minute. Add the eggs, one at a time, beating 30 seconds after each addition, scraping down the sides of the bowl as needed. Add the molasses and beat until well combined, about 30 seconds longer. Add the buttermilk and half of the flour mixture and beat on low for 30 seconds. Add the rest of the flour mixture along with the bran and the raisins and beat on low for 30 seconds or until combined. Finish mixing with a spatula.

2. Using an ice cream scoop or a large spoon, evenly distribute the batter among the muffin cups. The batter will completely fill the cups. Bake until the muffins are lightly browned and spring back slightly when poked in the center or a toothpick inserted into the center comes out clean, 18 to 25 minutes. Cool on a rack for 5 minutes before removing from the muffin tin. Serve warm.

Quicker Cinnamon Rolls

Fancy breakfast breads are part of our family's holiday tradition, especially on Christmas morning. Yeasted breads, however, take too much advance planning, so I set out to make quick cinnamon rolls using baking powder or soda, the sort of recipe that could be slapped together in just minutes and popped into a hot oven just in time to satisfy an itchy first grader. ▶◀

The basic recipe is a biscuit—there are two different types: a biscuit made with cold shortening such as butter and one made with cream. The latter is easier and somewhat lighter, so I started there. I tested both milk and buttermilk in place of the cream and preferred buttermilk; it added flavor and made the biscuits lighter. I also wanted large rolls, so I increased the recipe to 3 cups flour from 2 cups, adding a small amount of sugar for flavor. The addition of melted butter was not necessary, but ½ teaspoon baking soda added to the 2 teaspoons baking powder already in the recipe gave the biscuits more lift. In my original biscuit recipe, I called for 30 seconds of hand kneading (this actually provided a higher-rise biscuit), but I found that between the rolling and shaping of the dough for cinnamon rolls, the kneading was not necessary.

As for the filling, a combination of white and brown sugars was best. I was cautious with the cinnamon—1½ teaspoons was fine—but I also used 2 tablespoons melted butter for brushing on the dough before sprinkling with the sugar and spice.

As for working with the dough, I found that a 10-by-12-inch rectangle was ideal; anything larger made the rolls too fat but not tall enough. Once the dough is rolled out, excess flour is brushed off, the surface is coated with melted butter, and the filling is evenly distributed, leaving about ¾ inch at one short end to form a seam. (The dough seals beautifully when dotted along the seam with a bit of buttermilk.) Starting at the opposite short end, the dough is rolled up as tightly as possible. Once the log is formed, it should be lightly dusted with flour, making it easier to pull the rolls apart. Next I trimmed the ends, clipping just enough to expose a neat spiral. I found that the best way to slice the rolls is to use a thin, serrated knife and a sawing motion, applying very little pressure. The log is then cut in half, halved again, and each quarter cut in half again, forming eight rolls.

I tried using cake pans, springform pans, and pie plates to bake the rolls. A 9-inch deep-dish pie plate was my favorite, because the baked rolls are easy to remove.

(The sides of a regular pie plate are a bit too sloping, which makes odd-looking rolls.) However, you can also use a cake pan, although it is best to remove the rolls before glazing, otherwise they can be tricky to get out.

Most confectioners' sugar glazes are truly awful, packing a bitter, off flavor. However, the *Cook's Illustrated* test kitchen discovered that a combination of confectioners' sugar, buttermilk, and cream cheese makes a terrific topping. I added the sugar to a small bowl, whisked in the buttermilk until the glaze was smooth, and then whisked in the softened cream cheese.

Oven temperatures were tested: 425 degrees was too hot — the rolls got a bit too browned and tough on their exterior — but at 400 degrees, the problem was solved. Lastly, I found that the rolls should cool for five minutes before glazing and another five minutes more before serving.

Quick and Easy Cinnamon Rolls

MAKES 8 ROLLS

You can make these rolls in less than an hour, including assembling the ingredients.

Softened butter for greasing pie plate

FOR THE FILLING

2 tablespoons brown sugar, light or dark
2 tablespoons granulated sugar
1½ teaspoons ground cinnamon

FOR THE ROLLS

3 cups all-purpose flour, plus more for dusting work surface
2 teaspoons baking powder
½ teaspoon baking soda
1 tablespoon sugar
1 teaspoon table salt
1½ cups plus 1 tablespoon buttermilk
2 tablespoons unsalted butter, melted

FOR THE GLAZE

¾ cup confectioners' sugar
1 tablespoon plus 1 teaspoon buttermilk
1 tablespoon cream cheese, softened

1. Adjust an oven rack to the upper-middle position and heat the oven to 400 degrees. Lightly butter a 9-inch deep-dish pie plate or a 9-inch cake pan.

2. For the filling: Stir together the sugars and cinnamon in a small bowl; set aside.

3. For the rolls: Whisk together the flour, baking powder, baking soda, sugar, and salt in a medium bowl. Add 1½ cups of the buttermilk and stir with a fork or wooden spoon until a shaggy dough forms, about 30 seconds. Turn the dough out onto a countertop and work until it comes together, about 15 seconds longer. On a well-floured surface, roll or pat the dough into a 10-by-12-inch rectangle. Remove the excess flour from the surface. Brush the melted butter onto the dough leaving a ¾-inch seam allowance on one

continues

STEP-BY-STEP: CINNAMON ROLLS

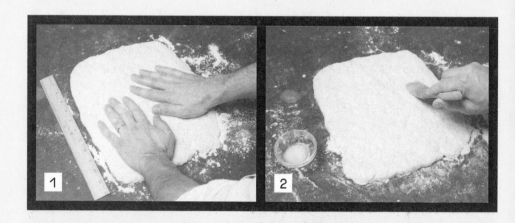

1 On a floured work surface, pat the dough with your hands into a rectangle that measures about 10 by 12 inches. **2** Brush 2 tablespoons melted butter over the entire dough, except for a ¾-inch seam along the far short side. **3** Sprinkle the cinnamon-sugar mixture evenly over the buttered area of the dough, leaving the ¾-inch seam uncovered. **4** Starting from the short side closest to you, begin to roll the dough into a log, making sure the log is as tight as possible.

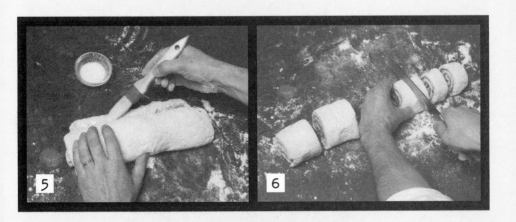

5 Dot the seam area of the dough with 1 tablespoon buttermilk and then seal the log tightly. **6** With a serrated knife, slice off a bit of each end of the log to reveal a neat spiral. Slice the log in half. Slice each half in half again. Finally, slice each quarter in half, resulting in 8 rounds. **7** Place the rounds in the buttered pie plate, with 1 round in the middle and 7 around the perimeter of the pan. Bake as directed. **8** After the rolls cool for 5 minutes, drizzle the glaze from a spoon directly over the warm rolls. Cool for 5 minutes more and then serve.

10-inch side. Evenly distribute the sugar-cinnamon mixture over the buttered area. Beginning at the buttered 10-inch side, roll into a log as tightly as possible. Dot the unbuttered edge with the remaining 1 tablespoon buttermilk and seal the seam. Even out the thickness of the log if necessary and lightly dust with flour. Slice off a bit of each end to reveal a neat spiral. (The log is best sliced with a serrated knife using a sawing motion and very little pressure.) Slice the log in half. Slice each half in half again. Slice each quarter in half, resulting in 8 rounds. Place the rounds in the prepared pie plate, flat-side down, and bake until light golden brown, 25 to 30 minutes.

4. For the glaze: While the rolls are baking, whisk together the confectioners' sugar and 1 tablespoon of the buttermilk. Add the remaining 1 teaspoon buttermilk a couple of drops at a time until the glaze is thick and smooth and glossy. Whisk in the cream cheese until well combined. Remove the rolls from the oven and cool on a rack for 5 minutes. Drizzle or spread the glaze over the hot rolls. Cool for an additional 5 minutes before serving.

A Cup of Flour

I have found eight different ways to measure flour. The most common choices include dipping the measuring cup into the bag and then sweeping off the excess (the "dip-and-sweep" method), sifting the flour and then pouring it into the measuring cup, and spooning it into a measuring cup from the bag. I decided to measure the weight of each cup of flour using all eight methods, and the results were astounding. All of the methods that used sifted flour ended up weighing up to 25 percent less than the methods that did not use sifted flour. In addition, the dip-and-sweep method produced about 10 percent more flour than when one spooned the flour from the bag into the measuring cup.

The conclusion? If a recipe calls for sifted flour, you have to sift it, because the difference in weight will be substantial. Second, you have to read the recipe ingredients carefully. One cup of *sifted* flour is *not* the same thing as 1 cup of flour, sifted. The former requires that the flour be sifted *before* measuring, and the latter suggests that one measure out the flour and *then* sift it.

As a general rule, I use the dip-and-sweep method for measuring flour—but you should always sift it when my recipe says to do so.

Quick breads, specifically Irish-style soda breads, are plenty fast, because they use baking soda instead of yeast for leavening. But having tested a number of soda-bread recipes, I soon discovered that they were often bland, lacking both salt and sweetness. In general, the more traditional Irish soda-bread recipes were leaner than their American cousins, the latter using butter, eggs, and sugar along with flour, salt, soda, and buttermilk. I decided that a richer bread was in order to provide a lot more flavor, which is more in keeping with modern palates. I also decided to work with white flour only, although many Irish and American soda breads also call for whole-wheat flour. ▶◀

The first issue was which type of white flour to use. For a more delicate crumb, one can use bleached all-purpose flour or a combination of cake flour and all-purpose, but I found regular unbleached all-purpose to be best, as I prefer a bit of chew to my bread. However, for a lighter, finer texture I used a bleached flour such as Pillsbury. Next, I played with the leavener. Although this is a "soda" bread, I also tested baking powder but found that baking soda was actually better in this recipe for a full rise. I then decided that I did want to add butter for flavor — soda bread can be very dull without it — but the addition of eggs was just too much. Although I wanted more flavor, soda bread should still be relatively lean. I also increased the amount of salt from standard recipes, using 2 teaspoons for 4 cups of flour. I settled on 2 tablespoons sugar to enhance flavor. Buttermilk as the liquid provided a texture similar to yeast bread with a slightly softer texture than many soda-bread recipes I have tasted.

I am a huge fan of cast-iron skillets, and, as I use one for baking powder biscuits and cornbread, I decided to try it with soda bread. It worked nicely, because the cast iron is a great heat conductor, which helped to form a nice crust. I also found that brushing the bread with melted butter after baking helped to soften the crust and give it more flavor. Irish soda breads often have a tough, thin crust, and this was an easy remedy.

You can use this recipe as a blueprint for other similar soda breads by substituting 1½ cups whole-wheat flour for the white all-purpose. (Whole-wheat graham flour is best.) This version will require slightly more buttermilk and a bit more cooking. The whole-wheat version should reach 190 degrees on an instant-read thermometer rather than the 180 degrees for the regular recipe. You can also use different sweeteners such as honey or molasses or, for the whole-wheat version, try substituting ¼ cup wheat germ for the same amount of white flour.

Rich, American-Style Soda Bread

MAKES 1 ROUND LOAF

This is a quick bread, as it depends on baking soda, not yeast, for leavening. Many soda-bread recipes use no butter and sugar and too little salt, which yields a dull loaf of bread indeed. The interesting aspect to this recipe is the use of a cast-iron skillet for baking. Cast iron is a wonderful heat conductor and also serves to shape the dough as it bakes.

  4 **cups unbleached all-purpose flour, plus more for dusting work surface**
  2 **tablespoons sugar**
  1 **teaspoon cream of tartar**
  1 **teaspoon baking soda**
  2 **teaspoons table salt**
  4 **tablespoons unsalted butter, softened**
1¾–2 **cups buttermilk**
  1 **tablespoon unsalted butter, melted**

1. Adjust an oven rack to the center position and heat the oven to 400 degrees. Whisk the flour, sugar, cream of tartar, baking soda, and salt together in a large bowl. With a fork or your fingers, stir the softened butter into the flour mixture until fully incorporated. Add 1¾ cups buttermilk and stir the mixture with a large rubber spatula or your fingers until the dough starts to come together. Add more buttermilk if necessary to produce a cohesive dough. Turn onto a lightly floured work surface and knead for 30 seconds or until the dough comes together. The dough should still be rough textured and lumpy.

2. Shape the dough into a round and place it in a 9- or 10-inch cast-iron skillet. Score the top of the dough with a knife or razor blade, making 2 or 3 slashes. Bake about 40 minutes (it may take longer; the key is to check the internal temperature) or until an instant-read thermometer indicates an internal temperature of 180 degrees. (Note that yeast breads usually have to be cooked to more than 200 degrees; this bread is done at a much lower temperature.)

3. Carefully remove the skillet from the oven (the handle is VERY hot), place it on a cooling rack, brush the bread with the melted butter, and let it cool for 30 minutes before serving.

HOMEMADE BREAD IN JUST 60 MINUTES

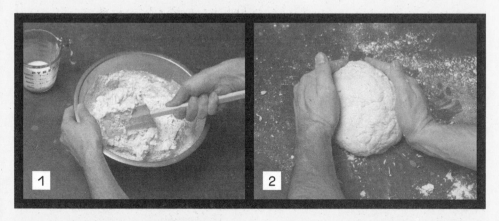

Elapsed Time: 10 MINUTES

Whisk 5 dry ingredients together in a bowl. Work in the softened butter with your fingers, then add the buttermilk and stir to combine with a rubber spatula.

Elapsed Time: 12 MINUTES

Turn the dough onto a lightly floured work surface and knead until it comes together, about 30 seconds.

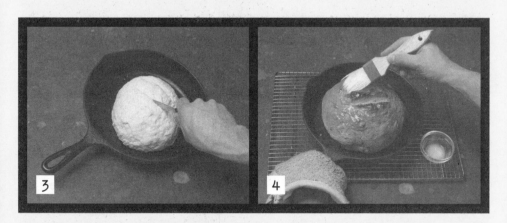

Elapsed Time: 15 MINUTES

Shape the dough into a round loaf and transfer it to a cast-iron skillet. With a knife, make several slashes across the top of the dough. Put the pan in the oven.

Elapsed Time: 55 MINUTES

Transfer the skillet with the baked bread to a cooling rack and brush with melted butter. Cool and serve.

Homemade Granola Bars

Once in a great while I come across something in a bakery that is so good it reminds me of my first croissant — rich, addictive, and, well, deadly. When I first tasted one of Joanne Chang's fruit-filled granola bars at her bakery, Flour, in the South End of Boston, I knew that I had hit pay dirt. The filling was rich with flavor but not jammy, and the granola layers were moist, chewy, and deeply satisfying. The question was how to adapt her recipe for a home cook. ▶◀

The basic notion is that dried fruit is hydrated in water and sugar. A dough of flour, oats, nuts, coconut, etc. is made in a food processor. The bottom crust is prebaked, the fruit filling added, the top crust pressed on top, and the whole thing is then finished in the oven. Simple enough, except that the recipe I was given called for 10 pounds of ingredients, enough to provide for a family of 12.

Starting with a 9-by-13-inch pan, I found that 3¾ cups dried fruit did the trick. A mix of dried, unsweetened cranberries, apples, and apricots produced an intense flavor when hydrated with sugar and water for about a half hour. The apples are absorbent and soften the filling; the cranberries and apricots provide an intense flavor and plenty of chew. I also tested sweetened cranberries as well as dried blueberries, strawberries, and cherries. The original trio was the winner.

For the dough, I started with flour and oats in equal parts. For the sugar, I tested all kinds and finally settled on light brown. Joanne also adds sweetened (not unsweetened) coconut flakes that add a nice burst of flavor and chew. Nuts are an essential addition to any granola bar; I preferred pecans and almonds to walnuts, which were bitter. (Toasting the nuts adds flavor but is not essential.) Sunflower seeds, part of the original recipe, were also good, but I preferred to add them with the other dry ingredients instead of pressing them into the bottom crust. Spices quickly became overwhelming, but a bit of cinnamon and salt, an ingredient missing from the original recipe, was called for.

Butter and honey were the other two key ingredients. Two and a half sticks of butter was just right—any more and the bars became greasy; any less and they became tough.

(And you thought that granola bars were healthy!) Honey added both flavor and moisture; 3 ounces (a generous ⅓ cup) was just right.

The method is simple enough: The dry ingredients are pulsed in a food processor, and then the butter and honey are added and the mixture is pulsed again until the butter is about the size of small peas. (Do not overprocess; the dough will bake up greasy and heavy.) This mixture is reserved in a large bowl while the nuts are pulsed with the coconut. The two mixtures are then combined by hand.

About two thirds of the mixture is baked in the bottom of the pan, the fruit compote is spread on top, and the bars are finished with the leftover dough. The pan is returned to the oven for 20 minutes. Heaven on earth.

Granola Bars with Fruit Filling

MAKES ABOUT 24 BARS

Do not overprocess the flour-oats-butter mixture, or the bars will turn out greasy. If you cannot find unsweetened dried cranberries, use sweetened and reduce the sugar to ⅓ cup, or you can try substituting dried cherries. Toast the nuts in a 375-degree oven for about 8 minutes or until lightly colored and fragrant. Cool completely.

FOR THE FRUIT COMPOTE

1¼	cups dried apricots, coarsely chopped
1¼	cups dried apples, coarsely chopped
1¼	cups dried cranberries, unsweetened preferred (see note)
½	cup granulated sugar

FOR THE DOUGH

2	cups all-purpose flour
2	cups quick-cooking oats
1	cup packed light brown sugar
½	teaspoon table salt
¼	teaspoon ground cinnamon
20	tablespoons (2½ sticks) cold unsalted butter, cut into ½-inch pieces
⅓	cup plus 1 tablespoon honey
1½	cups sweetened flaked coconut
1	cup toasted pecans or almonds or a combination of both
½	cup roasted sunflower seeds (salted is best)

1. For the compote: Combine all the ingredients plus 2½ cups water in a medium saucepan and bring to a boil. Reduce the heat to maintain a simmer and cook until the liquid is absorbed and the fruit is fully hydrated, about 30 minutes. Set the compote aside.

2. Meanwhile, adjust an oven rack to the center position and heat the oven to 375 degrees. Line the bottom of a 9-by-13-inch pan with parchment.

3. For the dough: Place the flour, oats, light brown sugar, salt, and cinnamon in the bowl of a food processor. Pulse briefly to combine. Add the butter and honey and process until the pieces of butter are no larger than a small pea, about twelve 1-second pulses. (Do not overprocess!) Transfer the mixture to a large bowl. Place the coconut, pecans and/or almonds, and the sunflower seeds in the food processor bowl. Process until the nuts are well broken up, about eight 1-second pulses. Transfer the nuts to the large bowl. Using your fingers, gently mix the 2 batches of ingredients together until well combined. When fully incorporated, the dough will look like lumpy wet sand.

4. Spoon about two thirds of the mixture into the bottom of the prepared pan and gently pat down into an even layer. Reserve the remaining portion (about 3 generous cups) in a cool place until needed. Bake until medium golden brown, about 18 minutes. Remove the pan from the oven and evenly spread the fruit compote over the top. Sprinkle the remaining dough in an even layer over the fruit. Return the pan to the oven and bake for an additional 20 minutes or until the topping is dark golden brown. (Underbaked bars will be damp and greasy.) Cool completely before cutting into bars.

Better Oatmeal Scones

Oatmeal scones with pieces of dried fruit are common enough at coffee shops and teahouses but rarely get made at home. I discovered why when I made five different recipes, most of which turned out dry and heavy. I was looking for good oat flavor packaged in a scone that wouldn't gag the family dog. ▶◀

The basic concept is simple: Butter is cut into the dry ingredients (oats, flour, salt, sugar, baking powder, etc.), and then liquid is added, which can be buttermilk, milk, or heavy cream. The dough is mixed until it just comes together, pressed into a circle, cut into wedges, and then baked, usually at 350 degrees. One recipe toasted the oats first and then soaked them in buttermilk, which produced good flavor but a heavy texture. Only one of the recipes was reasonably moist — the rest were too heavy — so I began with that one as a starting point.

Since I like the notion of toasting oats for oatmeal (see page 232), and the scone recipe using toasted oats was very flavorful, I started with this technique. I tried toasting the oats in the oven, as it had to be heated for the scones anyway. They toasted well at 375 degrees in about eight minutes. I chose to toast them dry for a couple of reasons: First, the recipe includes lots of butter that is cut into the dry ingredients. Secondly, the dry-toasted oats make for minimal cleanup of the pan, which is used to bake the scones; you can do a simple pass with a towel instead of a thorough washing. The oats do have to cool completely before the scones are assembled. For our recipe, I settled on 1¼ cups each of flour and oats.

The scones were definitely on the dry side, and I knew that butter held the solution to this problem. After a few tests, I settled on two full sticks. This gave the scones a rich butter flavor, which nicely complements the nutty oats. (I found that if I added any more butter, the scones became greasy.) Next, I tested various dairy products. Heavy cream made the scones too heavy, milk and half-and-half were lackluster, but buttermilk was a winner, adding a light note and good flavor. Because I thought the scones were still a bit dense, I added an egg along with the buttermilk. This proved to be my favorite scone. The scones were moister and lighter with the egg. It turned out that ⅓ cup buttermilk and one egg was the perfect quantity.

As for the leavener, I had started testing with 1¼ teaspoons baking powder and

¾ teaspoon baking soda, which, after much testing, turned out to be the correct amount. Although a basic scone recipe may use only a tablespoon of sugar, I found that oatmeal scones need a bit more sweetener, ⅓ cup being my favorite quantity. I tried using granulated sugar, light and dark brown sugars, honey, and maple syrup. The best-flavored scones were made simply with light brown sugar.

As for the dried fruit, I found that apricots and dried cranberries were winners. Dried blueberries are hard to find, and raisins as well as currants were a bit dull in flavor, although the latter are traditional and taste perfectly fine. I used ⅓ cup roughly chopped dried apricots and ¼ cup cranberries in my favorite scones. Ingredients that did not make the cut were dried coconut, nuts, cinnamon, nutmeg, ginger, and wheat germ.

As for technique, the dry ingredients are placed in a food processor and mixed to combine. The butter is added and cut into the dry ingredients with six 1-second pulses. I then add the oats and fruit and pulse six more times. (If the oats were added with the rest of the dry ingredients, they became overprocessed and the scones were dry.) The contents of the food processor are dumped into a bowl, and the buttermilk and egg are added. After a quick mix with a fork, the mixture is turned onto a countertop. The dough is gently kneaded a few times and then pressed into a disk. The disk is cut into wedges and placed on a parchment-lined baking sheet.

I baked the scones at 400 degrees (higher than most other recipes I tested) for about 15 minutes. If the oven is hotter, the scones are likely to burn because of all the sugar and butter in this recipe. (If they are baked at a lower temperature, they take more time and don't brown quite as well.) As with most scones, they should be held for about 10 minutes before serving to give them time to firm up. These scones have a somewhat ragged appearance compared with many other recipes, the price I had to pay for eliminating the choking dry quality of their taller counterparts.

Oatmeal Scones with Dried Apricots and Cranberries

MAKES 8 SCONES

You can use all apricots, all cranberries, or even currants if you like.

1¼	cups rolled oats (not instant)
1¼	cups all-purpose flour
⅓	cup packed light brown sugar
1¼	teaspoons baking powder
¾	teaspoon baking soda
¾	teaspoon table salt
16	tablespoons (2 sticks) chilled unsalted butter, cut into ½-inch cubes
⅓	cup roughly chopped dried apricots
¼	cup dried sweetened cranberries
⅓	cup buttermilk
1	large egg

1. Adjust an oven rack to the center position and heat the oven to 375 degrees. Spread the oats in an even layer onto a jelly-roll pan or cookie sheet. Place in the oven and toast until golden brown and fragrant, 8 to 10 minutes. Remove from the oven, transfer the oats to a bowl, and cool completely. Wipe the pan, line it with parchment paper, and increase the oven temperature to 400 degrees.

2. Place the flour, sugar, baking powder, baking soda, and salt in the bowl of a food processor fitted with a steel blade. Blend briefly to combine. Evenly distribute the butter over the dry ingredients and process for six 1-second pulses. Add the oats and fruit and pulse an additional 6 times or until the largest piece of butter is about the size of a pea. Transfer to a large bowl.

3. Stir the buttermilk and egg together in a small bowl or large measuring cup until well combined. Add this mixture to the dry ingredients and mix with a fork or rubber spatula until the dough begins to form large wet clumps. Turn onto a countertop and knead by hand, incorporating any dry floury bits, until it comes together into a rough sticky ball. Pat the dough into a 6- to 7-inch disk and cut into 8 wedges. Transfer the scones onto the prepared baking sheet and bake until dark golden brown, about 15 minutes. Cool on a rack for at least 10 minutes before serving.

21 Minutes at 375 Degrees!

A friend of mine, Lionel Brown, who used to be a U.S. Navy pilot and who has logged thousands of hours in small planes, once flew me from Hanscom Field just outside of Boston to a tiny airport near the Restigouche River in Quebec and back for a fishing trip. The flight up was uneventful — he simply dialed in the coordinates of our destination and let the plane do the work. I commented that flying seemed pretty simple, and he immediately shot back, "There are lots of dead pilots who would have agreed with you."

On the way back, however, things were quite different. The weather report was excellent: sunny and clear, with scattered clouds. Halfway home, the coast of Maine got socked in with dense afternoon fog, and, in a manner of seconds, we were in a race against time. Planes were scurrying to the airports that were still open, so we had to keep a close visual lookout to avoid a collision. The casual chatter stopped immediately. Lionel was busy calculating alternate landing sites based on our fuel supply. Then we noticed the thunderheads looming in front of us. We had to call in to get permission to change altitude. We flew over most of them, but, at one point, the clouds were simply too high, so we found a hole and flew through it. It got bumpy, and the plane started to feel slightly smaller and less stable than my first car, a 1961 Volkswagen.

Finally, just as we were minutes from the airport, we hit cloud cover, so we had to rely on the instruments. When we came in to land, we couldn't see the runway until we hit 300 feet, about the last moment that was legal under FAA guidelines. (The pilot of a small plane has to make visual contact with the runway before landing.) When Lionel let me off, I hopped onto the wing, my face pale and drawn, and thanked him profusely. I hit the ground, my legs weak, and my view of flying changed forever.

So what does this have to do with cooking? Flying, like cooking, is about experience. It's about recognizing situations before they get serious. It's about advance planning. It's about keeping your eyes peeled for trouble. It's about not relying on the advice and predictions of others — an incorrect weather report can kill you. In cooking, an incorrect recipe can also spell disaster. In other words, flying and cooking are not precise arts. The pilots who live to a ripe old age use their experience and sound judgment to make the right decisions. The same could be said of a good cook. He or she relies on common sense, a good pair of eyes, a light touch, and an independent palate. If you can only follow directions, you'll end up in disaster, sooner than later.

I know a very good cook for whom time does not exist. She is easily distracted (and rightly so) with children, the telephone, neighbors, the odd household disaster, and a long list of "to-dos." So, when muffins go into the oven, she sets the timer and goes away, relying on the baking time listed in the recipe. When the results are less than satis-factory, she blames the recipe. After all, it did say 21 minutes at 375 degrees!

The reason for this is simple. Different pans, different stovetops, different ovens, different ingredients, even different weather (flour behaves differently depending on the humidity and temperature) can substantially affect cooking times. So, let's step into the time machine and go back a hundred years to when we were cooking on woodstoves, and ovens were either hot, medium-hot, medium, or low. The same is still true today in England. Many ovens are adjusted using different "gas marks," which gives one less of a sense of precision than a precise number of degrees does. In fact, that is a better way to cook. Don't be lulled into a sense of exactitude just because your oven has a seemingly infinite number of settings. Think big. Think of your oven as being either hot, medium-hot, medium, medium-low, or low. Think of it as an imprecise art. Know that the recipe you are about to make was almost certainly tested in an oven, a skillet, or on a stovetop that was quite different from yours. Don't trust any times given in a recipe. Try to read between the lines to understand what the food should feel and smell like when it is done, and then use your own judgment.

More specifically, here are some tips to help you better manage cooking times: First, if you are baking, set one timer to the proposed entire baking time and another timer to half that time. At halftime, check the item, turn it in the oven, and then set the timer for, say, five minutes. (This amount of time varies based on the length of the total cook-ing time.) Check it again and set the timer at five minutes. Check it again, and so forth. I check any baked good at least four or five times. Never, ever, simply set the timer to the stated baking time and walk away. This is a recipe for disaster.

What about stovetop cooking? The same rule applies. A $165 All-Clad skillet cooks very differently from a $15 bargain pan bought at the hardware store. The All-Clad will cook evenly, rarely burning the food in the pan. The thin-gauge pan requires constant supervision and heat adjustment. It will develop hot spots, the food will stick and burn, and the cooking times will be quite different. By the same token, if you have a weak, 7,000 BTU burner on your stovetop (BTUs are British thermal units, a measurement of heat output), the steak or frittata will cook very differently than if you are using a professional-style stove that cranks out 15,000 BTUs.

So, just remember one simple rule. Never, ever trust cooking times in a recipe. Don't trust my recipes, Julia Child's recipes, or your mother's recipes. They will almost *always* be wrong!

Rediscovering Oatmeal

Since most of us are most familiar with the instant variety of oatmeal, the notion of oatmeal as anything other than a stomach-filler may seem like tilting at windmills. Yet, steel-cut oats make for a serious breakfast and are more than worth the trouble when properly prepared. I wanted to find the best method for preparing both steel-cut and rolled oats, both avoiding a gummy, pasty texture and enhancing the natural flavor of the oats themselves. ▶◀

Let's start with the different types of oats, as that is where most of us go wrong. *Whole-oat groats* are the whole oat kernel with just the outer hull removed. They have to be cooked almost forever and are very toothsome. *Steel-cut oats* (also known as Irish oats) are simply groats that have been cut into smaller pieces, thereby reducing cooking time. *Rolled oats* have been steamed and flattened, which reduces cooking time to about five minutes. Compared with steel-cut oats, they lack flavor and texture, and the porridge is mushier. *Quick-cooking oats* are similar to rolled oats but are cut into smaller pieces for quicker cooking. *Instant oatmeal* is precooked, rolled, and dried. Add boiling water, and it is ready to go. Unfortunately, instant oatmeal resembles a paste more than a good bowl of oatmeal. In my opinion, this form of oatmeal is virtually inedible.

My recipe research turned up two recipes I liked very much, one from *Cook's Illustrated* and the other from Alton Brown. They both used 4 cups of liquid to 1 cup steel-cut oats, a mixture of dairy and water, and an initial toasting step to enhance the flavor of the oats. I preferred the *Cook's* recipe, because it used salt and called for milk instead of a buttermilk-milk combination that tasted a bit odd.

My first question was whether toasting the oats was a necessary step. The obvious answer was a resounding yes — they were sweeter and better flavored. I preferred using a large skillet for this process and 1 tablespoon butter — the toasting goes quicker (two to three minutes), and they turn out more evenly browned. (The skillet can simply be wiped out without washing.) I also found recipes that suggest soaking the steel-cut oats overnight, but I preferred the texture of unsoaked oatmeal, so I skipped this step.

As for the liquid, 4 cups milk/water to 1 cup steel-cut oats was just right; more liquid made a soupy oatmeal and less did not give the oats sufficient time to cook properly. The next question was whether some of the water should be replaced by milk, cream, half-and-half, or buttermilk. Some dairy was called for, as all-water oatmeal tasted a bit bland. I finally settled on 3½ cups water plus ½ cup half-and-half.

For some reason, a few recipes did not call for any salt. I found that ½ teaspoon table salt was absolutely necessary to enhance flavors. However, the salt should be added after the first 15 minutes of cooking, otherwise the oatmeal turns out a bit less creamy. As for cooking technique, I tried starting the oats in both cold water and simmering water. The cold-water oats turned out mushy, but those added to simmering water were creamy with a bit of chew. I also found that the oats needed to cook uncovered for best results. (Otherwise they became too soft.)

As for managing the process, I found it best to heat the water-dairy mixture in a large saucepan while I was toasting the oats in the skillet. (Be careful when adding the oats to the water mixture — it can easily boil over.) I then simmered the oats for 15 minutes, stirring occasionally, and then added the salt. You will need to adjust the heat level constantly, as the oatmeal requires less heat as it thickens. In the last few minutes of cooking, you will need to stir frequently to avoid sticking. A heavy-bottomed saucepan is highly recommended. Some recipes suggest allowing the oatmeal to sit for five minutes covered before serving in order to make the oats creamier. I find that it takes about five minutes for everyone to add toppings and actually sit down to the table, so I skip this step.

Although most folks will opt for the usual toppings (very cold milk is traditional with hot oatmeal; I also use maple syrup), you might also try fruit compote. I take ½ cup each of dried apricots, cranberries, and apples, ¼ cup sugar, and 1½ cups water and simmer the lot for about 25 minutes over medium-low heat. This may seem like a lot of effort, but it's more than worth it for a special weekend breakfast.

Old-Fashioned Irish Oatmeal

SERVES 4 ADULTS

Note that the cooking time will vary depending on the heat level and your saucepan. You do not need to stir very much for the first 10 minutes of cooking. As the oatmeal thickens, more attention needs to be paid to the oats to prevent sticking to the bottom of the pot. This recipe can be doubled or tripled, although the toasting and cooking times may need to be increased slightly for the desired results.

½ cup half-and-half
1 tablespoon unsalted butter
1 cup steel-cut oats
½ teaspoon table salt

Bring 3½ cups water and the half-and-half to a simmer in a large saucepan over medium heat. Meanwhile, place a 9- or 10-inch skillet (nonstick or regular) over medium heat. Add the butter to the skillet, and, once it has stopped foaming, swirl to coat the bottom of the skillet evenly. Add the oats and toast, stirring often with a wooden spoon or spatula, until golden brown and very aromatic, 2 to 3 minutes. Stir the oats into the simmering liquid (to avoid a boil-over, take the saucepan off the heat when you add the oats) and adjust the heat to maintain a simmer. Cook, uncovered, for 15 minutes, stirring occasionally. Add the salt and stir gently to combine. Continue simmering and stirring occasionally until the oats absorb almost all of the liquid and the oats are swollen and tender with a bit of chew, 5 to 15 minutes more. The oatmeal will be thick and creamy and almost pudding-like. Serve immediately with fruit compote (recipe follows) or cold milk plus brown sugar, maple syrup, honey, or cinnamon.

Fruit Compote for Oatmeal

If you cannot find one or more of these fruits, try your own combination.

½   cup dried cranberries
½   cup dried apricots, coarsely chopped
½   cup dried apples, coarsely chopped
¼   cup sugar

Combine all of the ingredients plus 1½ cups water in a medium saucepan and bring to a simmer. Cover and cook, stirring occasionally, until the liquid has been almost completely absorbed and the fruit is fully hydrated, about 25 minutes.

VARIATION
Rolled-Oats Oatmeal
Rolled oats do not have the texture and flavor of steel-cut oats, but they do cook in only 5 minutes.

Substitute 2 cups rolled oats for the 1 cup steel-cut oats in the recipe on page 233. Increase the butter to 1½ tablespoons. Add the salt along with the oats to the simmering water-milk mixture. Stir frequently and reduce the cooking time to 5 minutes or until the oatmeal is thick and pudding-like.

Strawberries Plain and Simple

In *Chez Panisse Fruit,* Alice Waters offers a wonderful recipe for strawberries and orange segments served with a light syrup that's infused with the flavor of orange zest. When strawberry season is in high gear, I turn to this recipe for its elegance and simplicity, it being far easier to make than a cobbler, shortcake, or pie. As usual, I wondered if I could make it either better or simpler. ▶◀

I quickly gave up on the "better" half of the equation — it's a simple and refreshing dessert, as long as the fruit is good. However, Alice calls for simmering the sugar syrup for 30 minutes, and segmenting the oranges, another step, is not the easiest thing for most home cooks. So I decided to stick with strawberries and simplify the syrup.

The recipe calls for ½ cup sugar to 1 cup water and a long simmering time to extract the flavor of the orange peel. I tested shorter cooking times, from five to 30 minutes, and found that the flavor was no less intense with a quick simmer. The benefit of the longer cooking time was a thicker syrup, but by reducing the amounts and changing the proportions (to ¼ cup sugar and ⅓ cup water), the syrup was plenty thick in record time. I also tested lemon instead of orange zest but was unimpressed with the flavor. Other flavors such as basil, thyme, lemongrass, and mint were less well suited than orange. However, I did like a bit of liqueur, and Cointreau came up a winner. It cut down on the sweetness and added another dimension to the syrup while maintaining a light, clean finish.

As for the berries, I tested adding them to the hot syrup, but they lost their fresh flavor and texture, so I allowed the syrup to cool before adding them. (Alice also tosses the berries with granulated sugar, but I found this step to be unnecessary.) I also discovered that this dish should be made at the last minute for best results. This way, the fresh berries will glisten with a thin coat of clear, sweet, orange syrup. If left to sit in the refrigerator, the strawberries will macerate, and their juice will combine with the syrup, resulting in something less elegant.

These berries are great with panna cotta, vanilla ice cream, zabaglione, whipped cream, shortcake, pancakes, or waffles. I also loved them combined with blueberries. For a crowd, the amounts can be doubled.

Strawberries with Orange-Infused Syrup

SERVES 4 TO 6

Use a very light hand in zesting the orange. Any trace of the white pith, and the syrup will have bitter undertones. A rasp or fine grater works best. Don't make this recipe unless the strawberries are first-rate. If you like, combine the strawberries with segmented oranges.

¼   **cup sugar**
    Finely grated zest of 1 orange
1   **tablespoon Cointreau or orange liqueur of your choice**
1   **quart strawberries, rinsed and dried**

Combine the sugar, ⅓ cup water, and the zest in a small saucepan. Stir to combine and bring to a simmer over medium heat. Reduce the heat to maintain a simmer and cook for 5 minutes or until syrupy. Off heat, add the Cointreau. Transfer to a small bowl or jar and refrigerate until cold. The syrup will thicken further as it cools. Meanwhile, cut the berries into bite-size pieces and place them in a medium bowl. Immediately before serving, add the syrup to the berries and toss gently to combine. Spoon the berries and syrup into glasses and serve.

VARIATION
Mixed Berries with Orange-Infused Syrup
Replace 1 pint strawberries with 1 pint blueberries.

How to Roast Peaches

There are many good reasons not to bake, sauté, grill, or roast peaches, the best one being that a perfectly ripe peach is as close to the Garden of Eden as most of us will get during our lifetimes. That being said, in late August, when our family is on our third bushel (we buy peaches shipped up from Pennsylvania), I get hungry for a bit of variety, so I start subjecting them to heat and introducing them to other flavors. ▶◀

I tried sautéing them, but they quickly fell apart and appeared ragged. Given the variety of pans and stovetops, this method is also a bit tricky to standardize, so I turned to the oven. A simple 2-quart baking dish (8 by 11 inches) and a 400-degree oven worked fine. I baked the peeled, pitted, and halved peaches covered (with aluminum foil) for the first 15 minutes to make sure that even a less-than-ripe peach would cook through properly. Then I removed the covering and continued cooking for about eight minutes or until the sauce cooked down to the proper consistency. Keep in mind that the cooking time is approximate, as peaches vary greatly in terms of quality and ripeness.

In terms of flavors, I tried ginger, bourbon, rum, vanilla, cinnamon, nutmeg, etc. The one spice that really stood out was cardamom, but a little bit goes a long way, so I settled on a mere ⅛ teaspoon. Butter was essential to carry the flavor, and I also liked the taste of bourbon.

As for serving, a splash of heavy cream mixes nicely with the sauce, but no one will object to vanilla ice cream either.

Baked Peaches with Cardamom and Bourbon

SERVES 6 (HALF A PEACH PER PERSON)

As is often the case, too much sugar (and sometimes bourbon) was used in older recipes, detracting from the fresh flavors of the fruit. Here is a simple, lower-sugar recipe. The juices from the peaches make a simple sauce with the brown sugar. Note that the size and ripeness of the peaches will affect both the baking time and the quality of this dessert. To peel a peach, place it in boiling water for 30 seconds, remove it to ice water, and let it sit for a couple of minutes. Remove it and use a paring knife to remove the peel (which should come off easily at this point). Unripe peaches will be hard to peel and are not worth eating anyway.

	Softened unsalted butter for coating baking dish
¼	cup packed light brown sugar
⅛	teaspoon ground cardamom
3	large peaches, peeled, halved, and pitted
1	tablespoon unsalted butter, cut into small pieces
1	tablespoon bourbon
	Vanilla ice cream or heavy cream for serving

1. Adjust an oven rack to the center position and heat the oven to 400 degrees. Butter a 2-quart baking dish and evenly coat with the sugar, sprinkling the cardamom on top. Place the peaches in the dish, cut-side down. Scatter small butter pieces on top. Add the bourbon.

2. Cover the baking dish with aluminum foil and bake for 15 minutes. Remove from the oven, remove the foil, and check to see if the butter and sugar are forming a sauce at the bottom of the dish. Stir, if necessary, to combine. Continue baking, uncovered, for 8 minutes (peaches should be tender but not mushy). Remove from the oven and cool for 5 minutes. Invert each peach half into a bowl and top with a scoop of vanilla ice cream or a splash of heavy cream. Spoon the sauce from the baking dish over the top and serve immediately.

Poaching perfectly ripe fruit is insane. Why would any-body want to subject a perfect peach to a cooking process, when it is outstanding eaten out of hand? Instead, I find that full-flavored, ripe fruits such as peaches or berries require only a cooked but cold poaching syrup poured over them rather than immersion in a simmering poaching liq-uid, the method that is best suited for more resilient winter fruits such as pears. ▶◀

Peaches have an affinity for ginger; I love the convenience of crystallized ginger. There is no grating or mincing involved. I made a light poaching syrup ("heavy" or "light" depends on the ratio of sugar to water—I like my poaching syrups on the light and refreshing side), added white wine, ginger, and lime juice. When chilled, this syrup is poured over the peeled, pitted, and sliced peaches. Nothing could be simpler.

Peaches with Lime and Ginger

SERVES 4

This recipe requires perfectly ripe peaches, as they are not really poached; the flavored syrup is cooled before it is added to the fruit. If your peaches are underripe, I suggest pour-ing the hot syrup over them and then chill-ing. Crystallized ginger is found in bottles in the spice section of supermarkets. This dessert can be served with ice cream, a dense cake such as the Polenta Pound Cake on page 282, or cookies such as biscotti or shortbread. To peel a peach, place it in boiling water for 30 seconds, remove it to ice water, and let it sit for a couple of minutes. Remove it and use a paring knife to remove the peel (which should come off easily at this point).

½   cup sugar
1   cup white wine
¼   cup crystallized ginger
1   lime, juiced
4   ripe peaches, peeled, pitted, and sliced

1. Combine the sugar, 1 cup water, the wine, and ginger in a saucepan. Bring to a boil, reduce the heat to a simmer, cover, and cook for 7 minutes. Remove from the heat and add 1 tablespoon of the lime juice. Chill for 1 hour and then strain.
2. Toss the peaches with the remaining lime juice in a nonreactive bowl.
3. Pour the syrup over the peaches and toss. Refrigerate for 1 hour. Serve slightly chilled but not cold.

Plums for Dessert

There are many recipes for poached or baked fruit that include white wine, sweet wine, or fortified wine. In my opinion, one of the best fruit-wine combinations is plums and Marsala — the plums have enough flavor and tartness to stand up to the sweet Marsala. I started with a recipe from a cookbook that called for 3 pounds plums and 2½ cups Marsala and set out to get just the right balance between fruit and wine. ▶◀

The first issue was the plums themselves. Anything but perfectly ripe fruit is a waste of time; the plums bake up mushy, not tender, and the flavor is second-rate. Some recipes suggest baking the fruit whole, but I found that I could save cooking time by quartering them. As an added bonus, it is then easy to remove the skins from the baked plums, a step that dramatically improves the dish.

As far as the baking goes, I tested a variety of oven temperatures, but 350 degrees was best; higher temperatures turned out unevenly cooked fruit. Covering the baking dish for some or all of the cooking time simply made the plums softer, and I preferred the texture when baked uncovered.

As for the liquid, I added white wine, vermouth, red wine, and fruit juice. The white wine and vermouth thinned out the Marsala syrup; the red wine wasn't bad, although no better than the all-Marsala version. Fruit juice made the liquid too sweet. I also tested dry versus sweet Marsala and preferred the latter — it had more flavor and body.

Other ingredients tested were cinnamon sticks, vanilla beans, lemon peel, almond extract, and orange peel. The only winner was orange peel; the others were either overpowering or unpleasant. I also liked a bit of orange liqueur added after cooking. I did find that the liquid needed to be reduced in a separate saucepan after the plums were baked to thicken it and to concentrate the flavors. I tested using thickeners such as cornstarch, but by reducing the liquid by half, it was clean tasting and just right in terms of a syrupy consistency.

Baked Plums
with Marsala and Orange

SERVES 6 TO 8

Only make this dish with ripe, delicious plums, the sort you would eat out of hand. I prefer to serve this dish the same day it is made, either warm, at room temperature, or cold. The plums are nice on their own or served with vanilla ice cream.

6	sweet, ripe plums
1	cup sweet Marsala wine
⅓	cup sugar
3	strips orange peel, 1 by 3 inches, with the bitter white pith removed
1	tablespoon orange liqueur such as Cointreau or Triple Sec

1. Adjust an oven rack to the center position and heat the oven to 375 degrees. Quarter the plums, removing the pits. Arrange them in a single layer in a small baking dish. (An 8-by-11-inch glass pan works well.) Mix the Marsala and sugar and pour over the plums. Bake until tender, 25 to 30 minutes.

2. Pour off the liquid into a small saucepan. Add the orange peel to the liquid and bring to a boil over high heat. Simmer briskly for about 5 minutes or until the liquid is reduced by half. Remove from the heat and add the liqueur.

3. When the plums are cool, remove the skins with a small paring knife. (They should slip off easily.) Serve the plums with the syrup spooned over the top. If serving later, pour the syrup over the plums, cover with plastic wrap, and refrigerate.

Rethinking Fruit Salad

Fruit salad is, to our discredit, a lackluster after-thought, a recipe that is thrown together willy-nilly with little or no consideration for the proper dressing. Indeed, fruit salads do need to be dressed properly in order to heighten flavors, providing both depth and contrast. Simply put, there is nothing with more potential than a bowl of cut-up fruit — it cries out for a splash of sophistication. ▶◀

I immediately turned to a simple dressing referred to as a *gastrique*, a reduction of an acid (e.g., vinegar) and sugar. It is most often used to accompany savory dishes such as duck, but *Cook's Illustrated* turned to this recipe as a dressing for fruit salads. The basic method is to take 4 parts liquid (wine, champagne, or citrus juice) to 1 part sugar and reduce it in a saucepan for about 15 minutes or until slightly thickened. I tested this approach on champagne, red wine, and white wine with good results; vinegar and fruit juices (orange, lemon, and lime) were too severe and sour. I did uncover one big problem in my tests: The cooking time reduced the fresh, complex flavor of the wines, a result that was disappointing.

The solution to this problem was discovered on a Web site that suggested lightly caramelizing the sugar first and then adding the wine. In a small saucepan, I placed ¼ cup sugar with 2 tablespoons water and 1 teaspoon lemon juice, the latter included to prevent crystallization. Once the sugar had cooked for about five minutes, I added 1 cup wine, which turned out to be excessive. I eventually cut back the wine quantity to a mere ⅓ cup, which reduced nicely in just a few minutes and maintained its delicate flavor.

A second discovery evolved from a mistake. I let the sugar overcook in one test— it turned a dark amber color— and the resulting flavor was deep and wonderfully complex, especially when married to the wine. The final touch was flavorings; orange, lemon, or lime zest worked well with champagne, as did a bit of orange liqueur. When using red wine, either vanilla bean or cinnamon is a nice addition. (They should steep in the hot liquid for at least 10 minutes but not more than a half hour.)

As for the fruit, it has to be both fresh and full-flavored. This dressing will help, but it can't save tasteless melon or watery strawberries. Peaches, plums, or nectarines don't have to be peeled and can be sliced into ½-inch wedges. If you're lucky enough to find a mango or papaya, it should also be cut into ½-inch cubes. Halved seedless grapes as well as cantaloupe and honeydew melon are good candidates. Watermelon is best left to be eaten on its own, as it quickly becomes soggy. Bananas are another fruit best left for a different purpose. They rapidly turn soft and dark. The syrup dresses about six cups of fruit. The salad should be dressed very close to serving time, but the fruit may be cut and chilled hours ahead of time.

Fruit Salad with Caramelized Wine Dressing

SERVES 4

You can use strawberries, blueberries, blackberries, raspberries, seedless grapes, cantaloupe, honeydew, mango, papaya, peaches, plums, nectarines, or any combination. Strawberries should be halved or quartered, other berries left whole, grapes cut in half pole to pole, and other fruit cut into ½-inch pieces. Peaches, plums, and nectarines do not need to be peeled. The syrup may be made up to 5 days ahead of time and stored in the refrigerator, but the zest should be strained out if you're leaving it for more than a couple of hours.

¼	cup sugar
1	teaspoon lemon juice
⅓	cup champagne, dry white wine, or Prosecco
	Finely grated zest of 1 orange, lime, or lemon, optional
1	tablespoon orange liqueur such as Cointreau or Triple Sec, optional
6	cups prepared fruit (see note above)

Place the sugar, lemon juice, and 2 tablespoons water in a small saucepan over medium-high heat. Simmer until dark amber colored, about 5 minutes. (Once the syrup starts to color, it will turn dark quickly. Take the saucepan off the heat, swirl the contents, replace, and repeat to control the caramelization process.) Off heat, add the champagne. (Be careful; the sugar syrup may foam and splatter a bit.) Return to a simmer and cook until slightly thickened and reduced to just under ¼ cup, about 5 minutes. Stir in the optional zest and/or liqueur. Cool to room temperature. Toss the syrup with the fruit and serve.

VARIATION

Red Wine Dressing for Fruit Salad
Substitute red wine for the champagne in the above recipe. Instead of the lime or lemon zest (the orange still works in this variation), flavor the syrup with ½ vanilla bean or a 3-inch piece of cinnamon stick. The bean or stick should be removed before serving or after a half hour if preparing the syrup ahead of time.

Crisping Up Strawberry-Rhubarb Crisp

The problem with crisps is that they are usually anything but crisp. The topping is sodden or gluey and is matched to a fruit base that is overly sweetened. Strawberry-rhubarb crisps have the added burden of using fruits that vary tremendously in flavor, texture, and sweetness. Instead of a heavy, dull dessert, I was looking for a truly crisp topping married to a fresh-fruit base that tasted like fruit, not sugar. ▶◀

The first issue was the fruit. Rhubarb ribs vary from ¼ inch to 1¼ inches in width. For the sake of uniformity in cooking, I purchased fairly evenly sized stalks. I like using thinner ribs, ½ to ¾ inch thick, because they are easier to handle and make nice, bite-size pieces. One and a quarter pounds of rhubarb yields about 3 cups. I know that some cooks soak rhubarb in cold water before cooking it to tone down its acidity, so I made crisps using rhubarb that had been soaked for 60 minutes, 30 minutes, and not at all. The rhubarb that was soaked for an hour was remarkably less tangy than the unsoaked rhubarb, while the rhubarb soaked for 30 minutes was in between the two extremes. The soaking also dulled the color of the fruit. I preferred the unsoaked rhubarb, because it had the signature tangy finish and the trademark jewel tone. So for this application, soaking was out. (Soaked rhubarb, however, does taste better in the English dessert called a *fool*, where a soft, creamy flavor is preferred.)

I thought the strawberries would be a cinch, but they turned out to be troublesome. My first trip to the market provided me with small, perfectly ripe, sweet berries, and I found that ½ cup sugar for the fruit mixture was just right. During subsequent testing, however, I could find only very large berries that were white in the center as well as sour, and these required ⅔ cup sugar. (They also made an inferior crisp.) My conclusion was that a fruit crisp ought to be made with perfectly ripe strawberries, as they have a starring role.

The next question was how to thicken the fruit. The juice rendered from cooking the fruit is substantial, making the dish a bit on the soupy side. Nonetheless, when I tested Minute Tapioca and potato starch, I preferred the crisp without thickener. Since a crisp is spooned out of the baking dish (a slice of pie needs to stand on its own), and the juices marry nicely with a scoop of vanilla ice cream, I found the extra juice to be a good thing. As for other ingredients, I preferred orange juice and zest over lemon juice and zest, the latter being too sour when matched with the rhubarb. Six cups of the fruit mixture fit nicely into a 9-inch pie plate or an 8-inch-square baking dish.

Now I was on to the topping. I had done a good deal of work with simple flour-and-oatmeal toppings. Both yielded gummy crisps. My solution was to use a combination of nuts and flour, which make a truly crisp top layer. I found walnuts to be bitter and therefore preferred a combination of pecans and almonds, although either one by itself is fine. Most crisps use a heavy hand when it comes to spices, but I found a mere ⅛ teaspoon each of cinnamon and nutmeg to be plenty. (I often leave them out entirely if the fruit is top quality.) The basic method is to pulse the dry flour, sugars (light brown and granulated), spices, and salt in a food processor (a hand method is also included below), then add cold butter and pulse until barely incorporated. The nuts are added next, and the mixture is processed quickly until the texture resembles wet sand. Do not overprocess.

For baking, I start out at 375 degrees for 40 minutes and turn the heat up to 400 degrees for an additional five minutes to crisp up the top. Crisps are best served warm or at room temperature.

Best Strawberry-Rhubarb Crisp

SERVES 6

If you do not have a food processor, use finely chopped nuts and combine all the dry ingredients, including the nuts, in a medium bowl. Add the chilled butter chunks and pinch the mixture between your fingers until it looks like wet, lumpy sand. Serve the crisp with vanilla ice cream.

FOR THE FRUIT

- 1¼ pounds rhubarb ribs, ½ to ¾ inch thick, cut diagonally into ¾-inch lengths (about 3 cups)
- 3 cups ripe strawberries, hulled and cut into bite-size pieces
- ½ cup granulated sugar
- ½ teaspoon grated orange zest
  Juice from ½ orange

FOR THE TOPPING

- 6 tablespoons all-purpose flour
- ¼ cup packed light brown sugar
- ¼ cup granulated sugar
- ⅛ teaspoon ground cinnamon
- ⅛ teaspoon ground nutmeg
- ¼ teaspoon table salt
- 5 tablespoons unsalted butter, chilled and cut into ½-inch pieces
- ¾ cup coarsely chopped almonds and/or pecans

1. For the fruit: Adjust an oven rack to the center position and heat the oven to 375 degrees. Toss the fruit with the sugar, orange zest, and juice in a bowl. Place the mixture in a 9-inch glass pie plate or an 8-by-8-inch glass baking dish.

2. For the topping: Place the flour, sugars, cinnamon, nutmeg, and salt in the work bowl of a food processor. Add the butter and pulse 6 to 8 times or until the mixture resembles coarse cornmeal, with pea-size chunks of butter remaining. Add the nuts and pulse for about five 1-second bursts or until the mixture looks like wet, lumpy sand. Be careful not to overprocess.

3. Distribute the topping evenly over the fruit and bake for 40 minutes. Increase the oven temperature to 400 degrees and bake 5 minutes more or until the fruit is bubbling and the topping is deep golden brown. Serve warm or at room temperature with vanilla ice cream.

Home Baking, Buggy Whips, and Dodos

The media would have one believe that home cooking is going the way of the buggy whip and dodo bird. I read that consumers report that the "ideal" cooking time is 15 minutes and that the "ideal" number of pots used to make dinner is one. Restaurant sales have grown from $43 billion in 1970 to $354 billion in 1995. Those figures paint a grim picture.

But, I wondered, what about investigating the consumption of basic ingredients, the sorts of items one might use in home baking? I began by looking at egg consumption. Although the total number of eggs consumed per capita has dropped modestly from just over 300 per year in 1970 to 265 or so in 1997, the more interesting statistic is that eggs in the shell have dropped from 276 per capita in 1970 to 173 in 1997, while processed eggs have risen from about 40 in 1970 to roughly 75 in 1997. So home cooks are indeed cooking up fewer eggs per year.

The other, perhaps more telling, statistic is annual flour consumption per capita. Although the consumption of flour and cereal products is skyrocketing (from 136 pounds per capita in 1970 to 200 pounds in 1997), the consumption of flour purchased in a bag in the grocery store is not only falling but insignificant. (Although this amount seems low, this statistic was confirmed by the USDA.) Did you know that in 1998 the average American purchased only $2.64 of flour? (Adjusted for inflation, that is roughly a 50 percent decrease since 1980.) That says something about home baking!

So, although there are over 100 culinary publications in America, the Food Network is distributed to more than 78 million U.S. households, Emeril Lagasse is a household name, and Williams-Sonoma has over 200 stores, the fact of the matter is that cooking is destined to be primarily a spectator sport in the twenty-first century. Just like traditional Yankee values, we like the romance of it but not the hard work and dedication necessary to live the dream. Once again, convenience has carried the day.

Peach Kuchen is a recipe that graces the pages of community cookbooks but will never be found in slick food magazines. It's solid, no-nonsense fare — easy to make, unpretentious, and, when properly made, delicious. ▶◀

The first problem with peach Kuchen is defining it. Recipes call for everything from boxed cake mixes and refrigerated bread dough to yeast cake as a base. However, the consensus is that Kuchen (German for "cake") is a coffee or breakfast-style cake with fruit baked into the top and a garnish of cinnamon and sugar or streusel. Such a recipe appears in the new *Joy of Cooking*. It contains all-purpose flour, baking powder, salt, butter, sugar, and eggs for the cake and peaches, pecans, sugar, and cinnamon for the topping. As it turned out, the cake was dry and overleavened (1 tablespoon baking powder to 1 cup flour is extravagant), and it could have used a bit more fruit. My solution was to add milk to the batter for moisture, reduce the amount of baking powder, and increase the amount of fruit. Now I had a good working recipe — this Kuchen was sturdy but moist and had enough fruit to balance out the foundation of cake below.

Next, I tried using sour cream instead of milk, but, to my surprise, the texture of the cake turned tough. Cake flour produced a weak structure, one into which the sliced peaches happily dived during baking, so all-purpose was the winner. I fiddled with leavener quantities and settled on 1½ teaspoons baking powder and ¼ teaspoon baking soda, which balanced the cake's height with the moistness of its crumb.

Now I was on to the topping. I found that the peaches benefited from sitting out at room temperature for a couple of days to soften. After peeling and slicing them, I found lemon juice to be unnecessary for preventing discoloration. My first topping included cinnamon and sugar, but I preferred a more interesting streusel topping. After some experimentation, I settled on a topping made from flour, butter, sugar, and chopped nuts, which provided the crunch I was looking for. (Many streusel toppings are soft and too sweet.)

It is best to bake this cake in a 9-inch springform pan. In a pinch, it can be baked in a 9-inch cake pan and flipped out with minimal loss of topping, but it's much easier to work with a springform.

Peach Kuchen with Crunchy Streusel

SERVES 8

This recipe can also be made with apples or plums. The easiest way to peel peaches is to first immerse them in boiling water for 30 seconds and then plunge them into an ice bath. Do not use underripe peaches; they are tasteless and will be difficult to peel.

Softened unsalted butter for the pan
Flour for the pan

FOR THE STREUSEL TOPPING

2	tablespoons all-purpose flour
2	tablespoons light brown sugar
3	tablespoons chopped almonds and/or pecans
⅛	teaspoon ground nutmeg
⅛	teaspoon ground cinnamon
1	tablespoon unsalted butter, at cool room temperature

FOR THE CAKE

1½	cups all-purpose flour
1½	teaspoons baking powder
¼	teaspoon baking soda
½	teaspoon table salt
8	tablespoons (1 stick) unsalted butter, at room temperature
1	cup granulated sugar
2	large eggs, at room temperature
1	teaspoon vanilla extract
⅔	cup milk
3	cups peaches, peeled and cut into ½-inch slices, about 3 large to 6 small

1. Adjust an oven rack to the center position and heat the oven to 350 degrees. Butter and flour a 9-inch springform pan.
2. For the streusel: Combine all the ingredients in the bowl of an electric mixer and mix until crumbly and thoroughly combined, about 2 minutes. Set aside.
3. For the cake: Sift the flour, baking powder, baking soda, and salt together onto a piece of waxed paper. Place the butter in the bowl of an electric mixer and beat on medium-high for 1 minute. Add the sugar and gradually beat on high speed for 3 minutes, until the mixture is light and fluffy. Add the eggs one at a time, beating for 30 seconds after each addition. Add the vanilla and beat for 10 seconds. Add ⅓ of the flour mixture and ⅓ of the milk and beat on low speed until almost combined. Repeat twice, being careful not to overbeat. Using a rubber spatula, mix briefly, scraping down the sides of the bowl to make sure the batter is fully combined.
4. Scrape the batter into the prepared pan, smoothing the surface with the spatula. Top with an even layer of peaches. Sprinkle with an even layer of streusel topping. Bake for 20 minutes. Rotate the cake 180 degrees and bake for 20 to 30 minutes more or until the cake is golden brown and a cake tester or wooden skewer comes out clean. (The very center of the cake may appear a bit undercooked — this is okay. Check the cake about 2 inches in from the sides of the pan.) Let cool on a rack for 10 minutes before removing the sides of the pan. Serve warm or at room temperature.

Most of us are — excuse the expression — idiots when it comes to making a fruit pie. The bottom crust has to be rolled out, somehow lifted from the work surface, and transferred to a pie dish; then the filling must be added and a top crust rolled out and properly fitted over the pie with the edges neatly crimped. What one usually ends up with is not a Martha Stewart centerpiece but something out of the Addams family: cruelly shaped and tortured-looking. I also find that pies don't have enough crust for the fruit, the latter spilling out of a soft, half-baked crust, which doesn't do good summer fruit justice. I wanted a really crispy crust and plenty of it. ▶◀

In Europe, there is a tradition of simply rolling out dough, topping it with fruit, folding up the sides, and then baking. These doughs are often referred to as *galette* doughs, and they tend to be very soft, often made with cream cheese. I started my testing by trying five different galette doughs from various cookbooks, all of which used cream cheese as a key ingredient. For 1 cup flour, these recipes used anywhere from ¼ to ½ cup cream cheese plus 6 to 8 tablespoons butter. The doughs came together with very little water added and were smooth and easy to roll out. I soon discovered a few problems, however. The first was that many of these doughs were relatively soft, even when baked. I find this to be a disappointing partner for baked fruit. As with a pie, I wanted some crispness and flake to the crust to marry with the fruit. The more fat-laden recipes were so rich that I found them hard to digest. After a few more tests, I decided to go back to my basic pie dough recipe. This turned out to be a winner. It's simple, it's flaky, it's crisp, and it marries well with the fruit. If it works well with a two-crust pie, why not use it for this simple one-crust dessert as well?

For the fruit, I found that 2 cups was about right. Now, all of the other recipes I have come across called for the same ingredients: 2 tablespoons flour, 1 tablespoon white sugar, and 1 tablespoon brown sugar. I found this combination to be too heavy on the flour and too light on the sugar. In fact, I found that most fruit needs no flour at all.

If the fruit is cooked long enough, the juices mix with the sugar, and when cooled, it forms a thick syrup. The flour simply dulls the flavor of the fruit. I also found that white granulated sugar is better than brown sugar, because it doesn't interfere with the flavor of the fruit.

So I went back into the kitchen and tried my basic pastry dough recipe, used 2 cups fruit mixed with 3 to 4 tablespoons sugar, and baked it at 400 degrees for about 45 minutes or until the fruit was bubbling and the crust was nicely browned. I let it cool for at least an hour for the juices to set. The result was an intensely flavored filling (the fruit had cooked down with the sugar) married to a crispy, toothsome crust, and, best of all, even an idiot like me can make it!

One-Crust Fruit Pie

SERVES 6 HUNGRY ADULTS

This "pie" is much easier to make than a traditional 2-crust pie, because one layer of dough is simply rolled out; it doesn't have to be fitted into a pie dish, and there is no fussing with the edging. There is also a better ratio of crust to filling (this recipe uses 2 cups of fruit instead of 6 to 8 cups for a standard fruit pie), which makes it both an easy and also superior method for cooking up fruit. Note that the amount of sugar will depend on the fruit. Use 3 tablespoons with very ripe, sweet fruit and a full ¼ cup if the fruit is tart or less than perfectly ripe. Serve with either whipped cream or vanilla ice cream.

FOR THE CRUST

- 5 tablespoons cold unsalted butter
- 1¼ cups all-purpose flour, plus more for dusting dough and work surface
- ½ teaspoon table salt
- 2 tablespoons sugar
- 5 tablespoons all-vegetable shortening (Crisco), chilled
- 4–5 tablespoons ice water

FOR THE FRUIT FILLING

- 2 cups ripe summer fruit (berries, peaches, plums)
- 3–4 tablespoons sugar

Whipped cream or vanilla ice cream for serving, optional

1. For the crust: Cut the butter into ¾-inch pieces and place it in the freezer for 15 minutes. Mix the flour, salt, and sugar in a food processor fitted with the steel blade. Place the shortening in 1-tablespoon lumps into the food processor along with the frozen butter pieces. Pulse about 8 times (1-second pulses) or until the dough appears slightly yellow, pebbly in texture, and the butter is reduced to very small pieces, the size of peas or smaller. Check the dough after 5 pulses and every pulse thereafter. Turn the mixture into a medium bowl. (This dough can also be made by hand. Use your fingers to work the butter and shortening into the flour.)

2. Sprinkle 4 tablespoons of the ice water over the mixture. With the blade of a large rubber spatula, use a folding motion to mix, then press down on the dough with the broad side of the spatula until the dough sticks together, adding more water if the dough will not come together. (Do NOT worry about adding more water; add as much as you need to make sure that the dough easily comes together and is moist. If the outside of the dough becomes wet, simply flour it before you wrap it in plastic.) Work slowly, mixing the dough to evenly distribute the water. This should take about 1 minute. Shape the dough into a ball with your hands, then flatten it into a 4-inch-wide disk. Dust lightly with flour, wrap in plastic, and refrigerate for at least 30 minutes before rolling.

3. Adjust an oven rack to the center position and heat the oven to 400 degrees.

4. For the fruit: Prepare the fruit and place it in a medium bowl. (The berries just need to be washed and then dried with paper towels. Stone fruits such as peaches or plums can be skinned or not, pitted, and then sliced thinly.)

5. Roll out the dough into a 12-inch round on a sheet of parchment paper. (If the dough is hard to roll out—if it falls apart—place it in a medium bowl and add a couple of teaspoons of water. Mix gently with your fingers until the dough is moist. Add more water if you have to. Shape it into a disk and flour it lightly. Now roll it out again.) Or, roll it out on any lightly floured work surface and then transfer to a baking sheet. Toss the fruit with the sugar and place it in the middle of the dough, leaving a 2½-inch border all around. Drape the border up over the fruit in overlapping folds. Note that some of the fruit will remain uncovered.

6. Bake until the fruit is bubbling and the crust is very brown, about 45 minutes. Let cool for at least an hour before serving. Slice into wedges and serve with whipped cream or vanilla ice cream, if desired.

Dressing Up Vanilla Ice Cream

Although I am the author of *The Dessert Bible*, I often opt for a dead simple dessert, especially if I am serving an impromptu dinner to neighbors. The easiest of these desserts are quick sauces served over store-bought vanilla ice cream. Sound plain? Sure, but a homemade raspberry, caramel, or chocolate sauce is just enough to dress up an otherwise ordinary offering. ⋙◄

LIQUEUR

If I am really pressed for time, a splash of good after-dinner liqueur over a double scoop of Edy's Dreamery (NOT Edy's Grand) vanilla ice cream (the first-place winner in a *Cook's Illustrated* taste test) does the trick. I wondered, though, which liqueur would be best? Sherry, port, and Armagnac were all winners. But would they taste better if simmered first into a syrupy consistency? I tested this approach, even adding sugar, cinnamon stick, allspice berries, cloves, peppercorns, etc., but the liqueur lost both its bite and identity. The result? A splash of sherry, port, or Armagnac over vanilla ice cream works just fine on its own, with no recipe needed.

RASPBERRY SAUCE

Next, I investigated a simple fruit sauce. I opted for frozen rather than fresh, because I was aiming for an all-season recipe. Blueberries and strawberries were disappointing — they were either watery or flat-tasting. Raspberries, on the other hand, held their flavor and looked great to boot. Using a 12-ounce bag of frozen raspberries, I found that ⅔ cup sugar and 1 tablespoon lemon juice were just right. They required cooking for best flavor and consistency; a skillet cooked faster than a saucepan. A potato masher and a strainer smoothed out the sauce, and a touch of Cointreau or similar liqueur finished it off nicely.

CARAMEL SAUCE

Caramel sauce is made from caramelized sugar with the addition of cream and/or butter. The trickiest part of the sauce is caramelizing the sugar, so I decided to begin there. Sugar can be caramelized by either the wet or dry method. I have found that the wet method — water is added to the sugar at the outset of the process — is more foolproof and easier. I also found that the addition of lemon juice helps to avoid crystallization. My next concern was that once the sugar starts to color, it goes from golden to burnt in a very short amount of time. I found I could lower the heat at the point where the sugar starts to color, making the transformation from blond to dark amber more controlled. (I also take the pan entirely off the heat as the liquid begins to color, swirling the syrup as it cooks.) The time it takes to caramelize sugar will vary dramatically (from eight to 15 minutes) depending on the type of saucepan you are using.

As for other ingredients, cream and butter made for the smoothest and most balanced sauce. After several batches, I preferred ¾ cup heavy cream and 2 tablespoons unsalted butter to 1½ cups sugar. A healthy pinch of salt was also welcome. The cream needs to be added carefully in small additions. (It can be heated to minimize the bubbling, but the extra step and pan aren't really worth the effort.) Though the caramel sauce is already thick, intensely flavored, and delicious, a couple of tablespoons of rum or bourbon are a great addition.

Chocolate Sauce

For a chocolate sauce, I tested hot fudge sauce, ganache, a chocolate glaze, and a cocoa-based sauce. I felt that the ganache was the grandest of them all — thick and rich. For the working recipe, I started with 1 cup heavy cream and 12 ounces bittersweet or semisweet chocolate. In such sauces, the addition of corn syrup, granulated sugar, butter, and vanilla is common. However, adding sugar instead of corn syrup made the sauce thicker. Two tablespoons butter added shine and body, and ½ teaspoon vanilla offered balance. I borrowed a technique from Marcel Desaulniers's *Death by Chocolate* and added the chopped chocolate to the hot cream. I liked his method, because there is no chance the chocolate can overcook.

Raspberry Sauce

MAKES ABOUT 1 CUP

Add only a small amount of the liqueur at first and taste the sauce before adding more.

- 12 ounces frozen raspberries
- ⅔ cup sugar
- 1 tablespoon lemon juice
- 1–2 tablespoons orange-flavored liqueur, such as Cointreau, or liqueur of your choice, optional

Place the berries, sugar, and lemon juice in a heavy-duty nonreactive skillet over medium heat. Bring the mixture to a boil and reduce the heat to maintain an energetic simmer. Cook for about 5 minutes or until the mixture is thickened slightly, stirring occasionally. Halfway through the cooking process, press on the mixture with a potato masher to help break down the berries. Transfer the mixture to a mesh strainer (fine enough to capture the seeds) set over a bowl. Using a rubber spatula, work the juice and pulp through the strainer until only a sticky mass of seeds remains. Discard the seeds. Stir the sauce to even out the consistency. Add the optional liqueur. Serve at room temperature or chilled. Keeps in the refrigerator for several days.

Caramel Sauce

MAKES ABOUT 1¼ CUPS

The type and size of saucepan will dramatically impact the cooking time. For a chocolate variation, add 4 ounces finely chopped semisweet or bittersweet chocolate to the finished sauce and stir until melted and well blended.

1½	cups sugar
¼	teaspoon lemon juice
¾	cup heavy cream
2	tablespoons unsalted butter
	Pinch table salt
2	tablespoons dark rum or bourbon, optional

Place the sugar, ½ cup water, and the lemon juice in a small saucepan over medium heat. Stir to combine. Bring to a boil and cook until the mixture just begins to color, 6 to 12 minutes depending on your pan and stovetop. Reduce the heat to low and cook until dark amber, about 2 minutes longer, swirling the pan off the heat if the caramel colors unevenly.

Remove from the heat. Very carefully add the heavy cream, a little at a time, as it will bubble vigorously, stirring after each addition. Add the butter and salt and stir until the butter is melted and the sauce uniform. Add the optional rum and stir to combine. Serve warm. The sauce can be kept covered in the refrigerator for several days and reheated over low heat until warm.

Chocolate Sauce

MAKES ABOUT 2 CUPS

Use the best chocolate you can find. Callebaut is my first choice, but Ghirardelli is also very good.

1	cup heavy cream
2	tablespoons sugar
2	tablespoons unsalted butter
12	ounces bittersweet or semisweet chocolate, finely chopped
½	teaspoon vanilla extract

Place the cream, sugar, and butter in a small saucepan over medium-low heat. Bring to a simmer. Remove from heat, add the chocolate, and cover the pan. Let sit for 5 minutes. Add the vanilla and whisk the mixture until smooth and shiny. The mixture will look curdled until it comes together. Serve warm. The sauce can be refrigerated for several days and reheated over low heat until warm.

New Ways with Whipped Cream

I am sick and tired of lackluster whipped cream. It's as tasteless (and common) as a bad hamburger bun, a scoop of 2-day-old cole slaw, or the lifeless pickle that adorns most deluxe sandwich specials. I wanted flavor and lots of it, so that whipped cream really adds something to dessert rather than being a passive bystander. ▶◀

The first issue is the cream, which is sold as organic, natural, pasteurized, and ultra-pasteurized. I tasted them all, and the differences were subtle, although they all whipped into soft peaks. I enjoyed the fresh, sweet taste of the organic cream best and found that pasteurized cream whipped up much lighter and fluffier than ultra-pasteurized. In fact, 1 cup ultra-pasteurized whipped into 1½ cups, whereas 1 cup pasteurized whipped into a full 2 cups. So the winner was organic pasteurized heavy cream. Of course, the cream, the bowls, and the beaters should all be well chilled for the best results. As for the sugar, I found that granulated sugar worked best for a clean, sweet taste. (Confectioners' sugar left an aftertaste.) For 1 cup cream, I used 1 tablespoon sugar to produce a pleasantly sweet whipped cream. The cream and sugar are added to the bowl and beaten on medium until foamy, and then once the cream has started to thicken, the speed can be increased to high.

Next, I wanted to add flavor by using other dairy products. Mascarpone cheese has a sweet creamy taste, is rich, and should be left at room temperature for about 10 minutes before whipping. Four ounces added the right amount of flavor, but I needed to up the sugar by 1 teaspoon to compensate for the added cheese. Mascarpone should be added at the beginning of the whipping process, or it will turn out grainy. This combination is wonderful with baked or poached fruit.

Sour cream was a nice partner with whipped cream, turning out a very light but brighter-tasting mixture. As with the mascarpone, the sugar needed to be increased by 1 teaspoon. I also found it best to add the sour cream to the heavy cream at the beginning of the recipe instead of folding it in at the end. This variation is delicious with fresh berries, apple crisp, or blueberry cobbler.

I was prepared to dislike yogurt as an additive but ended up loving it. I added ¼ cup plain whole-milk yogurt for best flavor. As with the other variations, I found that I needed to increase the sugar and also that the best way to combine the ingredients was to mix them together at the outset. I liked this version with all of the serving suggestions above. Finally, I tried adding buttermilk and cream cheese to the heavy cream. The buttermilk was too watery and sour, and the cream cheese added little in the way of flavor.

As for specific flavorings, the winners included vanilla, orange liqueur, rum, brown sugar, and dark-amber maple syrup. Losers included cocoa, instant espresso, and spices.

Deluxe Whipped Cream

MAKES ABOUT 2½ CUPS

Try to find pasteurized rather than ultra-pasteurized heavy cream for this recipe. Organic cream has the freshest, sweetest taste and should be used if available. If you're making the sour cream or yogurt variation, these ingredients do not have to sit out for 10 minutes at room temperature — they may be added directly from the refrigerator. The mascarpone cheese is rich and sophisticated and is terrific with baked or poached fruit. The sour cream variation is lighter and great with fresh berries, crisps, and cobblers. The yogurt whipped cream is the lightest and lends itself to any fruit dessert.

- 4 ounces mascarpone cheese
- 1 cup heavy cream (organic pasteurized preferred)
- 1 tablespoon plus 1 teaspoon granulated sugar
- 1 teaspoon vanilla extract

Allow the mascarpone to sit at room temperature for 10 minutes. Chill a medium mixing bowl and beaters for a handheld mixer in the refrigerator for 10 minutes or in the freezer for 5 minutes. Add the heavy cream, mascarpone, sugar, and vanilla to the chilled bowl and mix on medium speed until foamy and beginning to thicken, about 45 seconds. Increase the speed to high and beat until smooth and shiny and soft peaks form, 30 seconds to 1 minute longer. If the cream becomes overbeaten and grainy, gently beat in a tablespoon of heavy cream to smooth it out.

VARIATIONS

Sour Cream Whipped Cream

Substitute ⅓ cup sour cream for the mascarpone cheese.

Yogurt Whipped Cream

Substitute ¼ cup plain whole-milk yogurt for the mascarpone.

Rum Whipped Cream

Decrease the vanilla to ½ teaspoon and add 1 tablespoon dark rum to the mascarpone variation.

Orange Whipped Cream

Decrease the vanilla to ½ teaspoon and add 1 tablespoon orange liqueur to the mascarpone or sour cream variation.

Brown Sugar or Maple Whipped Cream

Decrease the vanilla to ½ teaspoon and substitute brown sugar or dark-amber maple syrup for the granulated sugar in the sour cream or yogurt variation.

Better Rice Pudding

Bad rice pudding is inedible regardless of whether it is baked in the oven (heavy and custardy) or made on the stovetop (thick and indigestible). Rice pudding is also time-consuming; many recipes take up to two hours of simmering. I wanted to taste the rice, not just the dairy; I wanted some interesting flavors; and I wanted it quick — a half hour was my outside time limit. ▶◀

I started with the notion of stovetop cooking, using Arborio rice (it is starchy and available everywhere), a liquid (water and/or dairy), sugar, and flavorings. Some recipes (including one of my own) start by cooking the rice in water and then cooking it in milk. This tasted just fine but took an hour and a half. Instead, I combined the water and dairy (in this case, milk) and cooked it all at one time. The ratios of liquid to rice in the recipes I examined varied from 4 cups liquid to 3 tablespoons rice to 5 cups liquid to 1 cup rice. I decided on splitting the difference, using 4 cups liquid (3 cups milk, 1 cup water) to ½ cup rice. The good news was that I made rice pudding in 30 minutes by simmering it on the stovetop; the bad news was that it was much too thick and "milky," and I needed to infuse some flavors to punch up the dish.

My first thought was to add more rice. I tried ¾ cup and then settled on a full cup. I was surprised that I did not need to add more liquid, and, this time, the rice had a bit more tooth, although it was fully cooked. (I also tested long- and medium-grain rice, both of which rendered a thinner pudding; Thai sticky rice and sushi rice both produced a gooey dessert.) Next, I kept dropping the ratio of milk to water, finally ending up with 2½ cups water to 1½ cups milk. Now the texture was lighter. I ended up preferring half-and-half to milk (it was a bit smoother and creamier), although either is fine.

As far as sugar goes, I started with ¼ cup, increased it to 5 tablespoons, and finally settled on ⅓ cup — just enough to add flavor but not enough to make it sticky-sweet. Two teaspoons of orange zest added at the end gave this sleepy dish some bite, and vanilla extract rounded out the flavors. In an effort to add some texture, chopped pistachios sprinkled on top were just the thing, adding a lot more flavor than almonds. Still, this rice pudding tasted a bit flat, so I added ¼ teaspoon salt, an ingredient that turned out to be obvious but essential. Finally, I came up with a rum-raisin variation for those more traditional about their tastes in rice pudding.

Quick, Creamy Rice Pudding

SERVES 4

Pistachios can be toasted in a 350-degree oven for about 7 minutes or in a dry skillet over medium heat for about 5 minutes or until very lightly colored and fragrant. I prefer this dish served warm (it can be served cold as well); it can also be served as a porridge for breakfast.

1	cup Arborio rice
1½	cups half-and-half or whole milk
⅓	cup sugar
¼	teaspoon table salt
1	teaspoon vanilla extract
2	teaspoons finely chopped orange zest
¼	cup finely chopped toasted pistachios

Place the rice, 2½ cups water, the half-and-half, sugar, and salt in a large saucepan over medium heat. Bring to a boil and adjust the heat to maintain a gentle simmer. Cook uncovered for about 30 minutes, stirring occasionally, or until the mixture is quite thick but still wet. The pudding will thicken further as it cools. Off heat, stir in the vanilla and orange zest. Serve warm, at room temperature, or cold, topped with the pistachios.

VARIATION
Rum-Raisin Rice Pudding
Omit the vanilla, orange zest, and pistachios. Add one 2- to 3-inch piece of cinnamon stick to the saucepan along with the other ingredients. Meanwhile, soak ⅓ cup raisins in ¼ cup dark rum. Once the pudding has cooked for 25 minutes, add the rum-raisin mixture to the pudding for the final minutes of cooking. Discard the cinnamon stick.

The Julia Child One-Egg Rule

Once in a while, Julia Child would call and suggest that we cook dinner together. We both lived in Boston at the time, and Julia is the most inclusive person I have ever met. She invited everyone to her house at one time or another and was always generous with her food, wine, and attention.

Of course, Julia had her eye on you, much like one of her professors did her when she attended Smith College. She once asked me to shuck two dozen oysters, something that Jasper White, a well-known local chef and close friend of Julia's, might do in a few minutes. I froze them for 15 minutes; I tried using a church key; I pulled out two kinds of oyster knives; and I was still shucking after 45 minutes. I failed that test miserably.

I did have many opportunities, however, to return the favor. I have watched Julia cook a wide variety of dishes, almost all French, with nary a cookbook or timer at her disposal. She simply knows when things are ready, and, when she opens the oven door, they are!

One night, Julia was preparing a fresh corn custard, and she seemed to be making it up as she went. I asked her about the recipe, and she replied, "Well, dearie, you just use one whole egg per half cup of liquid." In essence, she was making a custard and telling me that most such recipes are based on a ratio of one egg to a half cup of milk, half-and-half, or cream.

The next day, I went through a bunch of my own recipes and, to my surprise, found that they were all based on Julia's simple formula. In some cases I used an egg yolk instead of an egg, but the basic principle remained intact.

So, if you want to throw away your cookbooks and start cooking without recipes, look for the underlying formulas. They're there if you take the time to look for them. And remember that you can make hundreds of different custards — savory or sweet — by simply using one egg per half cup of liquid. Just ask Julia.

Burnt-Sugar Custard

One of my favorite desserts is the classic crème caramel — the "burnt sugar" syrup, as it is sometimes called in American cookery, marries nicely to the light, rather bland taste and texture of the custard. I wondered if I could combine the two in order to make a "burnt-sugar custard" that would be richer and more satisfying than crème caramel and also show off the distinctive color and flavor of a caramelized sugar syrup. ▷◁

Traditional crème caramel uses a combination of milk and either light cream or half-and-half. This produced custard that was too light for this purpose. I wanted something richer, so I changed the mixture to milk and heavy cream in equal proportions. With 4 cups of liquid, I tried following a basic rule of custards told to me by Julia Child: one egg per half cup of liquid for thickening. This would mean eight eggs, but I found that four whole eggs plus four yolks was a better combination — it made for a silkier, almost lighter dessert. A touch of salt and some vanilla extract were also added to boost flavor. Now I had to make the sugar syrup.

My basic formula for any sugar syrup is 1 part water to 2 parts sugar; this helps the sugar dissolve. (The water evaporates during cooking.) I finally settled on 1⅓ cups sugar to ⅝ cup water. The trick is to cook the sugar syrup long enough to create flavor. If the syrup is too light, it is bland and too sweet, much like a fancy grade-A maple syrup. When cooked longer, it develops a slightly bitter flavor that has a lot of character. (Too much cooking, however, and the custard will indeed taste burnt.) The trick, I soon discovered, was to take the saucepan off the heat as soon as the syrup started to take on color and swirl the contents. Do this a number of times, putting the saucepan back onto the heat, removing it, swirling, and repeating. This way you can slow down and control the process, getting just the color you want. I prefer the syrup to be a rich mahogany color. Don't forget that the syrup will continue to cook after it comes off the heat, so watch it carefully.

My final adjustment was to add 3 tablespoons sugar to the eggs before adding the milk–sugar syrup mixture. This took the edge off the bitterness of the caramelized sugar and gave the dessert a nice boost of flavor. By the way, beating the eggs with the sugar in an electric mixer was not only unnecessary but created too much froth.

There is no need to unmold this dessert—it can be served directly in the ramekins. I prefer this dessert warm or at room temperature for best flavor. It will keep in the refrigerator overnight, but I find that the flavor is less intense the next day.

Burnt-Sugar Custard

SERVES 8

Make sure that the custard is barely set in the center before taking it from the oven. The very center should be slightly undercooked.

	Softened unsalted butter for ramekins
2	cups milk
2	cups heavy cream
¼	teaspoon (scant) table salt
1⅓	cups plus 3 tablespoons sugar
1½	teaspoons vanilla extract
4	whole eggs
4	egg yolks

1. Adjust an oven rack to the center position and heat the oven to 325 degrees. Put a kettle of water on to boil. Lightly butter eight 6- to 8-ounce custard cups and place them on a kitchen towel in a large roasting pan.

2. Heat the milk, cream, and salt together in a large saucepan over medium heat until the mixture reaches 160 to 170 degrees measured on an instant-read thermometer. (It should be very hot but not yet at a simmer.)

3. Meanwhile, place 1⅓ cups of the sugar and ½ cup plus 2 tablespoons water in a small saucepan over high heat. Cook until the mixture turns a rich mahogany color. (Swirl the pan a few times to remove any

sugar crystals from the sides. When the mixture starts to color, take the saucepan off the heat and swirl it for 10 seconds. This allows you to control the cooking process, slowing it down so the sugar syrup does not overcook. If the syrup is too light, it will not have much flavor. It should be a rich, deep mahogany color.)

4. Whisk the caramel syrup into the milk-cream mixture until well blended. (Some of the syrup may stick to the tines of the whisk; just keep whisking and most of it will eventually dissolve.) Whisk in the vanilla.

5. Whisk the whole eggs, yolks, and the remaining 3 tablespoons sugar to blend in a large bowl. Gradually add the hot cream mixture, whisking constantly. Pour the custard mixture into the prepared custard cups. Add the boiling water to the roasting pan until the water reaches about two thirds of the way up the sides of the custard cups. Make sure not to splash any water into the custard cups. Bake until the custards are set, 40 to 60 minutes, rotating the roasting pan after 20 minutes. (The baking time can vary a great deal depending on the size and shape of the ramekins.) They should be barely set in the center and still jiggle a bit when moved. Remove to a cooling rack. Serve slightly warm or at room temperature.

Keep on Cookin'

If you burn your finger, you are told to immediately run it under cold water. Of course, the cold water makes it feel better, but there is a more important reason for this step: It stops the cooking! Your finger has residual heat from the burn, and by reducing the temperature of the flesh, you are stopping any additional damage to the tissues.

This principle applies to many baked or roasted foods as well. Any custard-based pie (pumpkin is an example) continues to cook on the kitchen counter, as will crème caramel or crème brûlée. Have you ever noticed custard pies that are cracked around the perimeter? That's because they have been overcooked. The poor baker may have taken the pie out of the oven when it was perfectly set, but, to his or her great surprise, it kept on cookin'! That's why any custard-based dessert should be removed from the oven *before* the custard is set. The center of the pie should still wiggle and shake and be only partially set. After an hour of cooling, it will be just set, tender, and moist.

The same is true for meat. The internal temperature of a large pork roast can rise 15 degrees during resting. That's why I take roasts out of the oven when they are at only 125 degrees! If you wait until it reaches 145 degrees, the final roast may be 155 degrees or higher, too high for a moist piece of meat. A thick pork chop or any beef roast will also continue to cook out of the oven.

One exception to this rule is chicken. A roast chicken does not continue to cook out of the oven. (I know, because I have measured the temperature of a roast chicken as it sits on the cutting board.) The reason? Unlike a thick roast, a chicken is designed for quick cooling with a cavity and pieces of meat that are relatively thin. Air circulates around the bird and cools it off more readily than is the case with a pie or chuck roast.

SAME INGREDIENTS,

DIFFERENT RESULTS

DENSE CHEESECAKE

If you beat five whole eggs into the cream cheese batter,
the baked cheesecake will be dense and very rich.
This is called New York–style cheesecake.

LIGHT CHEESECAKE

If you add five yolks to the cream cheese batter,
beat the five whites separately, and then fold the fluffy whites into
the finished batter, the cake will turn out light and creamy.
This is how I prefer my cheesecake.

Light, Creamy Cheesecake

Reasonable cooks can come to blows about what constitutes the best cheesecake. Some like it thick, rich, and dense; others prefer a lighter texture, one that has plenty of tongue-coating silkiness but that is also more ethereal, dancing in the mouth before dissolving into a final burst of rich cream. I belong to the latter school, and my search for the perfect cheesecake carried me well off the culinary beaten path. ▶◀

To solve the issue of texture, the most obvious test was to separate the eggs, beat the whites separately, and then fold them back into the cream cheese mixture. This worked splendidly; the final texture was remarkably light. I tested adding cream of tartar to the whites as they were beaten, and in fact this did stabilize the whites, producing a somewhat higher and lighter cake. I did find, however, that a denser, more traditional New York cheesecake can be made by not separating the eggs, and I have included this variation below.

The next issues were oven temperature and baking time. Over many years, I have found that lower oven temperatures work best for cheesecake. Having tested everything from 200 degrees up to 350 degrees, I find that 275 degrees is in fact the winner; low enough not to toughen the egg proteins and dry out the mixture, yet high enough not to take all day. But, even with this low temperature, I found that the top of the cake would often come out cracked and overcooked. Although I prefer to make recipes as simple as possible, it turns out that a *bain-marie*, a hot-water bath, was essential. Unfortunately, this leads to complications. A cheesecake must be cooked in a springform pan, which can leak with water, ruining the crust. Therefore, aluminum foil is needed. An extra-wide piece is placed on top of the bottom of the pan, the pan is assembled, and then the foil is folded up around the sides. Finally, the pan is placed in a roasting pan and hot water is poured around the pan, enough to come up halfway. The water moderates the temperature around the pan and also provides a moister environment, one that produces a tender cheesecake.

After much testing, I determined that it was best to let the cake sit in the turned-off oven for two hours after baking. I also tested a variety of baking times from 50 minutes to one hour and 15 minutes. I found that a time between 60 and 70 minutes was best.

(All ovens vary. Never trust baking times; always check the contents of the oven during baking.) The flavors of the cheesecake were at their peak after the cake was thoroughly chilled, which will take three to four hours in the refrigerator. Slicing a cheesecake is difficult. It is made easier by running a sharp knife under hot water between slices.

Light, Rich Cheesecake

SERVES 12

The easiest way to make crumbs out of graham crackers is to place the crackers in a zipper-lock bag and then crush them with a rolling pin.

1	tablespoon unsalted butter, melted
3	tablespoons graham cracker crumbs (about 1 whole cracker)
2	pounds cream cheese, at room temperature
1¼	cups sugar
5	large eggs, separated
1	teaspoon grated lemon zest
1½	teaspoons vanilla extract
½	cup heavy cream
1	cup sour cream
½	teaspoon cream of tartar

1. Adjust an oven rack to the center position and heat the oven to 275 degrees. Remove the bottom from a 10-inch springform pan. To prevent leakage, cut a large piece of aluminum foil from an extra-wide roll and place it on top of the bottom, tucking the foil under around the edges. Reassemble the pan and then fold the foil up the sides. The foil should reach almost to the top of the pan. Wrap a second piece of foil around the outside bottom and sides of the pan. Brush the inside of the pan with the melted butter and then sprinkle with graham cracker crumbs, tilting the pan to coat evenly. Set the springform pan in a large roasting pan and bring a large kettle of water to a boil for the water bath.

2. Beat the cream cheese with an electric mixer or by hand until smooth. Gradually add 1 cup plus 2 tablespoons of the sugar and beat until smooth, about 3 minutes with an electric mixer or 6 to 7 minutes by hand. Add the yolks, one at a time, and beat until just incorporated, frequently scraping down the sides of the bowl. Stir in the lemon zest, vanilla, heavy cream, and sour cream with a wooden spoon or rubber spatula.

3. Beat the egg whites, remaining 2 tablespoons sugar, and cream of tartar in a clean bowl until they hold soft peaks. Fold the whites into the batter with a large rubber spatula. Pour the batter into the prepared springform pan and set the roasting pan on the oven rack. Pour enough boiling water into the roasting pan to come halfway up the sides of the springform pan. Bake for 60 to 70 minutes or until the cheesecake is puffy and slightly browned and the center is still a bit wobbly. Turn off the heat and let the cheesecake sit in the oven, door closed, for another 2 hours.

4. Remove the springform pan from the

water bath and set it on a wire rack to cool to room temperature. Cover and refrigerate until completely chilled, 3 to 4 hours. (You can make this recipe a day ahead of time if you like.) To serve, run a thin knife around the inside of the pan and remove the outer ring. Run the knife under hot water before cutting individual slices.

VARIATION

New York Cheesecake

For a denser, more traditional New York cheesecake, do not separate the eggs and beat in whole eggs instead of egg yolks.

Scalding Milk?

Do you scald milk (heating milk or cream to just below the boiling point) when making, let's say, a béchamel? Well, it turns out that you don't have to. The theory is that unpasteurized milk (the type that French cooks used when béchamel was invented) has enzymes in it that inhibit thickening. These enzymes are destroyed during pasteurization; in fact, the sign of successful pasteurization is the absence of enzymes. (Pasteurization is nothing more than heating to a specific temperature, usually 161 degrees, for a minimum of 15 seconds. *Ultra-pasteurized* means that the milk or cream has been heated to 280 degrees for at least 2 seconds. I should also note that milk is homogenized as well as pasteurized, a process that breaks down the fat globules, which, in theory, might also affect thickening.)

I had been spouting this enzyme theory for years, until quite recently when I borrowed a cup of raw milk from my Vermont neighbor. I made a medium béchamel (2 tablespoons butter, 2 tablespoons flour, and 1 cup milk) using cold, raw milk, and guess what? It thickened just fine, thank you very much. I did note, however, that the milk was briefly heated to over the 161-degree mark, so there were no active enzymes left in it anyway.

Then I got to thinking about this enzyme theory. After all, the flour in the béchamel can thicken just about anything, including water, so I seriously doubt that these enzymes could in fact prevent thickening (as I proved in my experiment). So why do many recipes still suggest that one scald milk before making a sauce? (The only viable reason I can suggest is that this step pasteurized the milk, thus destroying any bacteria. It may have been done simply as a food safety measure.) It doesn't really save much time. In fact, it is an added step. So, forget about the enzymes and forget about scalding. Flour will thicken anything.

The Problem with Ricotta Cheesecake

For some cookbook authors, ricotta cheesecake is nothing more than a New York–style cheesecake with the addition of ricotta and a few standard flavorings such as pine nuts, orange zest, and rum-soaked raisins. In my opinion, however, a really good ricotta cheesecake allows the unique texture of the ricotta to shine through by not drowning it in a cream-laden, custardy bath, as is often the case. With other recipes, the texture suffers, becoming dry and granular. In other words, the problem with ricotta cheesecake is the ricotta. ▶◀

I started with a few guidelines. I wanted to use an 8-inch springform pan (some recipes use odd sizes such as 6-inch pans), and I wanted to keep the recipe as simple as possible. I made four recipes to start, one each from Lidia Bastianich, Nick Malgieri, Carol Field, and the new *Joy of Cooking*. The differences were remarkable. Carol Field uses heavy cream and sour cream in addition to the ricotta, the *Joy* uses almost double the sugar plus chocolate chips, and there was no consensus about the number of eggs and whether or not the whites should be beaten separately.

The first issue to resolve was that of the eggs. Using 1½ pounds of ricotta, I found that five eggs produced a custardy cake, three eggs produced something akin to a cannoli filling, but four eggs was just right. I tried separating them and whipping the whites, but the resulting texture was on the dry side. However, when I separated only two of the eggs, I found the texture to be preferable. It was slightly drier and less "wet," an unpleasant feature of many ricotta cheesecakes.

Next, I tried adding 4 ounces cream cheese to the mixture; I found that the cake was pleasantly creamy. (The cream cheese has to be beaten with the sugar, not just added to the egg mixture, to properly blend it with the batter.) However, the addition of sour cream was unwelcome due to the added tang, and both sour cream and heavy cream resulted in a texture that was too wet.

I then sorted through all of the flavoring ingredients. Chocolate chips were revolting, cinnamon was overpowering, and pine nuts and raisins complicated the recipe without improving it. Orange zest, lemon zest, dark rum, and vanilla were a nice combination.

For baking times, I started with 375 degrees, which was a disaster: The center was puffy and cracked. At 350 degrees, the cheesecake was good but a bit on the wet side. I then tried a hot-water bath, which took forever and also produced a damp slice of cake. Finally, I started the oven at 375 degrees and then finished at 325 degrees, adding an extra 10 minutes or so in the oven for a drier texture, which I preferred.

Ricotta Cheesecake with Lemon, Orange, and Rum

SERVES 8

I like a relatively dry ricotta cheesecake, and that is why I suggest a relatively long baking time. If you prefer a moister, wetter slice of cheesecake, bake the cake a total of 55 to 60 minutes. With the longer baking time, the top of the cake will crack, which I do not find objectionable. Be sure to make this cheesecake well ahead of time, as it does require 4 hours of chilling before serving. This cheesecake is best served the day it is made.

	Softened unsalted butter for the pan
	Flour for the pan
4	large eggs, at room temperature
4	ounces cream cheese, at room temperature
½	cup plus 3 tablespoons sugar
	Finely grated zest of 1 lemon
	Finely grated zest of 1 orange
1	tablespoon dark rum
1	teaspoon vanilla extract
	Pinch table salt
1½	pounds whole-milk ricotta cheese

1. Adjust an oven rack to the center position and heat the oven to 375 degrees. Butter and flour the bottom and sides of an 8-inch springform pan. Separate 2 of the eggs. Beat the cream cheese in the bowl of an electric mixer on medium speed until smooth, about 1 minute. Gradually add ½ cup plus 1 tablespoon of the sugar and beat on medium for 2 minutes more. Add the 2 whole eggs and the 2 yolks, one at a time, and beat until each is just incorporated, scraping the sides of the bowl after each addition to avoid lumps. Add the zests, rum, vanilla, and salt and beat until incorporated. Add the ricotta and beat on low until fully mixed into a homogenous batter.

2. Beat the 2 reserved egg whites in a clean bowl on high speed for 20 seconds. Gradually add the remaining 2 tablespoons sugar and beat until the whites just hold a 2-inch peak. Fold the beaten whites into the batter.

3. Pour the batter into the prepared pan and bake for 25 minutes. Lower the oven to 325 degrees and bake for 40 minutes more or until the cake is lightly brown on top and just set in the middle. (See note at left for more information.) Remove the pan from the oven and set on a rack to cool to room temperature. Cover and refrigerate for about 4 hours or until chilled and firm. To serve, run a thin knife around the inside of the pan and remove the outer ring. Run the knife under hot water before cutting individual slices.

The Mystery of Sponge Cake

For many home bakers, sponge cake is no longer a simple
workhorse recipe. The reason? Many cookbooks direct
them to make sponge cake using the French génoise method,
which is finicky and prone to disaster. For a génoise,
whole eggs are beaten with sugar and then flour is very
gently folded in. This folding process can be trying —
especially for an inexperienced baker — because the delicate foam often collapses, and the result is a squat,
lackluster cake. I wanted to develop a better, more foolproof recipe. ▶◀

My first thought was to use a more American approach, one used for chiffon cake,
in which some or all of the eggs are separated and then beaten independently. Egg
whites, especially when beaten with sugar, are relatively sturdy and less prone to
deflating than a whole egg foam. By folding the egg white foam into the egg yolk
foam, I would be making the batter more stable.

I began my search for a light cake, one with a springy but delicate texture, not dry
or tough, one that would stand up nicely to a rich lemon custard filling. My working
recipe called for ¾ cup cake flour, ¾ cup sugar, and five eggs. I started by separating
out all five of the whites and found that the cake was too light, with insufficient structure. When I substituted all-purpose flour for the cake flour, the cake had more body,
but it was also a bit tougher. Next I tried different ratios of the two flours, finally settling on 2 parts cake flour to 1 part all-purpose.

Two other ingredients added fat and flavor: 4 tablespoons of melted butter and
2 tablespoons of milk. I thought that baking powder might be optional, but it turned
out to be essential; given my additions of butter and milk, the cake needed a boost
from baking powder to rise properly. By adding cream of tartar to the egg whites during beating, the cake became more tender and more evenly textured; it also had better
structure. The reason for these improvements? Cream of tartar is an acid, which
improves the performance of egg whites during whipping and baking. (See page 206
for more details on this phenomenon.)

I also played with the order of the steps. Beating the whole egg foam first and then the whites gave the relatively fragile foam time to deteriorate, producing a cake with less rise. I found that beating the whites first was vastly better. After much experimentation, I also found it best to mix together on low speed, all at the same time, the beaten egg yolks, the beaten whites, and the flour; once this mixture was about half-mixed, I added the warm butter and milk and finished folding with a rubber spatula.

I tested three baking temperatures—325, 350, and 375 degrees—and 350 degrees was the winner. I also discovered that this recipe could be made successfully in two 8-inch pans or two 9-inch pans. Determining when a sponge cake is properly cooked is a little more difficult than with a regular American layer cake. A sponge cake should show some resistance; however, it should not feel like the top of a soufflé. Another good test is color. The top of the cake should be a nice light brown, not pale gold, nor should it be a rich, dark brown.

Foolproof Sponge Cake with Rich Lemon Filling

SERVES 8

If you like, simply bake the sponge cake and fill it with jam such as blackberry and top with a sifted sprinkling of confectioners' sugar.

Softened unsalted butter for the pans
½ cup cake flour
¼ cup all-purpose flour
1 teaspoon baking powder
¼ teaspoon table salt
2 tablespoons milk
4 tablespoons unsalted butter
½ teaspoon vanilla extract
5 large eggs, at room temperature
¾ cup sugar
¼ teaspoon cream of tartar
1 recipe Rich Lemon Filling (see page 272)
Confectioners' sugar for dusting the cake

1. Adjust an oven rack to the lower-middle position and heat the oven to 350 degrees. Grease two 8- or 9-inch cake pans and cover pan bottoms with rounds of parchment paper. Whisk the flours, baking powder, and salt together in a medium bowl. Heat the milk and butter in a small saucepan over low heat until the butter melts. Off heat, add the vanilla; cover and keep warm.

2. Separate the eggs, placing the whites in the bowl of a standing mixer fitted with the whisk attachment (or a large mixing bowl if using a hand mixer or whisk) and reserving the yolks in another mixing bowl. Beat the whites on high speed until foamy. Gradually add 6 tablespoons of the sugar and the cream of tartar and continue to beat the whites to soft, moist peaks. If using a standing mixer, transfer the beaten egg whites to a large bowl and add the egg yolks to the standing mixer bowl (don't clean the bowl).

3. Beat the egg yolks with the remaining 6 tablespoons sugar on medium-high speed until the mixture is very thick and a pale lemon color, about 5 minutes. Add the beaten egg whites to the yolks, but do not mix.

4. Sprinkle the flour mixture over the egg whites and mix on low speed for 10 seconds. Remove the bowl from the mixer, make a well in one side of the batter and pour the melted butter mixture into the bowl. Fold gently with a large rubber spatula until the batter shows no trace of flour and the whites and yolks are evenly mixed, about 8 strokes.

5. Immediately pour the batter into the prepared pans. Bake until the cake tops are light brown and feel firm and spring back when touched, about 16 to 18 minutes for 9-inch cake pans and 20 to 22 minutes for 8-inch cake pans.

6. Cool completely on racks. Run a thin knife around the inside of the cake pans and then invert them onto the racks (or onto cardboard rounds or tart pan bottoms) to release the cakes from the pans. Remove the parchment paper.

7. Place one cake layer on a serving plate. Carefully spoon the filling over the layer and spread evenly to the cake edge. Place the second cake layer on top, making sure the layers line up properly. Dust the cake with confectioners' sugar and serve.

Rich Lemon Filling

MAKES ENOUGH TO FILL
AN 8- OR 9-INCH LAYER CAKE

I also use this filling for lemon meringue pie.

1	cup sugar
¼	cup cornstarch
⅛	teaspoon table salt
1⅜	cups cold water
4	large egg yolks
2	teaspoons grated zest from 1 lemon
½	cup juice from 2 lemons
2	tablespoons unsalted butter

Bring the sugar, cornstarch, salt, and water to a simmer in a large nonreactive saucepan over medium heat, whisking occasionally at the beginning of the process and more frequently as the mixture begins to thicken. When the mixture starts to simmer and turn translucent, whisk in the egg yolks, two at a time. Whisk in the zest, then the lemon juice, and, finally, the butter. Bring the mixture to a good simmer, whisking constantly. Remove the pan from the heat. Transfer the filling to another container to cool to room temperature, placing plastic wrap directly on the surface of the filling to prevent a skin from forming. The filling will thicken as it cools. To ensure that the filling does not thin out, do not stir it once it has set. (The filling can be refrigerated overnight.)

The $250 Chocolate Chip Cookie

America is chock-full of legends, rumors with lost begin-
nings that become part of the cultural landscape. Perhaps
the most intriguing food legend, other than the rumor
of spider eggs in bubble gum back in the 1970s, is the
$250 Neiman-Marcus cookie. Years ago, I had heard that
a customer had been charged $250 for the recipe for
Neiman-Marcus's chocolate chip cookie — not $2.50 as
she had assumed when requesting it — and was so furious
that she published the recipe on the Internet as a form
of revenge. I had not paid this rumor much attention until
my sister, Kate, an Internet maven, found the recipe and
the alleged story and forwarded it to me. Although it was
an unusual recipe, due to the use of oats, I made a batch
and fell in love with the cookies. They were thick and
chewy with plenty of chocolate taste. ▶◀

However, that was just the beginning. I felt that the original recipe was on the dry
side and also too sweet. I reduced the amounts of white and brown sugar and also cut
back on the amount of oats to 1½ cups. This made a better cookie, but I also increased
the salt level to boost overall flavor. Many cookie recipes call for both baking powder
and baking soda. In this case, I found that eliminating the baking soda entirely and
using only powder produced a good cookie. But it never browned sufficiently, so I added
back in ¼ teaspoon baking soda. (Baking soda promotes browning.)

The most interesting aspect of this recipe, in addition to the use of oats, is that it
uses both grated chocolate and regular chocolate chips. This delivers a lot of extra
chocolate punch. In terms of selecting chips, I recently participated in a chocolate chip
tasting, and my first choice was Guittard, which comes in large chunks, followed by
Ghirardelli, which was also good. Both have a clean, straightforward chocolate taste,
unlike most other brands, which abound with off flavors ranging from medicinal
(Hershey's) to highly perfumed (Nestlé) to dry and chalky (Baker's). Other chips were
too sweet or grainy or contained a strong note of imitation vanilla. I also taste-tested

the chips baked in a cookie and found, much to my surprise, that the chips made a big difference. For the most part, I could tell which chips were used in which cookie, and the differences were significant.

Note that this is a very stiff batter and hard to mix. I also find that, as with almost all cookies, these should be removed from the oven when they look undercooked and are still quite soft. They will harden as they cool.

Chocolate Chip Cookies with Oats, Pecans, and Grated Chocolate

MAKES 30 TO 36 LARGE COOKIES

To soften cold butter, you can use a microwave (see page 276) or, if you plan ahead, let it sit on the counter for about 1 hour. This recipe calls for both chocolate chips and grated semi-sweet chocolate. The easiest method of grating chocolate is to use a heavy-duty food processor fitted with the metal blade. I do not suggest that you use 2 baking sheets at one time, as this makes it difficult to achieve even cooking.

1½	cups rolled oats
2	cups all-purpose flour
1	teaspoon baking powder
¼	teaspoon baking soda
¾	teaspoon salt
16	tablespoons (2 sticks) unsalted butter, softened but still firm
¾	cup granulated sugar
¾	cup packed light brown sugar
2	large eggs, at room temperature
1	teaspoon vanilla extract
12	ounces chocolate chips
4	ounces grated or finely chopped semisweet chocolate
1½	cups chopped pecans or walnuts

1. Adjust an oven rack to the middle position and heat the oven to 350 degrees. Place the oats in a food processor and process until very fine. Add the flour, baking powder, baking soda, and salt and pulse 4 to 5 times until combined.
2. With an electric mixer (use the paddle attachment if you have one), beat the butter and both sugars until light, about 3 minutes. Add the eggs, one at a time, and beat 20 seconds after each addition. Add the vanilla and beat for 15 seconds to blend.
3. Add the dry ingredients to the butter-sugar mixture and beat on low speed until well mixed. Add the chocolate chips, grated chocolate, and nuts and mix on low speed until blended. (You can also mix by hand with a large, stiff rubber spatula if you do not have a standing mixer.)
4. Lay a sheet of parchment paper on a baking sheet; this is helpful for whisking the cookies off the sheet after they are baked. Form the dough into balls about 2 inches in diameter and place them 1 inch apart on the prepared baking sheet. (You will have dough left over.) Bake 7 minutes and then turn the baking sheet around in the oven. Bake an additional 7 to 9 minutes or until the cookies are puffy,

CHOCOLATE CHIP TASTE TEST

GUITTARD
Great flavor.
My first choice comes in large chunks.

GHIRARDELLI
A clean, straightforward flavor.
My second choice.

BAKER'S
Dry and chalky.

HERSHEY'S
An unpleasant medicinal flavor.

NESTLÉ
Highly perfumed, with off flavors.

soft, cracked on top, and light brown around the edges. (They will not spread very much and will look very undercooked. *Do not overcook or they will become hard and dry when they cool.*) Remove the baking sheet from the oven and let the cookies cool for 2 minutes on the baking sheet before transferring them to a cooling rack. Repeat with the remaining batter, using a second, room-temperature cookie sheet (not the hot one). Cool at least 30 minutes before serving.

Two Essential Microwave Shortcuts

We can argue about the usefulness of a microwave oven when it comes to actually cooking food, but we can't argue about its usefulness when it comes to recipe preparation shortcuts. It does two things really well, so well that it probably justifies its existence.

Softening Butter for Creaming
Butter needs to be pliable but still firm for creaming. (The temperature should be about 65 degrees.) Cold butter from the refrigerator can take well over an hour to come up to the proper temperature for creaming, so the microwave is a huge time-saver. Simply remove the wrapper and place the butter on a microwave-safe plate or bowl. Zap at 10 percent power for two minutes. Check the butter. If still too cold, heat for another minute at 10 percent (and so on) until it is ready. You can use this same technique for softening butter for the table. Just cook it longer (but always at 10 percent power).

Melting Chocolate
A double boiler is not necessary for melting chocolate. Simply zap the chocolate at 50 percent power for two minutes. Check it by stirring. (The chocolate won't look different— it will retain its shape even if very soft.) Continue cooking for one-minute intervals at 50 percent power until melted. This usually takes a total of three to four minutes. If you are also melting butter at the same time (many recipes call for this), add the butter after the first minute of cooking time.

Sugar Cookies Perfected

A sugar cookie stores well, is relatively easy to make, and is a clean slate onto which many different designs may be written. But, like all cookies, looks are deceiving. The right texture, the right flavor, and just the right icing are difficult to achieve, because even small changes in the ingredient list can yield large differences in results. ▶◀

I had already developed a sugar cookie recipe for *The Dessert Bible,* so that is where I started. I also looked to a recipe for sugar cookies in a recent issue of *Cook's Illustrated* for comparison. The two recipes were almost identical, except that the *Cook's* recipe used less flour in proportion to the butter. Testing the two cookies head to head, I agreed with the *Cook's* version and therefore upped the butter quantity to three sticks for about three cups of all-purpose flour. I tested adding milk, sour cream, and cream cheese; in all three cases the cookies had a weird aftertaste. Sugar cookies are pure and plain, and any foreign substance can be detected.

As far as the sugar goes, my version was a bit less sweet than other recipes, so I decided to increase the sugar just a bit. Taking a cue from a suggestion I had made to the *Cook's* staff during testing, I added 2 tablespoons brown sugar. (Since I was going to ice these cookies, I didn't want them too sweet, however.) I went back to the 3 cups flour and reduced it by 2 tablespoons to produce slightly crispier cookies.

I tested the ½ teaspoon baking powder, the one egg, the salt, and the vanilla and left the quantities the same, as they were right on. As for baking temperature, 375 degrees was indeed the correct temperature, as I had determined when testing my original recipe. The cookies baked until they were just starting to brown around the edges, about eight minutes. The flavor of the cookies was well balanced, with the butter, sugar, and vanilla at the fore. The texture was crisp with a hint of a chew.

I made these cookies using three methods: the traditional roll-and-cut, the drop, and the slice-and-bake. Originally, I thought the drop would be the easiest method. However, the cookies needed to be pressed in order to produce a thin uniform cookie and not a humped ball. This required a flat drinking glass to be pressed onto each cookie. This also left some of the cookies with jagged edges. I was able to produce neat-looking cookies with the slice-and-bake method. I formed the batter

ROTATE THOSE COOKIE SHEETS

UNEVENLY BAKED COOKIES

Most ovens heat unevenly, causing some cookies to bake
faster than others. As a result, some cookies brown (or even burn),
while others are perfectly cooked.

EVENLY BAKED COOKIES

Rotating the cookie sheet halfway through the baking
time compensates for uneven heating in your oven and ensures
that all the cookies are done at the same time.

into two 1½-inch logs using waxed paper. Once firm, the logs can be cut into ¼-inch slices. The recipe yields about seventy-five 2-inch cookies, which keep very well for several days.

The icing was the last problem to be solved. For this type of icing, the base ingredient is confectioners' sugar. It can be mixed with egg white (for royal icing), milk, buttermilk, water, or juice. Additional flavor may be added with citrus zest, extracts, booze, or wine. I tried every imaginable combination of the above but without a lot of success. The secret ingredient turned out to be cream cheese, which gives depth to the flavor and counteracts the slightly bitter taste of the confectioners' sugar. So, the icing recipe started with 2½ cups confectioners' sugar to which I added 5 tablespoons buttermilk and 1 tablespoon cream cheese. Once all of the ingredients were placed into a medium bowl, the icing needed to be whisked vigorously until smooth. An electric mixer made the icing too bubbly. The icing can be used as is or colored or sprinkled with holiday decorations. It may be flavored with vanilla extract or orange or lime zest.

Really Good Sugar Cookies

MAKES ABOUT 75 COOKIES

You will find that these cookies are a bit softer and slightly chewier than the usual brittle sugar cookies made around the holidays. I do not suggest using 2 cookie sheets in the oven at one time — it is likely that the cookies will not bake evenly. For more festive cookies, the icing may be colored and/or sprinkled with colored sugar or decorations.

FOR THE COOKIES

2⅞	cups all-purpose flour (3 cups minus 2 tablespoons)
½	teaspoon table salt
½	teaspoon baking powder
24	tablespoons (3 sticks) unsalted butter, softened but still firm
1	cup granulated sugar
2	tablespoons light brown sugar
1	large egg
2	teaspoons vanilla extract

FOR THE ICING

2½	cups confectioners' sugar
5	tablespoons buttermilk
1	tablespoon cream cheese, at room temperature
½	teaspoon vanilla extract, optional

1. For the cookies: Whisk together the flour, salt, and baking powder in a medium bowl. In a standing mixer fitted with the paddle attachment or using a hand mixer, beat the butter and sugars at medium speed until light and fluffy, about 3 minutes, scraping down the sides of the bowl as needed. Add the egg and vanilla and beat until combined, about 30 seconds. Add the dry ingredients and beat until just combined. Finish mixing with a rubber spatula to be sure the ingredients are well combined. Scrape half of the dough onto a sheet of waxed (or regular parchment) paper. Form the dough into a cigar about 1½ inches wide and 12 inches long using a spatula or dampened hands. Roll the paper around the cigar and then roll the wrapped cigar back and forth on a flat surface using very little pressure to help even out the shape. Repeat using the other half of the dough and another sheet of waxed paper. Chill until very firm, about 3 hours or up to 2 days.

2. Adjust an oven rack to the center position and heat the oven to 375 degrees. Line 2 cookie sheets with parchment paper. Remove one piece of dough from the refrigerator. Cut into ¼-inch slices and place 1 inch apart on one of the prepared cookie sheets. Bake the cookies until lightly browned around the edges, 8 to 10 minutes, rotating the cookie sheet 180 degrees halfway through baking. Cool on a rack for 5 minutes. Remove the cookies using a spatula and cool completely on a wire rack. Continue until all of the remaining dough is used, being sure to place the dough slices on a completely cool cookie sheet. (Use the second cookie sheet for the second batch; the first cookie sheet will be cooled by the time you are ready to make a third batch.)

3. For the icing: Combine the confectioners' sugar, buttermilk, cream cheese, and optional vanilla extract in a medium bowl. Whisk vigorously until completely smooth. Frost the cookies using a small icing spatula or a butter knife. Let them sit until the icing is set and then store them in an airtight container, where the cookies will keep for several days.

VARIATION
Orange or Lime Icing
Omit the vanilla in the icing and add 1 tablespoon finely minced orange or lime zest.

Investigating Polenta Pound Cake

Pound cake itself seems simple enough, but the basis of most recipes is creamed butter, and this process involves some precision. In addition, pound cake can turn out dry, greasy, or heavy because of small mistakes in preparation or recipe choice. To make matters worse, the addition of cornmeal or polenta (coarsely ground cornmeal) complicates the recipe, because using the wrong grind changes the outcome, usually not for the better. I was looking for a simple, foolproof recipe that would yield a tender pound cake with just the right amount of cornmeal texture and flavor. ▶◀

After a great deal of testing, I came up with two conclusions: I would use cake flour for a tender texture and baking powder to provide some lift. I was still stuck creaming the butter, until I decided to test melting it instead and then adding it to the other ingredients. To my surprise, this cake turned out better—less greasy and just as light! (At *Cook's Illustrated,* we had recently discovered the same phenomenon when making plain yellow cupcakes.) I was using polenta, not a fine-grain cornmeal, but, even so, the end result was on the heavy side. I went back and tried Quaker cornmeal (which is exceedingly fine-grained), but the cake wasn't much better. I even tried putting the polenta into a food processor to make it finer, but that had little impact as well. This recipe needed more work.

After testing just about every ingredient, I finally decided that perhaps the ratio of flour to butter should be radically increased. (I was using 1 cup cake flour at this point to two sticks of butter.) After much testing, I increased the flour to 1½ cups and cut the butter down to 14 tablespoons. Now I had a much less greasy product, one that was fine-grained as well. The next step was to revisit the polenta.

My original recipe called for ½ cup polenta to 1 cup cake flour. It turned out that the ½ cup polenta was right, even when the cake flour was increased. Now the question was what type of cornmeal to use. Real coarse-grain polenta was too heavy for this fine cake. Instant polenta, however, worked well, as did a typical fine-grain cornmeal. In my tests, Quaker did not have a lot of flavor, so I recommend using another brand.

Polenta Pound Cake

SERVES 8

Note that the batter will look very yellow and greasy when it is poured into the loaf pan. After baking, however, it will appear fine-grained and not greasy at all. This is a very simple recipe, because the butter is melted, not creamed, and the ingredients require very little beating.

	Softened unsalted butter for the pan
	Flour for the pan
1½	cups cake flour
½	cup instant polenta or fine-grain cornmeal
1	teaspoon baking powder
½	teaspoon table salt
1¼	cups sugar
5	large eggs
	Finely grated zest from 1 lemon
14	tablespoons (1¾ sticks) unsalted butter, melted and cooled slightly
1½	teaspoons vanilla extract

1. Adjust an oven rack to the center position and heat the oven to 325 degrees. Grease a 9-by-5-inch loaf pan with butter. Dust with flour, tapping out the excess.

2. Sift the flour, polenta, baking powder, and salt onto a piece of parchment or waxed paper.

3. Place the sugar, eggs, and lemon zest in the bowl of an electric mixer. Beat on medium until well combined, about 30 seconds. Add the melted butter and the vanilla and beat on medium-low until combined, about 10 seconds; increase the speed to medium and mix an additional 10 seconds. Decrease the speed to low and add the dry ingredients to the egg-sugar-butter mixture in 3 batches. Transfer the batter to the prepared pan.

4. Bake until golden brown and a skewer inserted into the center of the cake comes out clean, about 60 minutes, rotating the pan halfway through baking. Cool the cake in the pan for 10 minutes on a wire rack; invert the cake onto the rack and turn the cake upright. Serve slightly warm or at room temperature.

VARIATION
Almond Pound Cake

Omit the lemon zest, reduce the vanilla extract to 1 teaspoon, and add ¼ teaspoon pure almond extract along with the vanilla.

The $80 Cake Pan

One of the most surprising equipment-testing results at *Cook's Illustrated* was when an Ekco cake pan, priced at $3.99, performed as well as the expensive All-Clad, which will set you back $80. Not only did it perform as well, but we actually preferred it (slightly), because the cake rose a bit higher in the cheaper pan.

Now, that doesn't mean that the Ekco will hold up over time as well as the All-Clad, which is five-ply—made of three layers of aluminum and two of stainless steel. (The Ekco is made from one layer of tinned steel.) The All-Clad pan is clearly a superior product in terms of quality of manufacture. But does all this extra money produce superior cakes? No.

We have found similar anomalies when testing cookie sheets, chef's knives, loaf pans, etc. More money doesn't necessarily purchase a better product. True, a heavy-duty saucepan and a large skillet are good investments, even when that skillet sets you back more than $100. But, very often, a more expensive piece of cookware isn't better, it just costs more.

So, where should you spend your money? The four most important items are a 3-quart saucepan, a 12-inch skillet, a 9- or 10-inch nonstick skillet, and an 8-inch chef's knife. All-Clad makes the best saucepans and regular skillets, either Calphalon or All-Clad is fine for the nonstick skillet, and Wüsthof Grand Prix is the best knife on the market that I have tested (about $80), though the Forschner Victorinox, at about $40, is worth a serious look. In general, cheap bakeware is fine, a large stockpot (which is used to boil water) can be an inexpensive $25 model, and a cast-iron Dutch oven is a bargain at $40 or so.

The sturdy and attractive cake pan on the left costs $80 and delivered good results in my tests. The $4 cake pan on the right may not be quite as snazzy, but it performed just as well (if not slightly better) in kitchen tests.

A Simple Chocolate Cake

I was looking for a one-layer chocolate cake that was
rich enough to be served on its own with perhaps a dollop
of whipped cream. I didn't want to have to frost it or
soak it in sugar syrup, and, most of all, I didn't want
two layers. I was searching for a luxurious chocolate
taste and texture but well short of the damp, thick,
over-the-top flourless chocolate cakes that I find hard
to stomach. ▶◀

I started with a recipe that I had developed for *The Dessert Bible* that was an "almost fallen" chocolate cake. First of all, a real "fallen" chocolate cake is that ubiquitous dessert found at thousands of restaurants that is basically an undercooked chocolate cake, often served in a ramekin or small bowl. Chocolate tends to lose its flavor the more it is cooked, and therefore an undercooked chocolate cake has a lot of flavor. The problem with this type of dessert is that it has little structure, has to be served warm, and tends to be quite gooey in the middle. My "almost fallen" chocolate cake recipe was a big step in the right direction, but it still falls during cooling and the center is very soft and hard to manage. I wanted something a bit more cake-like without losing the great flavor and texture.

The basic recipe calls for a stick of butter melted with 8 ounces semisweet chocolate, ¼ cup flour, 6 whole eggs, ½ cup sugar, 1 teaspoon vanilla, and ¾ teaspoon salt. The eggs and sugar are beaten for 5 minutes, the flour and salt are folded in, the butter-chocolate mixture is folded in along with the vanilla, and then the mixture is baked in a springform pan. Simple enough. But I still wanted a bit more structure, so I increased the flour to ½ cup. This created a higher, more cake-like dessert, but it needed a bit more chocolate flavor, so I upped the chocolate to 10 ounces. Voilà! Now I had a cake that fell very little during cooling and had a light, chocolate-cake texture around the perimeter with a rich, thick chocolate texture in the center. This cake does not have to be served warm out of the oven, although it is at its peak about 20 minutes after baking. Best of all, it is rich enough to be served on its own without frosting and yet has the structure and feel of a real chocolate cake, not a warm pudding.

Simple Chocolate Cake

SERVES 8

The center of this cake will appear cracked and mottled when it is done, not smooth and high-rise like a regular chocolate cake. This is due to the low proportion of flour to butter and chocolate. Remove it from the oven when the center is just set (it doesn't shimmy and shake). Just shake the pan a bit from side to side to gauge whether the center is set. Don't press down on the center as you would with a regular cake to see if it bounces back. The cake will continue to set up out of the oven. Note that the center of the cake will be very rich and creamy, whereas the perimeter will be more cake-like.

    Softened unsalted butter for the pan
    Flour for the pan
 8 tablespoons (1 stick) unsalted
    butter
 ½ cup all-purpose flour
 10 ounces semisweet chocolate, chopped
    into small pieces
 6 large eggs, at room temperature
 ½ cup sugar
 1 teaspoon vanilla extract
 ¾ teaspoon table salt
    Confectioners' sugar for dusting the
    cake, optional
    Whipped cream or vanilla ice cream
    for serving, optional

1. Adjust an oven rack to the center position and heat the oven to 350 degrees. Butter and flour (or dust with cocoa) an 8- or 9-inch springform pan.

2. Heat 8 tablespoons butter and the chocolate together in a heavy-bottomed saucepan over very low heat until the chocolate is just about melted. (This can be done in a microwave oven: Heat the chocolate for 2 minutes at 50 percent power. Add the butter and heat another 2 minutes or so at 50 percent until melted. Stir every minute.) Set aside to cool almost to room temperature.

3. Beat the eggs, slowly adding the sugar, until very light and thick, about 5 minutes with the paddle attachment of a standing mixer or about 12 minutes with a hand mixer or whisk. (The eggs should be the texture of underwhipped cream. The mixture should mound when drizzled back onto itself. Do not underbeat this mixture; give it the time it needs.) While the eggs are beating, add the vanilla to the chocolate-butter mixture and stir until smooth. When the egg mixture is ready, fold about 1 cup of it into the melted chocolate. Sift the flour and salt onto the remaining egg-sugar mixture and fold it in. (If using a standing mixer, sift the flour onto the egg mixture and mix at low speed for 10 seconds. Add the chocolate and also mix on low for 10 seconds. Then fold the mixture together with a rubber spatula.) Add the lightened chocolate mixture to the bowl with the egg-sugar mixture and fold until fully incorporated. Pour the batter into the prepared pan. (The batter will now be about half the volume it was at the outset and will fill about two-thirds of a 2½-inch-high springform pan.)

4. Bake 30 to 35 minutes for the 8-inch pan or 25 to 30 minutes for the 9-inch size. (Baking times will vary depending on the calibration of your oven.) The cake should be just set in the center (jiggle the pan back and forth to check). Don't press on the top of the cake to judge whether it is done. Let cool for 10 minutes. Run a thin knife around the edge of the pan and release the sides.

5. Dust with confectioners' sugar and serve with whipped cream or vanilla ice cream, if desired. This cake is best served warm but can also be served at room temperature.

Who Needs a Double Boiler?

I haven't used a double boiler in 20 years. Why? Because a microwave does a terrific job of melting things such as chocolate, and given the high-quality cookware available today, I can gently cook or melt foods on top of the stove in a heavy-duty saucepan over very low heat. When purchasing a stovetop, by the way, always ask how low it goes. You want less than 1,000 BTUs (British thermal units) on simmer; an output number under 500 is best. That way, you can gently heat foods without the risk of burning or overcooking.

Let's take a few examples: One Viking range has a maximum BTU output of 14,000 yet gets no lower than 900 for simmering. (It also costs $1,750.) A Wolf model that costs about $2,500 has a maximum output of 16,000 yet gets down to a low of 500. A Frigidaire model (a bargain at $600) goes up to 13,000 and down to 500. I have found that getting the "simmer" BTU outputs is sometimes difficult, because manufacturers seem more focused on the maximums, but be persistent. An expensive stovetop with a high simmer is no bargain.

The Secret of Lighter Linzertorte

Traditional linzertortes are relatively dense single-layer tortes made from sugar, eggs, flour, and nuts and filled with jam. (Torte is a term usually reserved for a cake made mostly with nuts, eggs, and little flour.) They are not hard to make, but many recipes turn out leaden desserts with dense, floury crusts. I wanted three things from a linzertorte: a relatively light crust, the strong taste of nuts, and just the right pairing of nuts to jam for perfect balance. ▶◀

As usual, I started by making a half dozen or so recipes to find out what I liked. The first recipe used a food processor to cut the butter into the flour, after which the rest of the ingredients were added in a large bowl. The dough was then kneaded using a smearing method common to many old-fashioned pastry recipes. For the second recipe, I did all of the mixing in the food processor with no kneading. The third recipe creamed the butter and sugar, much like a cookie recipe. From these three tests, I concluded that the cookie method was inappropriate, as the baked torte was crumbly and fell apart easily. I liked using a food processor, because it simplified the process considerably. The first recipe, which required "smearing," was a bit heavy, yet the all-in-the-processor recipe also had problems—the crust was a bit too smooth and floury.

I made a few more recipes, unsuccessfully, and then ran across a recipe that called for an unusual ingredient: hard-cooked egg yolks added to the dough. To my great surprise, this worked well, producing a lighter crust. (My scientist friends have yet to come up with a satisfactory explanation for this phenomenon.) Now that I had a good working recipe, I decided that a combination of hazelnuts and almonds would be best, and I did all of the processing in the bowl of the food processor. I then wrapped the dough in plastic, froze it for 15 minutes (to make rolling easier), rolled it out, fit it into a springform pan, and then baked the unfilled crust for 15 minutes on the lower rack of the oven. I then removed the torte, sprinkled it with ground almonds, filled it with raspberry jam, added a lattice cover, and then finished cooking it in a 350-degree oven for almost an hour. The torte was gorgeous, like something out of a fancy food magazine, and also tasted great. The texture was light, moist, and not at all floury. Finally, the perfect, easy-to-make linzertorte.

Light Linzertorte

MAKES ONE 9-INCH TORTE,
WHICH EASILY SERVES 8

*The beauty of this recipe is that even a
ham-handed baker can turn out a beautiful-
looking dessert, as the soft dough melts during baking and conceals any rough spots.
If you are familiar with other linzertorte
recipes, you will find that this one has a more
tender crust. (Many linzertortes tend to be
a bit tough and dry.) The easiest method for
chopping the nuts is to use a food processor.
I have also made this recipe with walnuts
instead of hazelnuts with good results.*

1½	cups all-purpose flour
½	teaspoon ground cinnamon
1	teaspoon grated lemon zest
2	hard-cooked egg yolks, mashed until crumbly
16	tablespoons (2 sticks) cold unsalted butter, cut into pieces
½	cup sugar
2	raw egg yolks, lightly beaten
1	teaspoon vanilla extract
1	cup plus 2 tablespoons coarsely chopped toasted hazelnuts
¼	cup plus 2 tablespoons coarsely chopped almonds
2	tablespoons very finely ground almonds or dry bread crumbs
1	cup thick raspberry or currant jam (or a mixture of the 2)
1	egg, lightly beaten
1	tablespoon cream
½	cup slivered almonds, optional
	Confectioners' sugar, optional

1. Adjust the oven racks to the upper-
middle and the lower-middle positions
and heat the oven to 400 degrees.

2. In a large food processor bowl, pulse
together the flour, cinnamon, lemon
zest, and hard-cooked egg yolks. Add the
butter and sugar and pulse about 6 times
or until the butter is in small, pea-size
pieces. Add the raw yolks, vanilla, 1 cup
of the hazelnuts, and ¼ cup of the
chopped almonds to the bowl and pulse
until well blended. Add the remaining
2 tablespoons each hazelnuts and almonds
and process steadily until the mixture
forms a ball. Wrap the dough in plastic,
pat into a disk, and freeze for 15 minutes
or until the dough is firm but not hard.

3. Break off about ⅓ of the dough, shape
it into a ball, and roll it between sheets
of plastic wrap to make an 8-inch circle.
Place on a cookie sheet and chill. Using
your fingers, press the remaining dough
to cover the bottom and 1 inch up the
sides of a 9-inch springform pan. (Use the
bottom of a drinking glass to press the
dough into place.) Bake on the bottom
oven rack until the dough is lightly colored, about 15 minutes. The sides may
fall in a bit, which is okay.

4. Remove the pan from the oven and
reduce the temperature to 350 degrees.
Sprinkle the shell with the ground
almonds. Stir the jam, and when it is
smooth, pour it over the ground almonds,
spreading it evenly in the crust. (Do not
cover the sides with jam, even if they
collapsed while baking.)

5. Take the dough from the refrigerator

and remove the top sheet of plastic. Cut the dough into ½-inch-wide strips. (You will have about 8 strips of sufficient length.) Lay the strips over the jam in parallel rows about 1½ to 2 inches apart, starting with the longest strip in the center and working your way out. (Use every other strip of dough, reserving the others for the second set of latticework.) Attach the strips at the sides of the crust by pressing them lightly. Rotate the pan ¼ turn and repeat with the remaining strips to form a lattice. (It is okay if the strips break when transferred to the torte; repair them by loosely overlapping the cracks.) Use any leftover dough to overlap the ends of the strips, forming a neat edge. Note that during baking, the dough will melt a bit, smoothing out any rough spots.

6. Beat the egg lightly with the cream. Brush the dough with the egg-and-cream mixture and sprinkle the optional slivered almonds over the top. (The almonds add texture, but I prefer the look of the torte without them.) Bake the torte on the top rack of the oven until golden brown, 45 to 60 minutes. (The sides may brown more quickly than the top.) Let cool 5 minutes before removing the sides of the pan. Cool to room temperature and dust with confectioners' sugar, if desired.

Grease This!

Have you noticed that some recipes suggest preparing baking pans by "greasing" them, whatever that means? Other recipes suggest butter and flour, some instruct that one "line the pan with parchment paper," while others opt for the use of Crisco or vegetable oil. The question is, which method is best?

To answer that question, I tested 10 different methods, from using no grease at all to butter, Crisco, Baker's Joy, combinations of flour and shortening, and the use of parchment paper as well. Here is what I learned:

I quickly discovered that baking pans do need to be greased, even if they are "nonstick" pans. The big reason for this is not so much the difficulty in removing the baked goods; it is the lack of an even rise. You want the batter to climb up the sides of the pan easily to produce a nice flat top.

Second, dusting the greased pan with flour is a good idea as well, because this provides for better release. The last discovery I made is that parchment paper on the bottom of the pan does provide for a slightly more tender bottom, but a buttered and floured pan will release just fine.

Some bakers swear by Crisco instead of butter, saying it does a better job of providing release from the sides of the pan. This is, sad to say, true, but butter does provide better flavor. The choice is yours.

Chocolate Pecan Pie Worth Eating

A good pecan pie is hard to find, but a great chocolate
pecan pie is even harder. I wanted a crisp crust, a
creamy (not greasy) filling, pecans that have some snap,
and good balance between all the different flavors and
textures. I thought that the best place to start was with
a good pecan pie recipe, and then I'd figure out how to
add the chocolate. ▶◀

I tested five recipes of regular pecan pie, including my own from *The Dessert Bible*, and, predictably, liked mine the best. How was my recipe different? Well, it uses less butter and less sugar, and it adds ½ cup heavy cream and 1 tablespoon of bourbon. This results in a creamier, less candy-store confection. I also found that I preferred dark corn syrup to light, as well as dark brown sugar to either light brown sugar or white granulated sugar. One recipe even added flour for thickening, an unnecessary and unwelcome addition. Finally, I toasted and chopped the pecans so that they were crisper and the pie was easier to slice. (Have you ever tried slicing through a soggy pecan half?)

Reviewing my recipe, I tested all the ingredients one more time and came up with only a few minor adjustments. I increased the pecans to 2 cups from 1½ cups, bumped the salt from ¼ teaspoon to ½ teaspoon, and went with a full teaspoon of vanilla instead of a mere half. Now I had to figure out the best way to add the chocolate.

I tested three methods of converting my pecan pie to a chocolate pecan pie: I added chocolate chips, I stirred in melted chocolate, and I spread melted chocolate on the bottom of the crust. The chips were too random. Sometimes you got a big hit of chocolate, and sometimes you didn't. Brushing the bottom crust provided a two-tier flavor experience that I didn't care for. The best method was simply to add melted chocolate to the filling. In terms of type of chocolate, I settled on semisweet or bittersweet chocolate rather than either sweet chocolate or unsweetened. Milk chocolate was lackluster, and cocoa powder tasted flat. I ended up melting the chocolate with the butter and then proceeding with the master recipe.

As for baking the pie, my original recipe calls for a hot, prebaked pie shell into which is poured a hot filling. The filled pie is then put back into the oven and baked quickly. The result is a very crisp crust. However, I found that by using a very hot oven to start, 425 degrees, and baking the pie on the bottom shelf, I could get an excellent result without the fuss of prebaking. Finally, a chocolate pecan pie that was good enough for Thanksgiving.

Chocolate Pecan Pie

SERVES 8 TO 10

Note that this pie needs to be fully cooled to avoid messy, difficult-to-cut slices. If you are not handy with pie dough, it is best to make the dough the day before you intend to roll it out. Be sure to remove this pie from the oven before the center is set.

FOR THE CRUST

5	tablespoons cold unsalted butter
1¼	cups all-purpose flour, plus more for dusting the dough and work surface
½	teaspoon table salt
2	tablespoons granulated sugar
5	tablespoons all-vegetable shortening (Crisco), chilled
4–6	tablespoons ice water

FOR THE FILLING

2	cups pecan halves
4	ounces semisweet or bittersweet chocolate
2	tablespoons unsalted butter
3	large eggs
1	cup dark corn syrup
½	cup packed dark brown sugar
1	teaspoon vanilla extract
1	tablespoon bourbon or dark rum
½	cup heavy cream
½	teaspoon table salt

1. For the crust: Cut the butter into ¾-inch pieces and place it in the freezer for 15 minutes. Mix the flour, salt, and sugar in a food processor fitted with the steel blade. Place the shortening in 1-tablespoon lumps into the food processor along with the frozen butter pieces. Pulse about 8 times (1-second pulses) or until the dough appears slightly yellow, pebbly in texture, and the butter is reduced to very small pieces, the size of peas or smaller. Check the dough after 5 pulses and every pulse thereafter. Turn the mixture into a medium bowl. (This dough can also be made by hand. Use your fingers to work the butter and shortening into the flour.)

2. Sprinkle 4 tablespoons of the ice water over the mixture. With the blade of a large rubber spatula, use a folding motion to mix, then press down on the dough with the broad side of the spatula until the dough sticks together, adding more water if the dough will not come together. (Do NOT worry about adding more water; add as much as you need to make sure that the dough easily comes together and is moist. If the outside of the dough becomes wet, simply flour it before you wrap it in plastic.) Work slowly, mixing the dough to evenly distribute the water. This should take about 1 minute. Shape the dough into a ball with your hands, then flatten it into a 4-inch-wide disk.

Dust lightly with flour, wrap in plastic, and refrigerate for at least 1 hour before rolling. (Overnight is best.)

3. For the filling: Adjust the oven racks to the lower and middle positions and heat the oven to 375 degrees. Spread the pecans on a baking sheet and toast on the middle rack until slightly darker and fragrant, about 7 minutes. Check frequently to avoid burning. Chop coarsely. Increase the oven temperature to 425 degrees.

4. Melt the chocolate and butter in a microwave oven at 50 percent power for 2 minutes. Stir to mix. (Heat in additional 30-second increments if necessary.) In a large bowl, beat the eggs with a whisk until blended. Whisk in the corn syrup, brown sugar, vanilla, bourbon, heavy cream, salt, and the melted butter-and-chocolate mixture.

5. Roll out the pastry dough and fit it into a 9-inch Pyrex pie plate. Trim, leaving a ½-inch overlap. Fold the excess dough back under the crust and crimp with your fingers or a fork.

6. Fold the pecans into the filling and pour the filling into the pie shell. Bake on the lower oven rack for 10 minutes. Reduce the heat to 375 degrees and bake until the edges are puffy and cracked and the center 3 to 4 inches is still slightly wobbly, about 20 minutes. Do not overbake; the pie will become tough. Cool to room temperature (about 4 hours) before serving.

Crispy Pie Crust

The bane of most pies is the bottom crust. It is invariably half-baked and soggy. This is especially true with custard pies such as pumpkin or pecan. The remedy—at least the one I often used—was to partially prebake the crust without the filling (this is called blind baking), add a hot filling (which is cooked on top of the stove), and then finish the pie in the oven for 15 to 20 minutes or so. It works, but you have to refrigerate the crust and then freeze it before blind baking to ensure that it does not shrink. With a pie such as apple, of course, this is less practical, because precooking the filling is a lot more work than most people wish to invest in what is already a time-consuming process.

When working on the recipe for Chocolate Pecan Pie, I discovered that if you start with a hot, 425-degree oven, a Pyrex pie plate, and the oven rack at the lowest setting, you could produce a very good, crisp bottom crust. I baked the pie for 10 minutes at 425 degrees and then turned the oven down to 375 degrees to finish.

Sure, this is a compromise, but I'll take a crust that is 80 percent as good any day for about half the work.

Modernizing Trifle

Christmas in my household is a time for trifle. It is the ultimate holiday dessert, one that can be made ahead of time, and one that easily serves a crowd. The traditional recipe with jam and lady fingers was never a hit with my kids, but when I switched over to a rich chocolate trifle, I hit pay dirt. A combination of chocolate cake, cream, and glaze — it was heaven. ▶◀

Now the question was how to perfect the recipe. I tried a variety of cakes: chocolate genoise, buttermilk chocolate cake, devil's food cake, and an all-purpose chocolate sheet cake. The buttermilk cake was the winner, because it was both moist and chocolatey and was also the easiest recipe of the four. And it was light enough for a trifle (a really heavy cake turns trifle into something akin to a dense Christmas pudding), but it was still moist, not dry like a genoise. I baked the cake in an 8-by-8-inch square pan that made trimming and slicing a breeze.

Next on the list was the pastry cream. I had created a recipe for *The Dessert Bible,* and it used flour instead of cornstarch, the latter being a bit finicky. (A cornstarch-thickened pudding can break if stirred too vigorously.) I found that the pastry cream by itself (it is spread between the layers of the cake) was too thick, and whipped cream was too thin, so I folded the two together for an improved texture. Many trifles brush the cake with either amaretto or sugar syrup to add flavor and a bit of moisture as well. I combined these two ideas, making a sugar syrup and then adding liqueur.

So far, so good. I felt, however, that my trifle was lacking chocolate punch, as the only chocolate in the recipe at this point was the cake itself—both the pastry cream and the whipped cream were vanilla. I tried using chocolate pastry cream, but it offered too little flavor contrast to the cake. I tried using chocolate shavings, but they were lackluster. Finally, I drizzled chocolate glaze over the top of the trifle, and that did the trick. (I didn't like adding the glaze to the layers of the trifle, because it bled onto the white cream. For additional chocolate flavor, the glaze can be puddled under or drizzled over each serving.)

Assembling the trifle was simple. Using the square cake, I trimmed off ¼ inch from the edges and then cut the cake in half and then into ½-inch slices. I filled the serving bowl with alternating layers of cake and cream, starting with cake and ending with cream. I found that trifle is best when allowed to sit for several hours or overnight. The flavors meld, and the cake absorbs the syrup more evenly.

Chocolate Trifle

Don't be put off by the length of this recipe. The components are not hard to make, and it is fun to assemble. For best results, the trifle should be allowed to set up in the refrigerator for several hours or overnight. The pastry cream should be prepared first, because it takes the longest to chill. While it cools, the other components can be prepared, except for the chocolate glaze, which should be made shortly before serving. If you like, you can add the chocolate glaze to the top of the trifle ahead of time and then reheat the remaining glaze just before serving for drizzling onto individual servings.

FOR THE PASTRY CREAM

1²/₃	cups half-and-half
5	large egg yolks
7	tablespoons sugar
2½	tablespoons all-purpose flour
	Pinch table salt
1½	teaspoons vanilla extract

FOR THE CHOCOLATE CAKE

	Softened unsalted butter for the pan
	Flour for the pan
1½	cups sifted cake flour
½	cup Dutch-processed cocoa
¼	teaspoon baking powder
½	teaspoon baking soda
½	teaspoon table salt
12	tablespoons (1½ sticks) unsalted butter, softened
1¼	cups sugar
2	large eggs, at room temperature
1	large egg white, at room temperature
1½	teaspoons vanilla extract
1	cup buttermilk

FOR THE SYRUP

⅓	cup sugar
2	tablespoons dark rum or amaretto

FOR THE WHIPPED CREAM

1½	cups heavy cream, very cold
¼	cup sugar

FOR THE CHOCOLATE GLAZE

1	cup heavy cream
¼	cup light corn syrup
8	ounces semisweet chocolate, chopped into small pieces
½	teaspoon vanilla extract

1. For the pastry cream: Heat the half-and-half in a small saucepan until it just begins to simmer. Meanwhile, whisk the egg yolks, sugar, flour, and salt together in a medium heavy-bottomed saucepan until light and fluffy, about 1 minute. Add about half of the hot half-and-half to the egg mixture, whisking constantly but gently. When mixed, pour in the remaining half-and-half, whisking slowly to incorporate.
2. Place the pan over low heat and cook, whisking gently but constantly, until the mixture thickens, 4 to 7 minutes, being sure to get into the corners. (You can use a heatproof rubber spatula for this.) Continue whisking over the heat until the cream loses its flour taste, about 3 minutes more. (The mixture should not bubble or steam heavily or the eggs might cook.)

3. Strain the pastry cream into a small bowl. Stir in the vanilla. Smooth the top with a spatula and place waxed paper directly on the surface. Refrigerate until well chilled, 2 to 3 hours.

4. For the cake: Grease the bottom of an 8-by-8-inch pan with butter. Line the bottom with parchment and grease and lightly flour the paper and sides of the pan. Adjust an oven rack to the center position and heat the oven to 350 degrees.

5. Sift the flour, cocoa, baking powder, baking soda, and salt onto a sheet of waxed paper. Beat the butter in the bowl of an electric mixer for 1 minute. Add the sugar gradually and beat on medium-high speed for 3 minutes, until the mixture is light-colored and fluffy. (Scrape down 2 to 3 times.) Add the whole eggs and the egg white one at a time, beating for 20 seconds after each addition. Add the vanilla and beat for 10 seconds.

6. Add the flour mixture in 3 parts, alternating with the buttermilk. Beat on low speed to incorporate, and scrape down the sides of the bowl with a rubber spatula. Stir by hand to finish.

7. Pour the batter into the prepared pan and bake for about 30 minutes or until the top of the cake springs back when gently pressed and a cake tester or toothpick comes out clean. Cool for 15 minutes, remove the cake from the pan, and cool completely on a wire rack.

8. For the syrup: Place the sugar and ¼ cup water in a small saucepan over medium heat. Cook until the sugar is completely dissolved, 3 to 5 minutes.

Remove the pan from the heat and add the rum. Cool to room temperature.

9. For the whipped cream: Chill a large bowl and a whisk or the beaters from an electric mixer. Add the cream and sugar to the bowl and beat on low speed, gradually increasing speed until the mixer is on high. Beat until the cream is thick and can hold a 2-inch peak.

10. To assemble the trifle: Trim ¼ inch off each side of the chocolate cake. Cut the cake in half and cut each half into ½-inch slices. Fold the whipped cream and the chilled pastry cream together.

11. Select a clear glass bowl with straight sides or any other bowl that holds about 16 cups. Arrange ⅓ of the cake slices in a fallen domino pattern around the bottom of the bowl. Brush the syrup on the cake slices, giving each piece a generous amount and using ⅓ of the syrup. Spread ⅓ of the cream over the top of the cake. Repeat the above steps 2 times more, ending with a layer of cream. Cover and refrigerate for several hours or overnight.

12. For the chocolate glaze: Combine the cream and corn syrup in a heavy saucepan. Bring to a simmer. Add the chocolate, stir, and remove from the heat. Cover and let sit for 8 minutes. Add the vanilla and stir gently until the mixture is smooth and shiny. Allow the glaze to cool until tepid. Drizzle a spoonful of glaze back into the pan. If it mounds a little, the glaze is ready.

13. Drizzle a little more than half the glaze over the trifle. Serve, drizzling remaining glaze over individual portions.

Lighter Holiday Punch

Although *punch* originally described a British colonial drink in which five ingredients had to be included (*panch* means "five" in Hindu), punch has come to describe any combination of fruit juice and spirits. The problem with latter-day punches is that they are either intolerably sweet, boozy, or just plain overbearing. I wanted something light and refreshing but with enough warmth and kick to qualify as a legitimate holiday drink. ▶◀

I started by making five different punches, each one based on a different base ingredient: cider, booze, tea, wine, or fruit juice. Spiked or mulled cider quickly becomes sickening; it is heavy, spicy, and thirst-provoking. Punch based on booze is heavy-handed. (The Thin Man may have approved, but, these days, lighter fare is in order.) Spiked tea—hot or cold, fruity or otherwise—was heady and not refreshing. If using wine, I would stick to sangria. Fruit juice, unlike all of the other ingredients, can be at once thirst-quenching, refreshing, and, if not spiked too much, quite easygoing.

I started with a basic recipe that included a "base" juice, a stronger-flavored juice, ginger ale, and either rum, wine, or liqueur. I also wanted to play with the addition of grenadine, an ingredient found in many of the punch recipes I had researched. I quickly ruled out the ginger ale. It adds the taste of flat soda, because it doesn't have enough gas to carbonate the entire pitcher. I also decided to leave out the wine and liqueur, at least for now, as the mixture was too confusing.

After much testing, I settled on white cranberry juice as my base juice. It was lively and refreshing compared with other juices such as apple and white grape juice. Next, I moved on to strong-flavored juices, such as orange, lemon, lime, and pineapple. A combination of orange and pineapple juices was best. As far as liquor goes, dark rum was fine, as was bourbon. For added kick and interest, you can add a bit of orange liqueur. As for the grenadine, only a tiny bit was necessary to add color and a bit of sweetness, just a teaspoon when using a half gallon of white cranberry juice. The best thing about this recipe is that it is absurdly simple—no mashing of orange or lemon slices—and refreshing. Now that's something worth celebrating.

Quick, Refreshing Holiday Punch

MAKES TWELVE 1-CUP SERVINGS

Unlike so many others, this punch does not leave one the worse for wear. It is light and refreshing, but also interesting. And it goes together quickly. Fresh-squeezed orange juice is preferable to the supermarket type.

8	cups (64 ounces) white cranberry juice
¾	cup fresh-squeezed orange juice
¼	cup pineapple juice
¾–1	cup dark rum or bourbon or a combination of the two
¼	cup orange liqueur such as Cointreau or Triple Sec
1	teaspoon grenadine

Mix all of the ingredients together in a large bowl or pitcher. Serve very cold. The punch can be made several hours ahead of time and kept refrigerated.

INDEX

A

Almond(s):
    Linzertorte, Light, 287–89
    Pound Cake, 282
Anchovy(ies), 90
    Caper, and Olive Sauce (for Fish), 182–83
    -Onion-Parsley Topping (for Mashed Potatoes), 42
    Salsa Verde, 168–69
Appetizers and first courses:
    Goat Cheese Soufflé with Thyme and Parmesan, 209–10
    salads
        Beet and Goat Cheese, with Raspberry Vinegar, 56–57
        Goat Cheese, Baked, 61–62
        Greek, 63–66
        Orange, Onion, and Fennel, 69–70
        Pear, Roasted, with Arugula and Goat Cheese, 67–68
    Tuna Steak with Spice Crust, Six-Minute, 193–94
    see also Pasta; Risotto
Apple(s):
    Cider, Chives, and Cumin Sauce (for Pork or Chicken), 183
    Granola Bars with Fruit Filling, 224–26
Apricots, dried:
    Granola Bars with Fruit Filling, 224–26
    Oatmeal Scones with Cranberries and, 227–29
Arugula:
    Pasta with Goat Cheese, Raw Tomatoes and, 93–94
    Pasta with Quick Tomato Sauce and, 97–98
    Risotto with Tender Greens, 111
    Roasted Pear Salad with Goat Cheese and, 67–68
Asparagus, 36–37
    French-Style Boiled Dinner with Salsa Verde (Pot au Feu), 167
    Frittata, 204
    High-Roast, 36–37
        with Fresh Tomato-Basil Sauce, 37

Asparagus (*continued*)
        with Tomatoes, Anchovies, Capers, and Olives, 37
    Pasta Primavera, 85–87
    Risotto with, 111

B

Baking pans, greasing, 289
Balsamic Vinegar, Tomatoes, and Capers, Chicken with, 127–28
Basil:
    Pasta with Raw Tomatoes, Mint and, 89–90
    Pesto, 16
    Rough, 34
    Tomato Sauce, Fresh, High-Roast Asparagus with, 37
Bean(s):
    Cassoulet, Quick, 132–33
    Clam, and Potato Soup with Bacon and Tomatoes, 24–25
    Minestrone, Hearty, 14–16
    and Pasta Soup (Pasta e Fagioli), 18–20
        Quick, 20
    Pork Chili with Tomatoes, Cumin and, 177–78
Béchamel sauce, scalding milk for, 267
Beef, 156–67
    continuing to cook out of oven, 263
    French-Style Boiled Dinner with Salsa Verde (Pot au Feu), 165–67
    Salsa Verde for, 168–69
    short rib(s)
        Braised, 161–64
        Tomato Sauce, Pasta with, 101–3
    steak(s)
        au Poivre, Four-Ingredient, 159–60
        resting before cutting, 156
        selecting, 157
        with Sherry-Shallot Pan Sauce, 157–58
        Worcestershire Steak Sauce for, 183
    tough cuts of, making tender, 162, 165